ANAESTHETICS OF EXISTENCE

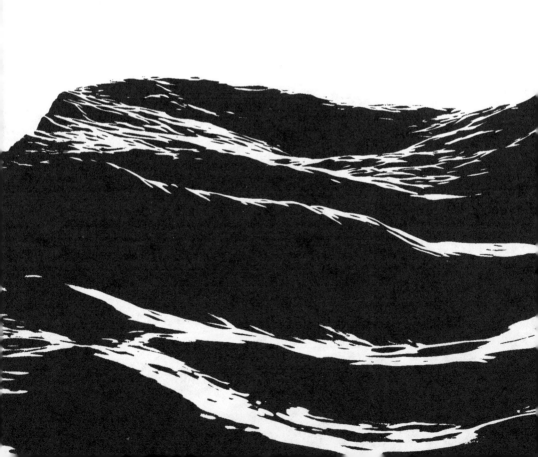

DUKE UNIVERSITY PRESS
Durham & London 2020

anaesthetics of existence

ESSAYS ON EXPERIENCE
AT THE EDGE

CRESSIDA J. HEYES

Printed in the United States of America on acid-free paper ∞
Designed by Aimee C. Harrison
Typeset in Portrait Text by Westchester Publishing Services

Library of Congress Cataloging-in-Publication Data
Names: Heyes, Cressida J., author.
Title: Anaesthetics of existence : essays on experience at the edge / Cressida J. Heyes.
Description: Durham : Duke University Press, [2020] | Includes bibliographical references
and index.
Identifiers: LCCN 2019033494 (print) | LCCN 2019033495 (ebook) | ISBN 9781478007814
(hardcover) | ISBN 9781478008262 (paperback) | ISBN 9781478009320 (ebook)
Subjects: LCSH: Experience. | Consciousness.
Classification: LCC B105.E9 H49 2020 (print) | LCC B105.E9 (ebook) | DDC 128/.4—dc23
LC record available at https://lccn.loc.gov/2019033494
LC ebook record available at https://lccn.loc.gov/2019033495

Cover art: 目 [mé], *Contact*, 2019. Installation at *Roppongi Crossing 2019: Connexions*,
Mori Art Museum, Tokyo.

CONTENTS

ACKNOWLEDGMENTS

I STARTED WORK ON THIS BOOK IN 2011, after taking a break of several years from monograph writing following the publication of *Self-Transformations* in 2007. My son was born in 2009 and the pause was deliberate—in part a privileged choice to allow me to focus on the process of having a child, and in part because I was exhausted and ill after he was born. Nonetheless, I didn't expect this book to take this long, because I didn't expect—could not have expected—the litany of painful and disheartening professional disasters that struck between 2009 and 2017. Raising a young child while negotiating an amicable end to a twenty-year relationship was plain sailing compared with all that, and I am eternally grateful to David Kahane for his generosity and commitment to easing us through. My colleagues in the Political Science Department at the University of Alberta welcomed a shell-shocked philosopher into their ranks very warmly, and I owe a special debt to Lois Harder and Catherine Kellogg, who both helped in different ways with that difficult transition, and have buoyed me with their supportive friendship and commitment to feminist intellectual life and politics.

Colleagues too numerous to list engaged this work in its various public presentations, while others talked to me, or to my classes, about ideas behind the scenes, or shared their own work—and/or (vital academic task) wrote letters of support. I would like in particular to thank Amy Allen, Alia Al-Saji,

Ann Cahill, Lorraine Code, Jon Goldberg-Hiller, Lise Gotell, Lisa Guenther, Jack Halberstam, Ami Harbin, Sally Haslanger, Karen Houle, Meredith Jones, Joe Latham, Natalie Loveless, Robert Nichols, Fiona Nicoll, Johanna Oksala, Alissa Overend, Lanei Rodemeyer, Gayle Salamon, Alexis Shotwell, Gail Weiss, Bronwyn Wilson, and Anna Yeatman. I have been blessed with terrific graduate students, old and new, and although it's a cliché to say it, I've learned a huge amount from them. My special thanks to Catherine Clune-Taylor, Lucas Crawford, Megan Dean, Kristin Rodier, and Joshua St. Pierre, who have particularly influenced this work. When I was first formulating the idea of a method that drew on both feminist phenomenology and Foucault's genealogy, I taught a senior seminar called "The Politics of the Body," and I much appreciated the talented and thoughtful undergraduates in both itera-tions of that course who helped me pull together some key ideas.

Parts of this book have been presented as papers or keynotes at meetings of the Foucault Circle, the Canadian Society for Women in Philosophy, the Ca-nadian Political Science Association, the American Political Science Associa-tion, the Canadian Philosophical Association, the American Philosophical Association, the Canadian Society for Continental Philosophy, the Society for Phenomenology and Existential Philosophy, Feminist Ethics and Social Theory, the Somatechnics conferences, and the Institute for Philosophical Nursing Research, and to audiences at Appalachian State University, Durham University, John Carroll University, Miami University, McMaster Univer-sity, Scripps College, the University of Adelaide, the University of Calgary, the University of Uppsala, and the University of Victoria. I'd like to thank my hosts and interlocutors at these events, especially Yuval Avnur, Michelle Bastian and Lisa Baraitser, Chris Beasley, Elisabeth Gedge, Kim Hall, Ada Jaarsma, Jennifer Koshan, Scott Marratto, Caitríona Ní Dhúill, Gaile Pohlhaus, Elizabeth Stephens and Karin Sellberg, Susan Stryker, Chloë Taylor, Dianna Taylor, Jim Tully and Jeremy Webber, and Kristin Zeiler and Lisa Folkmarson Käll. I am also grateful to everyone who attended these talks and asked ques-tions and provided feedback and constructive criticism.

This book could not have been written without the financial support of the Social Sciences and Humanities Research Council of Canada, who awarded me a Standard Research Grant to enable me to be part of a scholarly community as I wrote it and who supported my career (and feminist philoso-phy in Canada) through the award of a Tier II Canada Research Chair. While I held the CRC in Philosophy of Gender and Sexuality I taught fewer classes, and the bill for that teaching release was paid in part by the Faculty of Arts at the University of Alberta headed by Dean Lesley Cormack, to whom I am grateful for support in hard times.

I will always be indebted to the two anonymous reviewers for Duke University Press who provided me with such remarkably generous and generative feedback on the first draft of the whole manuscript. This book is a lot better—if also unfortunately quite a lot longer—because of their careful and serious reading. Thanks are also owed to Jeanique Tucker, who copyedited that first draft with great care. Duke University Press created a beautiful product, and I am grateful to all those who worked on it.

For found family in far-flung and chilly Edmonton, thank you to Gillian Colquhoun, Michel Figeat, Amy Kaler, Eddy Kent, Deborah Shiry, Terri Tomsky, and Heather Young-Leslie. Jonathan Leggo, friend and indexer, was witness to some particularly painful final stages of writing, and his patient listening and reliable tea-based solutions made the last year much more tolerable. For my parents, Vivien and David Heyes, and my brother Rod Heyes, outlaw-sister Lucy Rix, and niblings Albi and Frida, thanks for the vacation time and for keeping the kid busy at key moments.

My wonderful mentor and friend Marguerite Deslauriers was kind enough to say, on learning I was pregnant, that this undergoing would be a great gift to philosophy. I was deeply touched by that feminist sentiment, but still a tiny bit skeptical. I could never have imagined how my life would be changed by the experience of giving birth, or by the fascinating and humbling journey of parenting. This book is for my extraordinary, brilliant, argumentative, funny, stubborn, and loving son, Solomon.

Chapter 2, "Dead to the World: Rape, Unconsciousness, and Social Media," was first published in *Signs: A Journal of Women in Culture and Society* 41, no. 2 (January 2016): 361–83. Parts of chapters 3 and 4 were published as "Anaesthetics of Existence" in Lisa Folkmarson Käll and Kristin Zeiler, eds., *Feminist Phenomenology and Medicine* (Albany, NY: SUNY Press, 2014). An earlier version of chapter 5 was published as "Child, Birth: An Aesthetic" in Lisa Folkmarson Käll, ed., *Dimensions of Pain: Humanities and Social Science Perspectives* (London: Routledge, 2012).

INTRODUCTION

It was a question of knowing how to govern one's own life in order to give it the most beautiful form (in the eyes of others, of oneself, and of the future generations for which one might serve as an example). That is what I tried to reconstitute: the formation and development of a practice of self whose aim was to constitute oneself as the worker of the beauty of one's own life.—Michel Foucault, "The Concern for Truth" ([1984] 1988a, 259)

To continue to counter the moral science of biopolitics, which links the political administration of life to a melodrama of the care of the monadic self, we need to think about agency and personhood not only in normative terms but also as activity exercised within spaces of ordinariness that does not always or even usually follow the literalizing logic of visible effectuality, bourgeois dramatics, and lifelong accumulation or fashioning.—Lauren Berlant, "Slow Death" (2007, 758)

I ONCE ATTENDED A CONFERENCE on the implications of Michel Foucault's philosophy for ethics and the body. Fogged with lack of sleep and the nervous exhaustion that comes from sitting in fluorescent-lit rooms and trying for hours to focus on read-aloud presentations, I heard one speaker repeatedly talk of "anaesthetics of existence." I dozily turned this mysterious phrase over in my head, wondering what it could mean, and how it fit with the rest of the paper. Eventually, of course, I realized that the speaker was talking too fast, running together her words, and actually saying "an aesthetics of existence," a phrase that Foucault and his interpreters often used to describe a kind of self-styled ethical life and that made perfect sense of the rest. But the idea of "*anaesthetics* of existence" stuck with me. As Joan Scott recounts being provoked by a student essay in which "fin de siècle" became the enticing phrase "fantasy echo," I wanted to know more about this productive mishearing.[1] It was confusing and oblique—a mix-up that I couldn't quite make sense of, and that I was tempted to dismiss as merely an artifact of my own cerebral deficits. But the ethical work of the *aesthetics of existence*, with its implication of making oneself as art, in that moment felt grand and really tiring, while "anaesthetics" seemed more passive, curative, restful. So much of academic life is organized around the subjectivity I was trying to sustain at that conference: a self-mobilizing gumption, a sitting-up-and-paying-attention, an attitude of thinking hard about one's work and preciously representing the work as emanating from a carefully curated self. This life is both very privileged and very depleting—an interesting paradox. To have toyed with the idea of taking a cognitive vacation through some imagined *anaesthetics of existence* felt, briefly, transgressive (or perhaps, a "preface to transgression" [Foucault 1998])—transgressive enough, at least, that I held fast to the possibility and the phrase that seemed to capture it.

In a powerful and complex essay, Susan Buck-Morss argues with Walter Benjamin that the development of the human sensorium under modernity is characterized by attempts to cope with shock (1992, 16).[2] From the battlefields of the First World War to the much more everyday public spaces of shopping arcades, factories, amusement parks, casinos, and even crowded streets, our senses are neurologically overloaded. Do we attempt consciously to process this shock experience, or do we, at a certain point, need to rely on our ability to parry the bombardment of our senses, to protect ourselves as sense-perceiving subjects from the technological overwhelm of modern experience? To do so is always to manage an experience that is simultaneously objective and subjective, a set of stimuli emerging from a situation external to us and an interpretive attitude to that situation: "In order to differentiate our description from the more limited, traditional conception of the human nervous system which artificially isolates human biology from its environment, we will call this aesthetic system of sense-consciousness, decentered from the classical subject, wherein external sense-perceptions come together with the internal images of memory and anticipation, the 'synaesthetic system'" (13).

Under such conditions, Buck-Morss suggests, the synaesthetic system "reverses its role. Its goal is to *numb* the organism, to deaden the senses, to repress memory: the cognitive system of synaesthetics has become, rather, one of *an*aesthetics" (18). "Aesthetics," she reminds us, is a term that derives from the Greek *aisthetikos*—that which is perceived by feeling. The five senses form an interface between subject and world; together, they are a physical-cognitive apparatus serving "instinctual needs—for warmth, nourishment, safety, sociability" (6). The gradual appropriation of the term into modern philosophy to mean that branch of philosophical inquiry concerned with (evaluative judgments about) sense perception, and in particular our exercise of taste, thus represents an attempt to recommend the acculturation of our senses and transpose the focus of inquiry from sense perception itself to objects of art. The antonym *an*aesthetic is that which deprives us of sensibility, renders us incapable of perception. Its common usages are almost always medical, and it too is usually associated with its objects—namely, anaesthetic agents (drugs that render the patient insensible or numb).

Buck-Morss points out that the aesthetic shock of modernity coincides with the development of technologies of anaesthesia. Opiates, nitrous oxide, ether, chloroform, and cocaine entered widespread and everyday use through the 1800s (Snow 2006), developing their own economy (both within and outside formal medical practice) as varied tools for coping with synaesthetic overload. No longer dependent on anaesthetic habits as quaint as daily laudanum or ether frolics, we now have an amazing array of drugs aimed at managing the ubiquitous depression, anxiety, insomnia, and other synaesthetic diseases that thrive in contemporary Western cultures. We also have addictions (in some cases to those same drugs), which have increased in both their scope and their severity. Psychotropics are used in a systemic, involuntary or pseudovoluntary way to manage daily life for whole populations—the criminally incarcerated, those in psychiatric facilities, or elders in residential care, for example. Technologies that enhance, control, deaden, or eliminate sensation are ever more central to a wide range of lives and deaths.

"Aesthetics of existence," by contrast, the phrase I originally misheard, occurs in Foucault's last work on ethics and care of the self. Volumes 2 and 3 of *The History of Sexuality* evoke an ancient Greek and Roman understanding of ethics as a project of self-making in which the self is understood as an aesthetic product, a result of practicing the "arts of existence"—that is, "those intentional and voluntary actions by which men [*sic*] not only set themselves rules of conduct, but also seek to transform themselves, to change themselves in their singular being, and to make their life into an oeuvre that carries certain aesthetic values and meets certain stylistic criteria" (Foucault [1984] 1990, 10–11). This is an ethic that contrasts with Christian asceticism and morality as obedience to a code of rules (Foucault [1984] 1996a, 451). Returning to the ethical practices of antiquity, Foucault is writing a new genealogy of morals ([1984] 1996a, 451; [1983] 1997a, 266), which will reveal "the genealogy of the subject as a subject of ethical actions" in which "we have to build our existence as a beautiful existence; it is an aesthetic mode" ([1983] 1997a, 266). In his response to Kant, "What Is Enlightenment?," Foucault suggests that we think of modernity less as an epoch and more as an ethos—"a mode of relating to contemporary reality; a voluntary choice made by certain people; in the end, a way of thinking and feeling; a way, too of acting and behaving that at one and the same time marks a relation of belonging and presents itself as a task" ([1984] 1997g, 309). For my purposes, what's important in Foucault's characterization of this attitude is the relation to oneself to which it is tied: "To be modern is not to accept oneself as one is in the flux of the passing moments; it is to take oneself as object of a complex and difficult elaboration" (311). An aesthetics of existence, then, is a practice of ethics that takes the self as a commitment, to be made as one would make a work of art, where the project of making is paradoxical because the thing being made is also that doing the making. As Daniel Smith puts it,

> When Foucault says we should treat our life as a work of art, we should not understand him to be saying that "we" are something separate from and transcendent to this object "life" which we ought to use as the material for an aesthetic work of art. This would re-introduce exactly the kind of dualism Foucault tries to get away from in this essay. The distinction is not one of two different levels, a transcendent author-principle opposed to the substantial work of art which it produces, but one whereby the two things, the author and the work, remain strictly immanent to one another. (D. Smith 2015, 141)

The aesthetics of existence Foucault defends has a political goal: it resists the "will to knowledge" (in the context of sexuality in particular, but also more broadly) that causes us to inquire after our authentic truth, to try to work out what kind of subject we really are, particularly as defined by expert discourse. Instead, our freedom lies in being open to unanticipated transformation, including of the very identities we have come to hold dear (Heyes 2007, ch. 5). Foucault's method here, which has behind it all his genealogical work, constitutes a "critical ontology of ourselves"—a way of bringing into question the sorts of things we previously imagined ourselves to be. This ontology "must be considered not . . . as a theory, a doctrine, nor even as a permanent body of knowledge that is accumulating; it must be conceived as an attitude, an ethos, a philosophical life in which the critique of what we are is at one and the same time the historical analysis of the limits imposed on us and an experiment with the possibility of going beyond them" (Foucault [1984] 1997g, 319). This last work is part of a Kantian tradition solely in the sense that Foucault understands autonomy as the practice of critique of all things presented to us as necessary (including a transcendental subject) (Allen 2008, esp. 22–44).

Other critics have long implied that Foucault in his aesthetics of existence assumes a bourgeois modernist subject, and these criticisms have persisted and morphed into the challenge that his emphasis on self-stylization resonates a little too much with the discourse of human capital of which he was also critical.[3] When Foucault represents self-making as the "task" of a "worker" who refuses to accept himself as he is, no matter his philosophical intentions, he deploys a vocabulary perilously close to the corruptions and reductions of individual agency that characterize life under neoliberalism. In an interview with Stephen Riggins in 1982, he says, in response to a question about the relation of his philosophy to the arts: "You see, that's why I really work like a dog, and I worked like a dog all my life. I am not interested in the academic status of what I am doing because my problem is my own transformation. . . . This transformation of one's self by one's own knowledge is, I think, something rather close to the aesthetic experience. Why should a painter work if he is not transformed by his own painting?" (Foucault [1982] 1997b, 131).[4]

Foucault probably understood, presciently, that globalized capitalism was starting to create and deploy a self whose individual autonomy is not the source of resistance to its subjection but rather is a key capacity in drawing it ever deeper into biopolitical power. The labor of being an agential subject (of which political resistance is part) is not outside the neoliberal regimes that incite it. Rather, the norms of agency that constrain and enable us are fully implicated in systems of postdisciplinary power. Our ambivalent commitment (I might say "attachment") to self-making remains a valuable part of our aesthetic ethics, but one of the reasons it is ambivalent lies in the anaesthetic desire for respite from the assaults of late modernity and, now, neoliberal postmodernity.

Foucault is, of course, neither resurrecting self-sovereignty nor endorsing the disciplined subjectivity biopolitics creates—quite the contrary. One of the reasons he turns to the lives of privileged Greek and Roman men is to examine the practices of daily life—sex, diet, maintaining health, exercise, writing, marital relations—in a predisciplinary age, the better to contrast care of the self with the normalization that follows it. He died before he could fully articulate the connection between these historical sketches and the interviews he gave on a contemporary art of living. This leaves us with the open question of how Foucault imagined the contemporary subject would practice his aesthetics of existence. What is it *like*—as a matter of everyday life, of lived experience—to be the subject of this always-becoming, exemplary, critical, beautiful life? For Foucault himself the aesthetics of existence was, as the term suggests, in part a sensory undertaking, connected in a way he never quite explained to the pains and pleasures of the technologies of the self available in our age. As I considered in the final chapter of *Self-Transformations* (Heyes 2007, ch. 5), Foucault's remarks on the role of pleasure in his own life in his last interviews are oddly ambivalent. Although he once commented lightly, "A good club sandwich with a Coke. That's my pleasure. It's true," he stresses that in general he had a hard time experiencing pleasure, especially the ordinary pleasures of everyday life (Foucault [1982] 1997b, 129; also Foucault 1996b, 378). He sought out limit-experiences at the extremes of pleasure (or even at the limit of his capacity to have experience of any kind) in order to encounter the edges of his possibilities—even, as when he was hit by a car while high, of the edge of his life at the border with death (Foucault [1984] 1997b, 129)—and be transformed (Foucault [1982] 1997c, 165; Foucault [1975] 1996c, 188–89; Foucault [1963] 1998; Wade and Dundas 2017).

As Ladelle McWhorter's brilliant book *Bodies and Pleasures* (1999) shows, the forms that our pain and pleasure take are closely hooked in to practices of normalization, which cultivate our capacity to experience them both in order that we might be better rendered as docile bodies. The intensification of sensory experience Buck-Morss describes, then, provides more opportunity for such ambivalence about the pleasures of everyday life or the dramas of the limit. It also helps to make sense of our desire for the anaesthetic, the withdrawal from sensory experience, as a mode of managing pleasure and pain. Even for an individual less committed to the project of living an aesthetics of existence than Foucault, it can sound like an exhausting ethical endeavor. The subject of late liberal capitalism is required to exercise his autonomy iteratively, expressing his individuality qua capacity to choose in an interminable series of self-determining moments. When presented in the language of political philosophy we can lose sight of the lived experience of this subjectivity: it can be exhausting, ego-driven, obsessed with irrelevant choices, and abusively self-disciplining, committed to the fantasy of organizing and rationalizing a life of freedom in political contexts in which freedom is systemically denied. As Lauren Berlant argues, in an essay with strong resonances with Buck-Morss's work, the "mass physical attenuation" that happens to working populations under late capitalism contrasts with the dominant account of autonomy, and thereby demands a rethinking: "Sovereignty described as the foundation of individual autonomy . . . overidentifies the similarity of self-control to sovereign performativity and state control over geographical boundaries. It thereby encourages a militaristic and melodramatic view of agency in the spectacular temporality of the event of the decision; and, in linking and inflating consciousness, intention, and decision or event, it has provided an alibi for normative governmentality and justified moralizing against inconvenient human activity" (Berlant 2007, 755).

By "inconvenient human activity," I take it that Berlant is referring in part to the activities that contribute to the "slow death" she theorizes: eating in particular, but also all of the compulsive, numbing, addictive activities that render working life under neoliberalism more tolerable.[5] In this light, she suggests, we need a better way of talking about ordinary life and its reproduction—the management of households; preparing and eating food; daily routines of traveling, working, caring for children, and so on (echoes of Foucault's *Care of the Self*). Ordinary life in the context of the pressures of postdisciplinary neoliberalism often feels compressed, demanding, teetering on the edge of possibility, utterly draining, yet also out-of-control, micromanaged by distant institutions and individuals. The response from even the most privileged individuals cannot always be to sit up, pay attention, work harder, work to change ourselves—indeed, this is a mode of subjectivation that neoliberalism itself generates and exploits (Tokumitsu 2018). Sometimes, as Berlant also points out, the only possibility of resistance (or even the only viable response) might be to detach from experience, to evade pain and fatigue, to slow down, and (although she doesn't say this) to alter or even to lose consciousness.

A recent issue of a popular men's magazine includes a tongue-in-cheek feature called "The New Status Symbols: How to Be Better Than Everyone Else in 2018." Next to a cartoon of a bearded white man with a bun doing a pretzel yoga pose on a tropical beach drinking a veggie juice while taking a selfie is a text box that reads,

> We're not exactly sure when it happened, but sometime in the past few years, all the old signifiers of wealth and prosperity got flipped on their head. Uber replaced the sports car, and running a bootstrapped start-up is cooler than heading a Fortune 500 company. Now status is all about experiences, man. And getting lots of sleep. To help you make sense of the newfangled yet hyper-competitive world of being better than other people, we drew up a field guide. Just remember: it doesn't count if you don't post about it on social media. (Schube and Hansen-Bundy 2018, 34)

On a street corner near my urban home, a young woman hands me a small folded card. "EXPERIENCE NOTHING," it declares on its face, over a simple graphic of a supine human body against a blue field. The card is advertising a "float tank"—the sensory deprivation experience that is all the rage—and it touts the many benefits of floating, which fall under the headings of relaxation and meditation, broadly construed. Some people, we learn, have "drafted whole portions of books while floating." This obviously piques my interest, but it seems contradictory with the claim that I could "experience nothing." What is this "nothing" I'll be "experiencing," and if I'm experiencing it, isn't is *something*?

These two moments from popular culture capture two key ambiguities in the concept of "experience." On the one hand, not everything that happens to us counts as experience. We build ourselves as special and distinctive subjects by doing special and distinctive things—only these count as "experiences." We also know, however, that the "hypercompetitive world" in which individuals vie for status and compare their formative experiences on Instagram is exhausting and a bit depressing. On the other hand, then, we can withdraw from experience altogether and give ourselves respite for an hour by lying in magnesium-saturated water, having no experience at all. Almost as if the float tank purveyors are hedging their bets against our reluctance to "experience nothing" (which could, after all, also be achieved by having a nap for free), they stress that this is a special kind of nothing—ironically, an experience of nothing that will help me finish my book or visualize my next artwork, thereby contributing to my personal cachet in a more round-about and restful way. These examples show that we all tacitly recognize that "experience" functions to sediment subjectivity, and that experience has a constitutive outside—things that happen to us that do not quite count *as* experiences (whether because they are not exciting enough, or because they involve forms of consciousness that don't meet the bar for experience). Experience, in other words, is a complex social and political category as well as a complex epistemic concept.

If "(an)aesthetics" is one of the keywords of this book, "experience" is the other. In one version of empiricism, experience is best understood as a stream of sensory inputs entering individual consciousness (see Janack 2012, chs. 1 and 2). I don't think this is all "experience" is, but it is one of its frames of reference, and when we look at Buck-Morss's analysis we can see how our experience itself may be radically different in a postmodern age—not only because of the fact of the internet or the electric car, but structurally, because of the speed, diversity, form of delivery, range, and potential modulation of those sensory inputs. Note that in the formations loosely and tendentiously described as identity politics, and their inheritors, the experience of injustice is central to the claims making of oppressed agents (Heyes [2002] 2016). As I outline in chapter 1, arguments about experience in this context have been largely organized around whose experience gets to count as representative for political purposes; a less well-known literature also focuses on what experience *is*—specifically, whether it is a product of discourse or an origin of subjectivity. Both these debates, in different ways, sidestep another question about how the transformation of conditions of experience also transforms possibilities for subjectivity. We are having a crisis of experience: bombarded with inputs, and undergoing a contraction of the present and a speeded-up world, we cannot so straightforwardly rely on experience anymore as the basis for an enduring subjectivity. Our experience itself is fragmented and continually receding. Thus, if experience motivates political action, the very basis of our common organizing is undercut. We cannot, however, turn to larger historical stories about the forms our subjectivity takes and dismiss experience out of hand as a basis for political knowledge. As Gayatri Spivak provocatively asked, can the subaltern speak? Not if she is merely a discursive product, the answer went. To reject the epistemic value of experience this wholeheartedly is to undermine important arguments in standpoint theory that show how social location matters to understanding political structures.

If the term "identity politics" seems a little passé, the testimonial impulse in the politics of gender and sexuality has not waned.

Indeed, having experience has become a task, or project—a demand of post-liberal postmodernity (and also of feminism) that we make ourselves through trial and challenge, that we accumulate exciting events, that we engage in the lifelong fashioning to which Berlant refers. On vacation in Mexico I see a shuttle bus covered with an image of beautiful thatched cabanas standing in tranquil cerulean water, with a stenciled message: "This is not a resort. This is an experience." In this vernacular, as in my first example, "experience" harks back to an archaic English usage as an experiment or test, one that will (presumably) enrich your personal archive and make you a more complex and worthier human than tourists who go to cheaper all-inclusives and spend the week lying on a crowded beach drinking anemic margaritas. Here, experience is yoked to agency. Experience is not just something I have but something I curate. I return to this theme in chapters 3 and 4 to show how normative temporality supports productive action and marginalizes inaction, including passive resistance. Here I'll preview one case analysis that brings together experience, agency, and (an)aesthetics, and to which I'll return.

In her book *Skintight: An Anatomy of Cosmetic Surgery*, Meredith Jones describes how cosmetic surgery devotee Lolo Ferrari loved the oblivion of general anaesthesia and its capacity to suspend her life during a fairy-tale "enchanted sleep," allowing her to wake up transformed without any further exercise of agency (Jones 2008, 129–49). Ferrari was an ordinary middle-class French girl turned porn star and minor celebrity who died in 2000 at the age of thirty-seven of a (possibly suicidal) overdose of prescription drugs, including painkillers. She was best known for having the largest breast implants in the world, and at her death her chest was said to measure seventy-one inches. In her challenging analysis, Jones comments on Ferrari's avowed love of general anaesthesia: "Like the stereotypical promiscuous woman who seeks out sex and enjoys it too much Ferrari is too vocal about her taste for unconscious-ness. In a culture where self-control is paramount and there is a growing cult of self-determination and self-awareness, the notion of willingly surrendering to an anaesthetic is something abhorrent, something definitely not meant to be pleasurable, but perhaps something very seductive as well."[6]

Jones contrasts Ferrari with ORLAN, the performance artist who once made having cosmetic surgeries into her art form: "Orlan and Ferrari, two extreme practitioners of cosmetic surgery, are opposites in relation to agency. Orlan remains determinedly conscious during her operations, directing the proceedings, talking to the audience. In stark contrast Ferrari completely gives herself over the surgeon, describing the loss of power via general anaesthetic as a joy that she 'adores'" (Jones 2008, 132).[7] ORLAN certainly considers herself transgressive and has been hailed as undermining the conformity of cosmetic surgery. As Jones implies, however, she is the more conventional feminist. Taking control over the surgical scene, insisting on consciousness (a necessary condition of agency, we assume), and confronting the nonnormative changes to her body as they occur, she is very much a practitioner of the aesthetic rather than the anaesthetic. Ferrari, by contrast, fails one feminist test: she is passive, surrendering to her (male) doctors' ministrations, embracing and enjoying the "black hole" of general anaesthesia. Yet Ferrari could also be seen as someone who took extreme risks with her life and body, engaging in the limit-experiences of general anaesthesia and powerful narcotics, practicing self-transformation of the most dramatic kind, and making herself into a transgressive work of art.

This example, I've discovered, upsets a lot of feminists. Some think ORLAN is a groundbreaking critic, while others think she's a mediocre sensationalist, but everyone agrees she's a go-getter, a game changer, a challenging person.[8] Ferrari's altered body, though, is typically treated—by feminists and nonfeminists alike—as an object of ridicule, disgust, or pity. No one really thinks she had anything to say, and the kindest interpretations of her life read her as a pathetic victim (of abuse, patriarchy, or celebrity culture). While she may be an object lesson for feminism, she is not a feminist subject. Nonetheless, Ferrari embodies, Jones suggests, a paradoxical relation to aesthetic existence. Transforming herself by surrendering her agency, she is both a victim of an utterly normative femininity, and a self-made woman. What could we learn from her? Specifically: we are all faced with demands that we prove our personhood by demonstrating certain capacities associated with agency. What are the genealogies of these demands? From what political contexts do they emerge?

I learned this from Marx and Foucault, although many other radical thinkers make the same point: historically, the emergence of the modern liberal self as an intellectual ideal comes hand in hand with the emergence of forms of power that diminish and manipulate human beings in new ways. The capacities with which this self is endowed—such as autonomy, reason, and critique—are not transcendental, nor are they universal gifts of progress. Instead they are historically and culturally situated capacities that are differentially available within contexts of serious (and in some cases growing) inequality and exploitation. This doesn't mean feminists should reject any of them. We have excellent grounds to cultivate greater autonomy for women, to defend our capacity to reason, or our ability to offer critique. It does mean, though, that we should ask about how the philosophical quest to cultivate a self is caught up with structures of power that also constrain and manage us.

ON METHOD

This quest—to cultivate an aesthetics of existence in the context of understanding our own histories—is intellectually perplexing and paradoxical, but most of all (I find) it is methodologically challenging. What kind of *science humaine* do we need to free us from dogmas of necessity while not fetishizing autonomy? I have long been interested, too, in related paradoxes of freedom: Could freedom live in accepting what is as well as in the exercise of the will? Could freedom be found in an as-yet-unknown (and in-principle-unknowable) future as well as in programmatic recommendations? Is freedom a quality of subjects, or a worldly practice (Heyes 2018)? I started thinking about these paradoxes because so many of the technologies of the gendered self institutionalized in Western culture offer themselves to us as liberatory yet ultimately rely on a painful and futile voluntarist individualism that eschews real political change. Drawing on Foucault's method, my last book detailed the genealogy (including the contradictions) of a certain understanding of the self—as an authentic inner substance that must be realized on the surface of the flesh (Heyes 2007). I was interested in that understanding as it manifested in several different technologies (changing sex, losing weight, and having cosmetic surgery) that clearly had historically and culturally specific meaning but that were often construed (both in a cultural imaginary *and* in the self-conception of individuals) as essential personal truths. I wrestled with the interaction of the structural and the individual: having done a genealogy of trans identities, for example, what follows for how any one of us—including but not only those who want to "change sex"—can and should relate to our own gendered subjectivity (Heyes 2003; Heyes 2007, ch. 2; Heyes 2009)? I construed such questions as ethical, and they are; they are, however, also questions within ethical frameworks that are (contra how ethics is often practiced in philosophy) historically minded, sensitive to relations of power, and that place ethical demands on individuals with full recognition of the conditions of possibility for those subjects to act—or even to exist (Butler 2004, 2006).

Because I took this approach, quite a lot of my work for that book and for subsequent projects has involved reading qualitative, ethnographic research on how and why people seek to change their bodies to accommodate various kinds of social demand, to achieve intersubjective validation or "recognition" (e.g., Latham et al. 2019). Sometimes I think I am an anthropologist manqué, a scholar whose love of personal stories and the contexts in which they gain meaning has been vicariously satisfied only through philosophical reflection one step removed from those stories. As my intellectual career has moved on, I have tacitly tried harder and harder to narrow that gap between philosophy and everyday life, to bring the kinds of structural analysis I learned how to do as a political thinker together with personal stories without doing violence to either. Working through this ethical endeavor, I realized that I needed a more robust philosophical method for describing embodied lived experience "from the inside." This need stemmed in large part from my feminist commitments: the articulations of experience provided by oppressed people are an important window onto the epistemic elisions of frameworks of understanding that pass as universal. If Foucault's genealogical method aimed to expose the posturing of histories with a priori commitments to an essential subject, the feminist emphasis on experience aimed to expose the partiality of masculinist history by showing that women's perspectives pointed toward alternate interpretive realities that are often marginalized or entirely overlooked.

At the same time, I found that feminist theory lacked what we might call a *method* for describing experience, and perhaps especially embodied experience. There are of course better and worse writers—philosophers with varying capacities for "thick description" of things that happen to us. When we think about such key feminist topics as childbirth, pregnancy, rape, objectification, or racist violence, they all have an embodied component that is a necessary part of fully understanding them as sites of injustice. Historical or structural analyses of such injustices are certainly key to making sense of the relations of power that undergird them, but to keep analysis only at that level is to ignore the texture of individual undergoing that conveys the wrongs done and respects the subjects of that experience. Neither level of analysis can be reduced to the other, but neither are they (in my view) incommensurable or necessarily contradictory. I certainly wanted to have effective descriptive skills and to be able to cite and create narratives that would capture the personal. More than that, however, I wanted a model for making sense of lived experience that included philosophical principles, a helpful vocabulary, an established set of insights, an intellectual tradition and literature, and arguments with forms

I could appropriate. I turned to phenomenology as the most obvious example of such a method. Phenomenology was not only a challenge to learn for an analytically trained philosopher with no background in the tradition but also a tricky balancing act for a scholar with a commitment to Foucauldian genealogical investigation (Stoller 2009).

Genealogy, recall, is Foucault's Nietzschean method as he implements it in particular in *Discipline and Punish* and in volume 1 of *The History of Sexuality*, and as he describes it in a number of essays and interviews. Genealogy offers a "history of the present" (Foucault [1976] 1978, 31) that, he argues in his key essay, "Nietzsche, Genealogy, History," renounces any claim to "suprahistorical perspective." The "historian's history," Foucault says, "finds its support outside of time and pretends to base its judgments on an apocalyptic objectivity. This is only possible, however, because of its belief in eternal truth, the immortality of the soul, and the nature of consciousness as always identical to itself" (Foucault 1977, 152). In other words, "history in the traditional sense" assumes a transcendental subject who is the author of progressivist narratives that organize the events of the past into a developmental story. This way of doing history likes to take a great distance on its object, articulating the origins and achievement of, for example, liberty. The "effective" history of genealogy, Foucault argues, is, by contrast, "without constants": "nothing in man [*sic*]—not even his body—is sufficiently stable to serve as the basis for self-recognition or for understanding other men" (153). Genealogy as a method opposes the idea of any single unity progressing through history— such as the free individual, who acts intentionally and systematically to increase his liberation—and instead focuses on accumulating accounts of those historical threads that, taken together, create the conditions of possibility for certain kinds of subjects to exist. For Foucault, as I'll describe in chapter 3, the very concept of evolutive time, for example, and the individual who lives in it, are produced by discipline rather than preceding it (160–61). What Foucault seeks to articulate via genealogy is typically the emergence of a discourse—a set of beliefs and practices that come together to structure the conditions of possibility for a particular subject position.

There is a large literature interpreting Foucault's genealogical approach (e.g., Gutting 2005, ch. 5; Sluga 2006), but in the context of the tension with phenomenology I need only ask, What does genealogy do for us? It shows us our contingency by demonstrating how subjects emerge historically, rather than existing prior to history and participating in it. Foucault's much more specific and local approach (compared with the grandiosity of Nietzsche's genealogy) is a way of disturbing our illusions of unity, and depriving "the self of the reassuring stability of life and nature" (Sluga 2006, 228). For example, *Discipline and Punish* shows how "the disciplines"—practices in disparate areas of life (education, the military, hospitals, prisons) that share common features—converge to create "docile bodies." Docile subjects did not emerge as a result of a single organized strategy, nor are they a political phenomenon that can be understood as only regressive (or progressive); rather, the painstaking archival work Foucault undertakes reveals how a particular politics of truth functions to organize and limit the self-understandings available. It thus gives us, as contemporary inheritors of disciplined bodies, a perspective on our own conditions of possibility. For Foucault, then, genealogy is one part of a larger commitment to *critique*, understood as a radical challenge to our certainties about ourselves, and to our ways of knowing those certainties (Foucault [1978] 1997f). As I and others have argued elsewhere, critique can be understood in this context as an ethical practice explicitly in contrast to judgment, which undergirds a distinctive understanding of freedom (Butler 2002; Heyes 2007, ch. 5; Heyes 2018). Genealogy is deeply relevant to the subject's understanding of itself, but that relevance comes from pulling the epistemic rug from under our feet, rather than relying on any certainty about descriptions of who we are.

If this is genealogy, phenomenology is something quite different. The term "phenomenology" and its cognates are used very loosely across a wide range of disciplines to imply any method that focuses on first-personal perspectives on experience; in its most capacious uses, some researchers call their work "phenomenological," meaning only that they value personal narrative, or quote the anecdotes of their research participants at greater length. Of course, phenomenology is a much more robust philosophical tradition than this, with a long reach, but which for my purposes has proved most useful in its post–Merleau-Pontian feminist articulations. Introductions to phenomenology typically characterize it as a philosophical method that attempts to identify the essential structures of consciousness, starting from a first-personal perspective—it is the undertaking of the conscious subject to find necessary truths about the meaning of things in our experience. This project famously requires a bracketing, or *epoché*, of our own unreflective immersion in our own lived experience, to shift our attention from what is experienced to how it is experienced, and what makes this experience possible.[9]

Foucault himself had a troubled relation to phenomenology—one of the schools of philosophy he was trained in, and was expected to embrace as part of his philosophical education and milieu. His early work on psychology evinces that training. In 1954 he wrote an extended introduction to Ludwig Binswanger's essay "Dream and Existence," the same year in which he published his own short book *Maladie mentale et personnalité* (Binswanger with Foucault [1930] 1993; Foucault 1954). The first part of that book argues that the claims of the natural sciences, and of physical medicine, cannot be mirrored in (or incorporated by) the human sciences, of which psychology is a part (Foucault [1962] 1987, xii), and disavows any continuity between "organic" and "mental" pathology (10, 13). Foucault repudiates the reductive explanatory techniques that natural scientific models imply (and especially the pseudoscientific account of mental illness offered by psychoanalysis), in favor of descriptive (i.e., phenomenological) language. This language recognizes the symptoms of "mental illness" as part of a mind-world context, in which a form or style of relating to certain difficult situations comes to pervade the whole of a person's Being-in-the-world. The second part, at least in the original edition, attempts to bridge the gap between phenomenology and Marxism—a project that, as Todd May (2006) points out, was in keeping with the intellectual environment (dominated by Sartre) in which Foucault found himself in postwar France. During Foucault's *Wanderjahren* between 1955 and 1959 he spent time in Sweden, Poland, and Germany working on his history of madness, first published as *Folie et déraison* in 1961. During this time, he came to repudiate his early work and dissociated himself from phenomenology as a method and a politics. As he said in 1966, "If there is one approach that I do reject, however, it is that (one might call it, broadly speaking, the phenomenological approach) which gives absolute priority to the observing subject, which attributes a constituent role to an act, which places its own point of view at the origin of all historicity—which, in short, leads to a transcendental consciousness" (Foucault [1966] 1970, xiv).

Foucault's first book was reissued in 1962 as *Maladie mentale et psychologie*, with an entirely different second part that is more a précis of the central arguments about the history of madness appearing in his other work than a logical extension of the project of phenomenological psychology (Foucault [1962] 1976). Foucault no longer takes mental illness for granted and attempts to politicize it but instead makes a more radical move: he questions the historical constitution of the very category "mental illness," in much the same manner as *Madness and Civilization* had the year before. As May describes, this period between 1954 and 1962 is marked by Foucault's turn to the work of Georges Canguilhem and Nietzsche and his development of his own genealogical method. The subject becomes "more constituted than constituting. It is not subjective experience, but rather the formative history of that experience, that now becomes the relevant subject matter" (May 2006, 302):

> It is no longer the experience of the subject that is to be interrogated, but the categories within which that experience is articulated. If, methodologically, archaeology and genealogy step back from the immersion in experience that characterizes phenomenology, by the same gesture they step back from the content of that experience in order to take as their own content the categories and structure of thought that phenomenology takes for granted. If phenomenology takes subjective experience as its object and description as its method, the later Foucault takes phenomenology (and other human sciences) as his object and history as his method. In this sense, the rejection of phenomenology could not be more complete. (306)

If Foucault's driving political belief was that there were no universal necessities about the human or about human existence, then the forms of phenomenology available to him were especially antithetical to his mature philosophical methods. Although he never returned to phenomenology, he did return to more explicit consideration of experience and the role of marginal individuals and their subjugated knowledges in politicizing human contingency. Foucault might have turned to his contemporaries for exemplars of existential-phenomenological thinkers putting their work to more radical uses: although he had a mostly antagonistic intellectual relationship with Sartre that ended with a rapprochement of sorts, he could have been reading and engaging Fanon (of whom he seems to have known nothing); Beauvoir (whom he allegedly treated with chilly politeness, even though they moved in the same political and intellectual circles in Paris); or even returning to Merleau-Ponty (who taught him as an undergraduate).[10] Instead, his early rejection of existentialism and phenomenology seems to have directed him away from the figures of his own day who were using these intellectual traditions in more political and self-reflexive ways.

More or less since Foucault's death, phenomenology in the English-speaking world has divided. If you attend the annual meetings of the US Society for Phenomenological and Existential Philosophy, for example, you can still find plenty of panels devoted to the minutiae of Heidegger's *Nachlaß* or the role of the transcendental ego in Husserl. In a strangely through-the-looking-glass way, however, you can also find a parallel conference of presentations focusing on feminist and queer phenomenology, phenomenology of sexuality or disability, Black or Latinx phenomenology, and so on. These latter established and emergent modes of thinking all start from the claim—explicit or implicit—that the phenomenological reduction is incomplete. Far from bracketing everything except the pure transcendental ego, the phenomenological tradition has allowed vestiges of privileged experience to remain attached to it, masquerading as human universals. Rejecting the idea that there is any form of subjectivity that could fully exclude the "empirical ego," "posttranscendental" phenomenology thus aims "not to try to find an ego unmarked by naturalizing and historicizing processes, but to use the reduction to critically reveal the naturalization and contingency of subjectivity—the way in which structures, meanings and norms of being are socially and historically sedimented so as to make our experience what it is" (Al-Saji 2010b, 16n9).

This was what I needed. I wanted to learn to describe lived experience in ways that perhaps rested in moments on the essentials of embodied cognition, but that was consistently alive to the diverse realities of culture and history—and in particular the cultures and histories of gender, race, disability, and sexuality—as they are felt in our bodies. I wanted to describe lived experience in a thoroughly political vein. I was uninterested in a transcendental phenomenology, in other words, but urgently needed an existential one. My models for this kind of phenomenology have thus been twentieth-century thinkers who deploy first-personal philosophy to understand sexual difference and colonial racism—most notably Simone de Beauvoir and Frantz Fanon—as well as *their* inheritors—the late twentieth-century scholars and my peers who, really only since the 1990s, have taken phenomenological work further afield to integrate its insights with political theory. Sandra Bartky's *Femininity and Domination* (1990), together with Iris Marion Young's early essays, especially her germinal "Throwing Like a Girl" ([1980] 2005) (as well as the responses this work came to generate [e.g., Bartky 2009; Chisholm 2008; Ferguson 2009; Mann 2009]), were my first connection to feminist philosophy that took the specifics of female embodiment as lived (rather than as represented) seriously. As this project evolved, I was especially influenced by Gayle Salamon's work on transgender, racism, and disability (2006, 2010, 2012, 2018); Lisa Guenther's (2013) book on solitary confinement; Alia Al-Saji's essays on veiling, touch, and the visual in racism (2010a, 2010b, 2014); Linda Martín Alcoff's work in critical race philosophy and on experience in the context of sexual violation (1996, 2000, 2006, 2014); and Sara Ahmed's (2006) "queer phenomenology"—a corpus that models how to understand "lived experience" using the rich methods of phenomenology without treating the political context of that experience as detachable.[11] I also read contemporary essays in phenomenological psychology, phenomenologically inflected work on the lived experience of time, and Drew Leder's (1990) Merleau-Pontian analysis of health and illness, all of which appear at various moments in the essays in this book. Their methodological unity, despite their varied themes, comes from their attempt to interweave analyses of the emergence of particular subject positions with close description of the lived experience of those subjectivities. That is, they approach *assujettissement*—the process of becoming a subject and being subjugated—from two directions, the genealogical and the first-personal, with the aim of showing how these levels of analysis inflect each other and are indispensable to political projects.

Within most social science research, such a dual approach might not be considered especially controversial: there are structures, and there are agents who act within them. Even here, however, the question of how much the structure dictates the agent (or vice versa) has a long intellectual half-life that motivates methodological controversies in social theory. Within continental philosophy, with its greater degree of abstraction, the methodological challenges tend to be approached as theoretical knots rather than as practical problems of how to account for experience. As I show in chapter 1, genealogy repudiates the transcendental subject by showing how the very idea of such a subject has its own history; phenomenology follows the intentional threads of lived experience back to their condition of possibility—a transcendental ego that makes such experience possible.[12] In this sense, phenomenology is starkly opposed to genealogy: genealogy is intended to show how certain kinds of person come into existence, and it is (in theory) irrelevant to its method how those persons experience their world, while phenomenology takes lived experience as an epistemic foundation. My goal in the first chapter is thus to set out these theoretical tensions and outline in principle how my method resolves them; the work of the subsequent chapters is to show how particular phenomena of time, space, and embodiment can be approached from simultaneously genealogical and phenomenological perspectives. This book, then, is an attempt to model a philosophical method that moves back and forth between registers—between the lived experience of an individual and her conditions of possibility; the constraints on what we can be and do, and how we engage and exceed those constraints. Genealogy models a constant interrogation of our conditions of possibility as the kind of subjects we find ourselves to be. Phenomenology, however, has a related critical depth, what Johanna Oksala calls "the phenomenological imperative of ultimate self-responsibility": "phenomenology must," she says, "be a self-critical and self-responsible practice, a movement of thought that turns back, again and again, to investigate its own conditions and origins" (2016, 71).

APPLYING THE METHOD

The examples in this book are worked through using this method, identifying what it can show us about particular embodied experiences that invite "the crosslighting of two irreducible perspectives," the subjective and the historical (Oksala 2010, 14). They are chosen with an eye to the way the term "experience" functions in contemporary political life. My cases are also about "experience at the edge"—a phrase I coined to capture those parts of our lives that resist inclusion within the frame of undergoings readily available for social and political interpretation. As I've flagged, some things happen to us but don't seem to count as our experience, exactly, whether in our own minds or in the opinions of others. In this light, chapter 2 examines popular focus on sexual assault cases involving targets who are unconscious—whether because drunk, drugged, anaesthetized, in a coma, or asleep—which has drawn attention to the role of social media in both exacerbating and gaining redress for the harms of sexual violence perpetrated against unconscious or semiconscious victims. To be violated while "dead to the world" is a complex wrong: it scarcely seems to count as a "lived experience" at all, yet it often shatters the victim's body schema and world. I situate political anxiety about women's unconsciousness and sexual assault while offering a phenomenological analysis of its harms: it exploits and reinforces any victim's absence from intersubjective life, and exposes her body in ways that make it especially difficult for her to return to the shared world as a subject.[13] It undercuts her capacity to sustain a body schema that persists across time, as well as her capacity to retreat from that body schema into what Maurice Merleau-Ponty called "anonymity." While this analysis is generalizable, the harm caused by exposure of the body's surface and the two-dimensional visibility it generates occurs within the contexts of the racialization and sexualization of bodies. Drawing on Fanon's account of the racial-epidermal schema in the context of Merleau-Ponty's analysis of "night," the chapter argues that sexual violation of one's body while unconscious can make the restful anonymity of sleep impossible, leaving only the violent exposure of a two-dimensional life. This consequence is doubled and redoubled for women in visibly racialized and sexually stereotyped groups—who are, contra media fixation on the tragic cases of middle-class white high schoolers, more likely to be sexually assaulted. Finally, the way the assault is sometimes played back to the victim after the fact through the digital circulation of photos, video, or commentary can draw out the experience in a way that forecloses her future.

Philosophy of time perhaps especially clearly invites a dual genealogical and phenomenological approach: there is objective time as it evolves historically, and there is *temporality*—or time as it is lived. In chapters 3 and 4 I show how these two registers for philosophizing about time come together in the attempt to manage a postdisciplinary, neoliberal experience of social acceleration and temporal fragmentation. Chapter 3 shows a commonality between E. P. Thompson's and Foucault's historical accounts of time discipline—a way of representing, organizing, and experiencing time. Writing in the waning days of Keynesianism, they both describe related historical processes (industrialization and the emergence of the disciplines) that generate a distinctive temporality in which the clock becomes sovereign and time becomes a currency to be invested, spent, wasted, or profitably used. This transition enables not wasting time to become an individual virtue, and leisure to be brought within the purview of time-discipline.

Both Thompson and Foucault wrote just before neoliberalism came into view. I therefore go on to articulate an account of *postdisciplinary time*, which, I argue, has developed along three additional axes. First, it reconflates work and life by introducing the potential for work into every moment—including (but not only) through new communications technologies. Rather than approaching demanding and complex projects sequentially and incrementally—as Foucault describes the process of disciplinary time—postdisciplinary time requires both that the lessons of disciplinary time be learned and that they be fractured and reapplied to the challenge of simultaneously managing multiple complex tasks. "Multitasking" presents well-known challenges of attention, which in turn feed into a temporal experience both ruthlessly linear and circling or repetitive. The conflation of work and life has a particular gendered tenor, and I review some examples from the literature on the "second shift" to show how public/private distinctions are reconfigured for women who do the most housework and childcare. Finally, I suggest that postdisciplinary time generates its own affects: most importantly, it remains radically future-oriented, but in the absence of the step-wise linearity of disciplinary time it generates a generalized anxiety (that form of uncertain worrying about what happens next that can float relatively free of any particular object).

I conclude by suggesting that postdisciplinary time should reconfigure how we think about agency, even further away from an individual account that is premised on a temporally extended self, and toward a much more skeptical analysis that recognizes the value of not-doing.

The phenomenological tradition has typically understood temporality as a central organizing axis of lived experience, and experience itself as always temporal. We construct experience around what has happened, is happening now, and will happen. Our past is known and organized and to some extent interpreted, while the future is unknown and open and full of possibilities. As embodied subjects we always exist spatially and temporally, with an interesting bent toward the future: our eyes look ahead, and we most commonly and easily move forward rather than back. More subtly, some phenomenological thinkers understand the typical lived experience of temporality to require activity—the self-conscious completion of various doings that fill in and provide a framework for grasping the passing of time. Indeed, this bare assumption appears in marked and often unquestioned form in the way postdisciplinary time is articulated. Chapter 4 picks up my account of postdisciplinary time to suggest that it requires an antidote, an inverse, a time out of time rather than an "experience." I call this nonexperience *anaesthetic time*, and I provide an account of it that parallels and complements my account of postdisciplinary time.

Anaesthetic temporality, I argue, is a sensical response to postdisciplinary time, as a way of surviving in an economy of temporality that is relentlessly depleting. Not exactly the same as boredom or daydreaming (both moods that have attracted phenomenological attention [e.g., Svendsen 2005; Geniusas 2015]), anaesthetic time is "addiction lite" (as I show through comparing and contrasting research in phenomenological psychology on serious opiate addictions). It is a diffuse, drifting, unpunctuated, unproductive, and unsynchronized temporality facilitated by everyday drugs such as alcohol, cannabis, or "benzos"—those common sedative prescription drugs that mitigate daily anxiety. Anaesthetic time loves the night and doesn't care about the future. It cannot contain experience that is temporally organized—maybe what happens during anaesthetic time doesn't even count as experience because it is not taken up with anything we might call activity. I show how anaesthetic time is gendered, and how it is sold to white, middle-class women, especially mothers, through cheap mommy wine represented as safely bourgeois. White femininity, on the one hand, is stereotypically read as docile or submissive, while on the other hand educated white women have been (and have been represented as) upwardly mobile within traditionally male-dominated labor markets. This political tension maps neatly to a drug that paradoxically lets you check out at the end of a hard day. In reality, anaesthetic time may be more imperative for women who are under financial stress, while drug use is disproportionately stigmatized and punished for racialized women. Extending this analysis, I point out that within a biopolitics of life and death, rather than using drugs to speed up or slow down in temporary ways aimed at maximizing productivity, some populations have been deemed postdisciplinary *postsubjects*—not worthy of managed life at all, so much as a drugging-toward-death. Finally, I argue that sleep is the limit case for anaesthetic time. We must sleep to live, but it's hard to grasp whether (or how) sleep is part of "lived experience." It represents an immediate and involuntary suspension of existence and a total respite from postdisciplinary time. This sensory void represents a limit, an encounter (for better or worse) with complete withdrawal from temporal experience, including from the exhaustion of contemporary fantasies of autonomy.

Chapter 5, finally, articulates some of the historical reasons that childbirth is so difficult to describe, and why those descriptions have in any case come to be epistemically discounted, while interspersing this genealogy with phenomenal description of my own experience of giving birth. Narrating a positive experience of pain in childbirth, as I (ambivalently) do is politically fraught: it risks being complicit with histories of Eve's punishment or feminine masochism. As Elaine Scarry (1985) argues, it is also constrained by the notorious impossibility of putting pain into language, and the way that intense pain destroys the possibility of linguistic expression and even of subjectivity itself.

It is this observation that reveals that the experience of the *Leiden* (passion/suffering) of childbirth can also be a limit-experience—an undergoing at the edges of the subject's own intelligibility to itself that breaks down the self in a way that permanently changes it. Freedom, for thinkers from Heidegger to Bataille, can be known only by finding the edges of our human subjectivity. A "limit-experience" describes a unique, possibly entirely unexpected event that puts the self's account of itself into radical question, and in doing so redraws the bounds of its self-imagining. Because a limit-experience is embodied and extralinguistic, there is no method for approaching it, nor any after-the-fact description that fully captures it. One can, however, describe the techniques that happen around limit-experiences, or that generate their conditions of possibility. This is what Foucault imagined when he alluded to S/M or his Death Valley trip, or some spiritual traditions imagine when they foster epiphanic practices. I am reliving birth post hoc by building a story about it that will necessarily reflect my historical and cultural moment, but there was, before, an inexpressible limit-experience in the moment of which there was no self nor speech. This last essay thus reclaims the limit-experience from its embeddedness in existential heroism for the more mundane and everyday in general, and for childbirth in particular. Through its narration of a birth, it shows the edges of intelligibility and how experience itself sometimes is interrupted, only to be taken up again "after the fact" in a reworking of oneself as a new ethical subject. Again, this theoretical intervention also speaks to a larger public debate about "women's voices" in the delivery of health care that often struggle to capture experiences of obstetric violence as well as the existential aspects of childbirth (Shabot 2016, 2017; Shabot and Korem 2018).

Anaesthetics of Existence, then, is a book about refusal, exclusion, and liminality. It has been written with a keen sense of the dangers of assuming the autonomous individual as the basic unit in political ontology, at the same time as it takes seriously our individuality as part of an irreducibly plural humanity, as Hannah Arendt might say. I want to talk about what different people experience, especially when this experience is put under erasure by a political field and denied to us as political subjects, but I am also wary of the impulse (including the feminist impulse) to treat testimony as unimpeachable, as if it did not have (and gain) meaning by appearing on to a particular political stage, always in a long-running drama. If, as these comments indicate, what counts as experience is always disputed, I also hope that this book will provide an analytic frame as well as some content about those undergoings that fall outside experience or happen at its limits. The case studies in this book track the three "edges" of experience I outline at the end of chapter 1: asking how the interruptions of unconsciousness can be thought for a politics of experience; revealing the normative constitution and exclusions of experience as temporal; and asking after the possibilities of experience at the limit of subjectivity. They follow various arcs, moving from a melancholic essay on sexual violence, through a sardonic reading of privileged forms of "checking out" of temporal discipline, to a joyful discussion of birth; or from the most obvious "outside" of experience—unconsciousness— through increasingly subtle erasures. Thinking about experience as a normative category with a constitutive outside in this way enables experience to be resituated in feminist philosophy as a less commonsense political category, and a more politically useful one. Rather oddly for a philosopher, perhaps, I tend to be better at showing than telling, so there is a lot more to say about the theoretical method I'm developing here than I do say (mostly in chapter 1). That will have to wait for another time. I have tried to keep this book short, pithy, and parsimoniously referenced, in the hope that the situations of depletion it describes might not be exacerbated by reading it.

CHAPTER ONE

Foucault's Limits

EXPERIENCE AT THE EDGE

What counts as experience is neither self-evident nor straightforward; it is always contested, and therefore always political.—Joan Scott, "The Evidence of Experience" (1991, 797)

THE INTERPRETATION OF Foucault's genealogical work as representing a methodological break from his very early phenomenologically influenced writing is unsatisfying to me, even if it is not entirely inaccurate. Unlike the turn from the genealogical to the ethical he made at the end of his life, in which Foucault justifies the continuity of his projects, as I indicated he repudiated phenomenology in interviews and by trying to suppress the publication and translation of his early work *Maladie mentale et personnalité*, which nonetheless subsequently became the heavily revised *Maladie mentale et psychologie*. But his work maintains a palpable political concern with the contexts of social injustice and the experience of the subjected—psychiatric patients, prisoners, perverts. Here, perhaps, is where a thread can be pulled through all of Foucault: the thwarted possibility that phenomenology might describe the experience of madness without reductive, pathologizing explanation; his desire to challenge forms of historical thinking that attribute a transcendental subject, bracket the constitution of that subject, and thus ultimately script our accounts of ourselves in advance; and his turn to technologies of the self and to how subjects relate to practices of power and might parrhesiastically speak against them. Foucault famously said in 1978, "I haven't written a single book that was not inspired, at least in part, by a direct personal experience" ([1978] 2000b, 244), and his *History of Sexuality* was "a matter of seeing how an 'experience' came to be constituted in modern Western societies, an experience that caused individuals to recognize themselves as subjects of a 'sexuality,' which was accessible to very diverse fields of knowledge and linked to a system of rules and constraints" (Foucault [1984] 1990, 4). Although Foucault puts "experience" in scare quotes, the perspective of the individual on their "sexuality" (similarly flagged) is not irrelevant to the work he is doing. Indeed, the main purpose of the project is to show us how we are historically constituted, not so that we can cease to have epistemic relevance as authors of ourselves but so that we can gain critical distance from the forms of unfreedom given to us as deep personal truths (Florence [1984] 1998). *This* reading might ground Foucault's desire and my own to keep both genealogy and, if not exactly traditional phenomenology, at least a feminist phenomenological inflection in the same philosophical frame.

My interest in this chapter is twofold: it is in a recent literature on Foucault as a philosopher of experience, and with feminist writing about women's experience as a source of subaltern knowledge. These two foci for philosophizing experience are often in productive tension. Central to feminist practices of critique has been the gesture of revealing a false universalism—man's experience wrapped up as everyone's truth—by introducing theoretical models that take as their archive women's accounts of our experience. "Telling one's story" to and with other victims of oppression has long been a central method of feminist epistemology and politics. The accumulation of experience from multiple contexts can, if shared, sediment across individuals into political analysis—this is perhaps a philosophical shorthand for whatever "consciousness raising" has been to feminism. Whatever method is recommended for this transformation of experience into politics, it carries risks. In its more identity-political moments, feminism has leaned too heavily on what Sonia Kruks calls an "epistemology of provenance": "the claim that knowledge arises from an experiential basis that is fundamentally group-specific and that others, who are outside the group and who lack its immediate experiences, cannot share that knowledge" (1995, 4). While it's not clear that anyone was ever quite this epistemically maladroit, the assumption that experience is only an origin of political truth, rather than being the product of an already-existing politics, is not one any scholar of Foucault will defend, as my methodological discussion in the introduction showed. Further, feminists now know to ask how experience is reported and whose account defines political reality. The problem is not just that experience itself doesn't automatically generate politics but that how experience is represented necessarily carries its own exclusions. "My experience as a woman" is no longer a credible ground in feminist philosophical vernacular.

This chapter sorts through the debates about Foucault's own account of experience alongside feminist engagement with his work and with experience as a ground of politics. I am working toward posing some neglected questions about experience "at the edge" in these debates (to be answered by the case studies in the later chapters): How should feminist philosophers think about those things that happen to people but are tacitly or explicitly excluded from being within their "experience"? What general norms structure the sensations and undergoings typically reported and included as experience, and what do these norms tell us about what we consider feminist subjects to be? Finally, how might experience not only motivate politics but also itself act as a medium of political change? What makes an experience— whether individual or collective—transformative of how one thinks about one's self or the world?

EXPERIENCE IN FEMINIST THOUGHT

As philosophers like to point out, until the 1700s the word "experience" in English had a double meaning: first, it signified something like "experiment"—a risky engagement, a test or trial; and, second (the meaning that we now associate more strongly with the word), an encounter with the world, a first-personal undergoing (Williams 1983). *Expérience* in contemporary French usage retains this double meaning, which helps to make sense of Foucault's interest in the term. Of course, experience is also a philosophical term with a weighty history within numerous traditions; in his epic book *Songs of Experience* (2005), Martin Jay elaborates in over four hundred pages how philosophers from Montaigne to Bataille have understood it. Central to the many philosophical distinctions "experience" provokes is that between the prereflective encounter with the world, and that encounter as expressed through an interpretive frame: in German, this is *Erlebnis* (that which is lived) versus *Erfahrung* (that which has been journeyed through). As Raymond Williams puts it, "At one extreme experience (present) is offered as the necessary (immediate and authentic) ground for all (subsequent) reasoning and analysis.

At the other extreme, experience (once the present participle not of 'feeling' but of 'trying' or 'testing' something) is seen as the product of social conditions or of systems of belief or of fundamental systems of perception, and thus not as material for truths but as evidence of conditions or systems which by definition it cannot itself explain" (Williams 1983, 128).

My somewhat paradoxical epistemic and methodological proposition is that all experience should be understood as always already both of these—as immediate to us in consciousness, yet, however it is apprehended, as formed by a larger context that gives it meaning to us. Our capacity to be reflexive about this process will be key to making political sense of experience. We have all encountered political moments in which experience is held up as an irresistible lodestone—a first-personal encounter with reality that discloses the truth of the subject, and sometimes the truth of her world. We've also seen, however, how irruptions of testimony can be dismissed as lies, manipulation, anecdote, or marginalia, in favor of a grand view of political reality that has a merely tacit connection to any standpoint. One need only look at the painful drama that unfolded in 2018 as Brett Kavanaugh was nominated to the US Supreme Court. A woman recalls the long-ago night he sexually assaulted her, and recounts this experience, drawing thousands of protesters to the public sphere to augment her evidence with their own. For her questioners, however, she is a political pawn, a tangential gadfly who is either fabricating or misremembering (and perhaps to them it doesn't much matter—an interesting epistemic twist in the unequal gender politics of experience) something that never involved this man, using counterfeit experience to undermine him. He, too, answers questions about his experience—of homosocial bravado, drinking beer, sexual assault—but these are a less important part of the epistemic weave that makes him (a privileged Yale Law School graduate, a middle-aged white man with a long history of conservative jurisprudence) into the right kind of subject for this appointment. That an understanding of who is the best person to be on the Supreme Court is also related to whose experience can matter ought to be a legible political claim, but it struggled to enter this fray. This might be taken as the best evidence that feminists should continue our parrhesiastic efforts, adding more and more voices to the cacophony, until an alternate reality becomes so pressing it cannot be denied, but this impulse is not politically straightforward (Valverde 2004). Christine Blasey Ford told her audience about the posttraumatic consequences of the assault and otherwise recounted her past in the language of science (the laughter of the young men "indelible in the hippocampus"); she had already (in this case, over many years) made sense of the events in a frame very specific to her educational and intellectual contexts. Commentators observed that Anita Hill—an African American woman testifying twenty-seven years earlier about sexual harassment by a putative Supreme Court nominee who was also Black—had used very different language and been received in a very different way. Unsurprisingly given how much was at stake, Ford was accused by some of lying, and this charge is especially dangerous when the evidence of experience is not scaffolded by an existing hermeneutic frame. Demands in response that we "always believe survivors" have their origin in the fragility of subaltern avowals of experience that are so readily denied, but when people do misremember, tweak, or exaggerate their stories, or outright fabricate accounts of sexual violence—as we have to allow that they sometimes, if rarely, do—this threatens to bring the epistemic edifice crashing down, in a way that lying about what happened in, for example, an individual car accident does not undercut public perceptions about the reality of dangerous roads.

Feminist theory thus faces a challenge in understanding this doubly constituted aspect of experience. The second wave placed an early emphasis on attempts to reclaim women's experience *simpliciter* from epistemic and political erasure. Susan Brownmiller's recounting of the case of Carmita Wood, an admin officer in a lab at Cornell University headed by physicist Boyce McDaniel, provides a famous example of how both repeated experience for one individual, and the sharing of similar experiences across individuals, can generate a political breakthrough:

> As Wood told the story, the eminent man would jiggle his crotch when he stood near her desk and looked at his mail, or he'd deliberately brush against her breasts while reaching for some papers. One night as the lab workers were leaving their annual Christmas party, he cornered her in the elevator and planted some unwanted kisses on her mouth.... She requested a transfer to another department, and when it didn't come through, she quit.... When the [unemployment insurance] claims investigator asked why she had left her job after eight years, Wood was at a loss to describe the hateful episodes. She was ashamed and embarrassed. Under prodding—the blank on the form needed to be filled in—she answered that her reasons had been personal. Her claim for unemployment benefits was denied. (Brownmiller 1999, 280–81)

Here Wood lacks any language for describing the "eminent man's" actions. He does things to her that provoke negative emotions (and, we also learn, physical symptoms), but she cannot parse a response for leaving that does not originate in her own free choice; she cannot find an ethical or political discourse to make his behavior wrong, and her reactions into an unjust harm. It's an indicator of how far the feminist approach to sexual harassment and assault has come since 1975 that a cognitive blank at this level is hard to comprehend, but then there was no language. As Brownmiller continues, "Lin [Farley]'s students had been talking in her seminar about the unwanted sexual advances they'd encountered on their summer jobs,' [Karen] Sauvigne relates. 'And then Carmita Wood comes in and tells Lin *her* story. We realized that to a person, every one of us—the women on staff, Carmita, the students—had had an experience like this at some point, you know? And none of us had ever told anyone before. It was one of those *click, aha!* moments, a profound revelation." (281). As taken up by Miranda Fricker, the famous Wood case is an example of hermeneutical injustice: "the injustice of having some significant area of one's social experience obscured from collective understanding owing to persistent and wide-ranging hermeneutical marginalization" (2006, 99). We are very familiar with this kind of marginalization and with consciousness raising as a response, which has developed a new life since the days of Carmita Wood with social media story sharing. Here the institutionalized, iterative experience of unwanted sexual attention from men at work is communicated in a context in which an inchoate sense of wrongdoing passes through what Brownmiller describes as "one of those *click, aha!* moments" that changes the hermeneutic frame. Today (mostly) women and genderqueer people are coming forward to speak out with #MeToo about instances of sexual violence, where this social experience is far less hermeneutically marginalized but still difficult to speak about for reasons of power and risk.

This key practice of gathering experience and speaking out comes out of the erasure of marginal experience as an epistemic resource for radical politics. As the Combahee River Collective put it in 1977,

> There is also undeniably a personal genesis for Black Feminism, that is, the political realization that comes from the seemingly personal experiences of individual Black women's lives. Black feminists and many more Black women who do not define themselves as feminists have all experienced sexual oppression as a constant factor in our day-to-day existence. As children we realized that we were different from boys and that we were treated differently. For example, we were told in the same breath to be quiet both for the sake of being "ladylike" and to make us less objectionable in

the eyes of white people. As we grew older we became aware of the threat of physical and sexual abuse by men. However, we had no way of conceptualizing what was so apparent to us, what we knew was really happening. ([1977] 1983, 211)

This quote displays the slippage between experience understood as "seemingly personal" events that defy explanation, and a more robust account of experience as the raw material of political interpretation. While gathering accounts of "what happened to us" is a start for standpoint-informed organizing, it is not, as the Combahee River Collective knew, the end. A politics of experience requires, first, a process in which the location and partiality of the "us" is kept in question, and, second, methods for turning personal narrative into political theory that will always exceed the content of that narrative. The experience of being a woman—whatever that could be—is neither universal nor a sufficient condition of feminist consciousness (Mohanty 1992).

The challenge of these two conditions led feminists of my generation to be skeptical of consciousness raising; we know that experiences get falsely generalized (especially those of members of dominant groups), and that patriarchy shapes what stories we tell even when we speak against it. In graduate school in the mid-1990s I read Joan Scott's influential article "The Evidence of Experience," in which she argues that Foucault's genealogy is the method par excellence for challenging foundationalism, especially the assumption that experience can be epistemically transparent and have meaning outside a hermeneutic frame (1991, 773). For Scott, the appeal to experience as an evidentiary ground for a radical politics of difference is question-begging: as she says, it reifies existing identities rather than asking after their conditions of possibility; it decontextualizes resistance and agency, casting them as qualities of individuals rather than historical fields; and accepts testimony rather than asking how it is shaped. In short, "the evidence of experience then becomes evidence for the fact of difference, rather than a way of exploring how difference is established, how it operates, how and in what ways it constitutes subjects who see and act in the world" (777). Rather than reject experience as an epistemic tool, however, Scott argues, it should be reclaimed as always both explanatory and in need of explanation; not as an unassailable ground of subjectivity, but as its historical product. In taking Foucault's genealogy as the radical challenge to foundationalism, Scott prefigures a debate in feminist philosophy about the epistemic origins and contours of experience itself, to which I now turn.

CHARLES JOUY, SOPHIE ADAM, MICHEL FOUCAULT

One of the most-discussed and controversial moments in Foucault's oeuvre is the passage in *The History of Sexuality*, volume I, in which he recounts the case of Charles Jouy:

> One day in 1867, a farm hand from the village of Lapcourt, who was somewhat simple-minded [*un peu simple d'esprit*], employed here and there, depending on the season, living hand-to-mouth from a little charity or in exchange for the worst sort of labor, sleeping in barns and stables, was turned in to the authorities. At the border of a field, he had obtained a few caresses from a little girl, just as he had done before and seen done by the village urchins round about him; for, at the end of the wood, or in the ditch by the road leading to Saint Nicolas, they would play the familiar game called "curdled milk." ([1976] 1978, 31)[1]

This marginal individual was identified, in turn, by the girl's parents, the mayor, the police, the judge, and thence a doctor and "two other experts," who ultimately published the account of the case to which Foucault is referring. In his recounting in *History of Sexuality*, Foucault critically comments on the physical and interrogative examination of Jouy: "The thing to note is that they went so far as to measure the brainpan, study the facial bone structure, and inspect for possible signs of degenerescence the anatomy of this personage who up to that moment had been an integral part of village life; that they made him talk; that they questioned him concerning his thoughts, inclinations, habits, sensations, and opinions" (31). In so doing, they made him the object of "a judicial action, a medical intervention, a careful clinical examination, and an entire theoretical elaboration" (31). Acquitted of any crime, Jouy was nonetheless confined to a psychiatric hospital for the rest of his life.

For Foucault in *History of Sexuality*, the case serves a historical bracketing function: taken together with Walter, the "Victorian gentleman" who, beginning in 1888, published a detailed account of his sexual exploits in eleven volumes, these examples bookend a key period in nineteenth-century Europe in which "sex became something to say," and became subject to "a whole machinery for speechifying, analyzing, and investigating" (32). As Foucault will go on to argue, the explosion of discourse about sex, coupled with the contradictory hypocrisy that sex was something "repressed" that could not be spoken about, was a key part of the emergence of sexual perversions—deviant practices solidified as sexual subjectivities that bear disproportionately the weight of social anxiety about sex in general. Jouy is an example of psychiatric power producing the very "abnormal individuals" it then treats. Exactly what kind of abnormal individual Jouy is remains unspecified, although for feminist philosophers who have read only the brief recounting of the case in *History of Sexuality*, he is typically understood as a sexual deviant.[2] Whatever the truth of his abnormality, it is found, according to those who examine him, not in the machinery of speechifying sex but rather in his body. "What is the significant thing about this story?" Foucault asks, rhetorically, and answers himself: "the pettiness of it all." "These inconsequential bucolic pleasures," he famously states, "these timeless gestures; these barely furtive pleasures between simple-minded adults and alert children" provoked (he implies) an excessive, punitive reaction, buoyed by its own pomposity and hypocritically enabled by the repressive hypothesis and the mantle of emergent "science." (At the same time as Jouy is being made an object of knowledge for the world, Foucault sardonically remarks, "one can be fairly certain" that "the Lapcourt schoolmaster was instructing the little villagers to mind their language and not talk about all these things aloud" [32]). He represents Jouy as a socially marginal, albeit recognizable, individual, newly rendered as an object of psychiatric knowledge through his attributed status as a "half-wit" (*niais* [Foucault 1976, 45]) or "imbecile" (*imbécile* [Foucault 1999, 210]) (Foucault [1999] 2003, 300).

For a number of years in the early reception of Foucault's work, feminist philosophers understood Foucault's account of experience and his relation to feminist politics primarily through this rendering of the Jouy case. Linda Alcoff's widely cited "Dangerous Pleasures: Foucault and the Politics of Pedophilia" (1996) provides the earliest and still best-known response, and includes two main objections.[3] Foucault, she argues, is indifferent to the experience of the little girl, preferring instead to define the encounter through his imagined account of Jouy's experience. This is part of a familiar and typical pattern of epistemic arrogance, especially in regard to sexual violence, in which the interpretation of an act offered by the perpetrator (which, as I've shown, frequently meshes with a dominant misogynist interpretation within patriarchal cultures) has greater epistemic standing than any counternarrative the victim might supply. This is triply so when, as is so often the case, the perpetrator is an adult male, and the victim a minor female. Those judging the meaning of such incidents ignore or trivialize the experiences of victims in order to make the act fit their existing political understandings; Foucault is thus no different than any other sexist victim blamer.[4]

Alcoff is also, however, making a second, deeper methodological point about Foucault's relation to experience: "My suggestion is that we need to supplement discursive accounts of the cultural construction of sexual experience with phenomenological accounts of the embodied effects on subjectivity of certain kinds of practices. The meanings and significance of sexual events inhere partly in the embodied experiences themselves, whether or not they can be rendered intelligible within any discursive formation" (2000, 55).

This gesture involves not only a recourse to more diverse perspectives on the same incident but also to embodied experience as outside discourse. In order to make her point Alcoff re-creates a possible alternative reading of acts like those Jouy asked or forced the girl to perform:

> In encounters similar to the one Foucault described, the child exhibits a need to be held or hugged, to have affection or attention, or perhaps to obtain some basic good like money for food or shelter. The adult complies but on the condition of genital stimulation. This misresponse produces in the child pain and fear mixed with compulsion and intimidation, a duress created by uncertainty and the disparity between soothing words and painful, uncomfortable invasions, by the command to be silent and the assurance that all that is happening is ordinary and based on affection. One is told by a trusted adult to take the thing in one's mouth, to allow groping explorations, to perform distressing enactments that feel humiliating and foreign. While the child gags and whimpers (or even screams and cries), the adult sighs and moans, holding tightly so the child cannot get away. (2000, 54)

To reconstruct this account, Alcoff appeals to "the phenomenology of sex itself, which involves uniquely sensitive, vulnerable, and psychically important areas of the body, a fact that persists across cultural differences" (1996, 127–28). Thus, for Alcoff, there is a form of experience that stands outside discourse and the constitution of the subject; the bracketing of, here, "cultural differences" enables us to identify the essence of embodied experience in the context of sexual abuse, in a way that sidesteps the constructions of cultural misogyny.

Foucault's lecture series given at the Collège de France in 1974–75 was published for the first time in English in 2003 under the title *Abnormal*—some years after the debate about his attitude to sexual violence and women's experience in anglophone feminist philosophy had established his negative reputation. The lecture given on March 19, 1975, focuses almost exclusively on the Jouy case and includes far more description and analysis of Jouy's interactions with his social milieu, including with the girl, here named as Sophie Adam (Foucault [1999] 2003, 291–318). Foucault alludes again to the game of curdled milk, about which Adam boasted to "a peasant who was returning from the fields," and then, "only a bit later, the day of the village festival . . . Jouy dragged young Sophie Adam (unless it was Sophie Adam who dragged Charles Jouy) into the ditch alongside the road to Nancy. There, something happened: almost rape, perhaps [*moitié viol, peut-être*]. Anyway, Jouy very decently gives four *sous* to the little girl who immediately runs to the fair to buy some roasted almonds" (292). Foucault is at pains to establish that Jouy has a "firmly established" social, economic, and sexual role, and that Adam's practice of masturbating boys is commonplace among her peers: "part of a social landscape that . . . was quite familiar and tolerated" (295). Where once the behavior of Adam and Jouy alike would have "seemed perfectly commonplace and anodyne" (296), now there is potential for an appeal to psychiatry.

As Jana Sawicki (2005) predicts in her review of *Abnormal*, this more extended treatment of the Jouy case might have been expected to fan the flames of feminist critique of Foucault on experience. Here he might be read as confirming Alcoff's worst fears: a forty-year-old man drags a girl into a ditch and rapes her, and this act is interpreted as mutual—perhaps even an act of violence against the adult—for which monetary recompense is an unproblematically ethical response. Things haven't exactly gone this way, as feminist interpreters have, variously, accepted Foucault's "epistemic arrogance" but valued his account of experience (Oksala 2016, 54); understood his ambivalent repetition of the Jouy case to exemplify his genealogical method without judging the experience of the actors (Ball 2013); or acknowledged his narrow approach to medical-legal power struggles while situating Jouy in the context of a diversity of case studies (Taylor 2013). Accompanying the allusion to Jouy in *History of Sexuality* with the extended analysis in *Abnormal*, in other words, has complicated feminist philosophical understanding of Foucault on experience. In her 2017 book *Foucault and Feminist Philosophy of Disability*, Shelley Tremain undertakes a lengthy reinterpretation of the Jouy case and criticizes feminist engagement with it for its lack of textual support and failure to situate the case in the context of the history of disability (129–57). Socially excluded, ridiculed, and then eventually medically abused, Jouy, she argues, was understood in his own historical moment not as a sexual deviant but rather as an "imbecile"—an emergent category of cognitively disabled person who resembles a child in developmental terms. Challenging feminist ortho-doxy that Adam is a victim of sexual violence and Jouy a sexual aggressor against children, she claims that "given the historically shifting constitution of the character of sexual practices and sex crimes . . . this representation of these incidents is by no means self-evidently true" (151). Tremain's approach is to recover a genealogy of cognitive impairment in order to show, among other things, that feminist critique of the Jouy case has failed to understand him as "the predecessor of the (post)modern-day isolated, disenfranchised, and unwanted disabled person." She writes, "I submit, therefore, that when Jouy asked Adam to masturbate him as he had seen her do with other boys with whom she played the game of 'curdled milk,' he did so to secure a sense of belonging and recognition, to be included in the game" (151–52). She goes on to suggest that Adam, far from lacking the capacity to consent, in taking money for sex might have "exploited his [Jouy's] gentle nature and his desire for social recognition" (152).

There is much of value in Tremain's careful alternative reading of this case and of Foucault's broader remarks on sexual violence (see esp. 153–54). His analysis of Jouy, she shows (as does Kelly Ball in her longer 2013 analysis), provides an archetype of the abnormal individual in the European psychia-try of the nineteenth century, bringing together Foucault's genealogy of the monster, the infantile masturbator, and the recalcitrant child (146). She also challenges previous feminist interpreters—in my view, rightly—for failing to incorporate a critical reading of the genealogy of (what we now call) disabil-ity, and for an epistemic a priorism about the experience of Jouy and Adam in particular, and sexual experience in general. There is a contradiction, how-ever, in Tremain's challenge to the feminist interpretation of Jouy as rapist and Adam as victim, and her insistence that she can read the case instead through a different experiential lens that imputes countervailing desires and beliefs to these same actors.

The hypothesis that a young girl (Adam's age is not given) in the mid-nineteenth century could masturbate an adult—"imbecile" or not—or even have intercourse with him, and that this could be a normal part of the fabric of village life that has no particular traumatic consequence for her (or him) is not one we can ever, exactly, validate. It is, however, one that a genealogical method suggests we should countenance, no matter what its political risks in a contemporary culture that trivializes sexual abuse of children. (Tremain is right on this.) But equally, if Jouy seems from another direction to be a cog-nitively disabled adult experiencing the kind of economic, social, and sexual marginalization all too familiar from our current ableist milieu, we have no particular ground for making these into first-personal ascriptions either. Foucault does consistently tend toward the assumption that the incident was "commonplace and anodyne" ([1999] 2003, 296), so that he can justify his thesis that its excessive treatment marked a completely new way for psychiatry to function (293). As Ball has argued in her close reading of the case, his rhetorical style is intended to create the impression of a fairy tale, an endearingly parochial narrative that assumes a sinister and absurd significance (to psychiatric technologies) (2013, 55–56). In each iteration of its telling, she points out, "Foucault keeps truth, cause, and judgment suspended. . . . Indeed, and perhaps most critically, the only truth Foucault asserts is that something happened, the only cause Foucault offers is chance, and the only judgment Foucault lodges without hesitation is that which legal psychiatry defined and declared as its own. . . . Foucault pushes us away from foundations, leaving us only to trace the effects of an overreaction: legal psychiatry's hyper-production of evidence in order to substantiate the absence of cause haunting its truth claims" (54).

The lived experience of Jouy or Adam is unknowable: the 1868 manuscript from which Foucault mainly draws is not in any way concerned with the first-personal perspectives of the imbecile (or the child), despite its claim to be preoccupied with *l'état mental* of Jouy.[5] Had Adam or Jouy been literate, they might have left us some personal reflection on what happened, but in a historical moment when the abnormal individual is being consolidated, such an account would raise precisely the kind of interpretive challenges that this book attempts to meet. It certainly could not constitute the transcendental truth of lived experience (and falling back on an understanding of experience as bodily sensation that has meaning outside cultural horizons will always fail the genealogical challenge). No memoir could do this—although Foucault's publication of and commentaries on the memoirs of Herculine Barbin ("a nineteenth-century French hermaphrodite") and Pierre Rivière (who, in 1835, "slaughtered his mother, sister, and brother") indicate his philosophical and political engagement with the genealogical and the first-personal together. They show that he wants to resurrect subjugated knowledges, not in order to affirm the epistemic merits of testimony— far from it—but rather to develop a method for understanding experience that conjoins analysis of how discourse produces subjects with how those subjects understand themselves (Oksala 2016, 62–66). In this rather precise way, his work can guide the project of this book.

In a later phase of Foucault scholarship, a flurry of new literature recuperating his understanding of experience has been published—Timothy O'Leary's *Foucault and Fiction: The Experience Book* (2009), Lynne Huffer's *Mad for Foucault* (2010), and, most pertinently for my purposes, Johanna Oksala's *Feminist Experiences* (2016). These authors all suggest, in different ways, that Foucault has a lifelong preoccupation with how the self-reflexive subject understands their own relation to history, with self-transformation, and with investigation of how experience is related to (rather than reducible to) knowledge and power. Authors in this field concur that Foucault's mature conception of experience incorporates all three themes of his corpus: *The History of Sexuality* was planned, he says, as "a history of the experience of sexuality, where experience is understood as the correlation, in a culture, between fields of knowledge, types of normativity, and forms of subjectivity" (Foucault [1984] 1990, 4). Thus *Erlebnis* is only one component of a larger field. Within this field subjectivity as constituted through norms and subjectivity as lived are in constant mutual implication:

> Refusing the philosophical recourse to a constituent subject does not amount to acting as if the subject did not exist, making an abstraction of it on behalf of a pure objectivity. This refusal has the aim of eliciting the processes that are peculiar to an experience in which the subject and the object "are formed and transformed" in relation to and in terms of one another. The discourses of mental illness, delinquency, or sexuality say what the subject is only in a certain, quite particular game of truth; but these games are not imposed on the subject from the outside according to a necessary causality or structural determination. They open up a field of experience in which the subject and the object are both constituted only under certain simultaneous conditions, but in which they are constantly modified in relation to each other, and so they modify this field of experience itself. (Florence [1984] 1998, 462)

In this context, Oksala has attempted to recuperate Foucault's account of experience from Alcoff's critique, even in the face of what she agrees is his "male and adult pattern of epistemic arrogance" (2010, 2). The particular epistemic leaning toward trivializing the encounters between Adam and Jouy in Foucault's texts does not necessarily speak against the theoretical inadequacy of his account of experience, and nor is it a point in favor of phenomenological approaches. Indeed, as Oksala mentions, Alcoff's early articles imply an attenuated definition of phenomenology as the articulation of personal narrative (2016, 67). Phenomenology is not telling stories (any more than feminist phenomenology is telling counterhegemonic stories) but rather trying (minimally) to maintain a critical distance on those stories, to bracket their specificity and our immersion in them to relate them to larger horizons of possibility. If "discourse" constitutes experience from a historical point of view, while phenomenology starts from the subjective, that is not to say that either method ends there. Even if we can only slacken the intentional threads that join our consciousness to the world and thereby come to understand them, we still reconstruct lived experience using a systematic method. Likewise, although we are constituted through discourse, this constitution is engaged by the sensing, feeling subject in a range of ways, including through critique. Genealogy offers a method from the other direction for identifying the conditions of possibility of our own subjectivity. Although there is always the iterative possibility—even eventually the certainty—that we will fail to grasp some element of our own constitution, the possibility of reflecting on ourselves is real, not least because we do it. As Oksala explains, if experience can be approached from either of two poles—the objective and the subjective—Foucault and phenomenology start from opposite ends, but neither thinks the other pole is irrelevant.

Indeed, Alcoff herself returns to the question, "How do we come to interpret our experiences in the way that we do?" especially when those experiences include such sensitive things as sexual violation (2014, 450). Her answer there includes a sympathetic recounting of Foucault's emphasis on his trilateral model of experience as well as a more systematic attempt to incorporate phenomenological method. As Alcoff represents feminist phenomenology, "This tradition is not about uncritical expression, much less an empiricist foundationalism, but actually, following roughly in Hegel's footsteps, about the constitutive conditions that make experience possible. These constitutive conditions come in two categories: the transcendental, on the one hand, and the immanent or contextual, on the other. Immanent or contextual conditions allow us to animate, and scrutinize, such socially variable experiences as racial fear or feminine bodily comportment. Experience is, however, at the center of this analysis—neither unproblematized nor merely epiphenomenal" (457). On this reading, Alcoff seems to entirely close the distance between her own position and Oksala's.[6] In her interpretation of Foucault, Oksala identifies an ontological gap between the subject's lived experience and the discourse that defined him: "Our embodied habits and sensations are constituted in a web of both discursive and non-discursive practices," and "experience always incorporates modes of self-awareness and critical self-reflexivity" (2010, 6):

> The tension between the objective and subjective dimensions of experience is only a contradiction in Foucault's thought to the extent that experience itself is paradoxical: it is irreducible to either its objective or subjective dimensions. It is constituted by practices of knowledge and power—as we know from Foucault's influential studies of madness, delinquency, and sexuality—but it also importantly contains a self-reflexive and meaning-constitutive dimension, the modes of self-awareness. Instead of a clearly defined prism, we might think of it as a series of foldings: the subject must fold back on itself to create a private interiority while being in constant contact with its constitutive outside. The external determinants or historical background structures of experience and the internal, private sensations fold into and continuously keep modifying each other. (Oksala 2016, 57)

In earlier work, Oksala (2004) gives philosophical depth to this conclusion, positing an understanding of the body's relation to discourse that is neither reductionist nor naturalist. The historical materialization of norms, she argues, cannot be understood as determining a subject "constructed" by a discourse with no constitutive outside. A key resource for transformative experience is what Foucault calls "subjugated knowledges," which "refer to forms of discourse that have been disqualified for being below the required level of erudition or scientificity: they are nonconceptual, naive, and hierarchically inferior. They are typically the knowledge of the patient, the pervert, or the delinquent, and they make possible the local critique of dominant discourses" (Oksala 2016, 62). The case of Jouy and Adam simply lacks any articulation of a subjugated knowledge. In feminist approaches to a politics of experience, however, we are building archives for future historians that will enable the methods of analysis this book defends.

EXPERIENCE AT THE EDGE

One does not drive to the limits for a thrill experience, or because limits are dangerous and sexy, or because it brings us into a titillating proximity with evil. One asks about the limits of ways of knowing because one has already run up against a crisis within the epistemological field in which one lives. The categories by which social life are ordered produce a certain incoherence or entire realms of unspeakability. And it is from this condition, the tear in the fabric of our epistemological web, that the practice of critique emerges, with the awareness that no discourse is adequate here or that our reigning discourses have produced an impasse.—Judith Butler, "What Is Critique?" (2002, 215)

Feminist discussion of the role of experience in politics has been accompanied—especially within feminist *philosophy*—with reflection on what experience actually is that has been circumscribed by debates about discursive production versus lived experience. In the context of the feminist debates on Foucault's legacy, I've showed how whose experience gets consideration, and what epistemic status it is afforded, became key questions. I've endorsed Oksala's position that Foucault's account of experience does not reduce it to discourse, without adopting Alcoff's early (later moderated) view that lived experience has universal forms found in bodily sensation (Janack 2012). Like them, my philosophical challenge is thus to make sense of experience on this intermediate terrain where dominant discourse is in mutual relation with subjective life even as the two are not fully contiguous. In the end, this literature has reached a loose consensus: whether it's by means of a prism, a folding, a chiasm, or a mutual implication, the genealogy of a particular subject position stands in some ontological relation to the subject's own excess—that distinctive individuality that puts each of us in different relation to the situations we share—without being reducible to it. I don't know how important the ontological metaphor really is here: we have the capacity, as the essays in this book and the intellectual tradition of which they are a part exemplify, to stand in reflexive relation to our own lived experience understood in this frame, although just how deep our capacity to offer critique goes is surely a matter of iterative engagement with accepted norms and interpretations as they rub against our collective epistemic discomfort with a current form of life, as Butler (2002) suggests.

The debate around the Jouy case focuses on the important questions of who gets to represent whose experience, and on what epistemic basis (Alcoff 2018). Although I've showed the contours of this debate in the context of the feminist Foucauldian literature, to answer these questions is not to resolve every methodological question it raises. Missing from this treatment is examination of how experience as a category includes norms of inclusion as well as a constitutive outside—what lies, in other words, at or beyond the edges of experience. I am interested not only in critically examining the epistemic origins of experience but also in tacit philosophical assumptions about the *form* it must take—questions that cannot be easily separated. Asking where the edges of experience are is important for a number of philosophical reasons, related in a deep way to the debate about how genealogy and phenomenology treat the subject. What does experience do? One answer is that it accumulates to make a subject. Therefore, those things that happen to the subject but are not considered to count as experience are not part of subjectivity. This is a straightforward enough thing to say, but, I suggest, the case studies in this book highlight moments when whether an undergoing will actually get into the category "experience" is cast into question, as Scott's epigraph to this chapter suggests. The idea that things happen to subjects that may or may not count as experience suggests a more fragmented and less transparent self than feminist philosophers typically admit. Revealing the constitutive outside of experience also reveals how our understanding of what it is to be a subject—in specific contexts, and in the most general terms of space, time, or embodiment—is normed.

We can thus think of experience as being "at the edge" in three senses. First, experience is something that is taken to happen within a specific form of *temporality*, or lived experience of time. There are many different contexts in which this claim has content, but in later chapters I suggest that the emergence of linear, disciplinary time (and the transition to what I call postdisciplinary time) in particular make time normative: a framework for having and interpreting experience that tacitly places things that happen in other, nonnormative temporalities out of experience, and hence out of subjectivity. Making good use of time becomes a task, and activities that happen within (or generate) temporalities not readily assimilable to a commodity account of time cannot be conceived as experience—with all the implications for self-building that I have described. Specifically, only certain kinds of action— those that are considered "productive," most centrally—are taken to fill time, constitute experience, and thus sediment subjectivity. Doing things that produce no outcome, or refusing to do things, are not only ways of being that are often described as "wasting time," they are also tacitly characterized as not-even-doing. When Melville's Bartleby famously starts refusing his scribing work ("I would prefer not to") and sits staring at the wall, he is compelling because we don't know whether he is melancholically sinking into self-destructive torpor, or cunningly refusing the work ethic that would see him exhausted and exploited. Possibly, of course, he is doing both. Both these interpretations—of failure to act as evidence of mental illness, and refusal to work as an ethical failure—involve tacit processes of norming experience. One of the projects of this book is to show how these norms invite deviation (as every norm must) and function to place certain genres of undergoing outside the realm of "experience." Given the cultural valuation of experience that I described in the introduction, this is a significant but typically occluded political gesture.

Sometimes we use the term "experience" to imply a kind of jaded repetition: being very *experienced* as a qualification for a job, for example, implies that one has been through multiple variations on the themes of the position, and can anticipate and handle work challenges as a result of having seen it all before. Especially as we age, experience has this quality: the same things come around again seemingly faster and faster, and my sense of self is sedimented through the repetition of my past in the present. As Beauvoir says, the older we get, the more aware we become of our finite nature: "The old person . . . knows that his life is accomplished and that he will never re-fashion it. The future is no longer big with promise: both this future and the being who must live it contract together" ([1970] 1972, 377). Thus, the second "edge" of experience is in those memorable times when the repetitions of experience abruptly break down, and an undergoing—whether entirely novel or the thousandth time something has happened, whether a lightning moment or a more durable period—transforms the subject. We might start by considering those undergoings that are so profound they wrench the self away from itself, or transform the self in unexpected ways. For thinkers interested in personal and political change, the experience that does not simply repeat and sediment an existing subjectivity but generates a novel self-understanding or perspective on one's own constitution is epistemically key. In the intellectual tradition Foucault inherited, one term for this is "limit-experience," and the reading of Foucault as a thinker who permits no gap between discourse and lived experience simply cannot account for his own interest in this phenomenon— those moments where the self runs up against the limits of its own possibility, or is compelled to contrast itself with an alternate way of being. The limit-experience can be a secular epiphany—that unavoidably Christian term that signifies a flash of instant comprehension of the true nature of something, inspired by divine revelation. In his recent book on psychedelic drug use, Michael Pollan describes mystical experiences produced by taking LSD or psilocybin mushrooms that lead, for example, the terminally ill to understand the unity of all things and lose their fear of death (2018). More prosaically, sometimes the accretion or collation of experience generates a flash of political insight—the *aha!* moment that Brownmiller describes. This is a moment in feminist politics that hasn't been much thought of philosophically; it just happens. But how might we think about transformative experience in the context of political life and its abruptions?

A limit-experience, as Timothy O'Leary and Lynne Huffer have pointed out, can for Foucault also be an experience that defines a cultural limit, or constitutive exclusion that defines a culture's interior and exterior—a limit on meaning, in other words. For both O'Leary (2009, esp. 77–88) and Huffer (2010, esp. 15–36), the exclusion of madness-as-unreason by reason as described in *History of Madness* is Foucault's classic example of this kind of limit-experience writ large. An individual limit-experience, by contrast, and as Foucault describes it in his later work, is the moment when the experience of a particular subject transgresses those cultural limits, and this is where I focus my attention, with the important acknowledgment that a personal limit-experience gains its meaning in part from the background—the context of culturally prescribed and possible experience—against which it happens.

The gap between discourse and experience is often most apparent to individuals at the point where "embodied habits and sensations" are torn from everyday experience; where the subject runs up against the limits of itself, especially against its own lived experience. The kind of experience I am most interested in pulls me away from my habituated practices and customary inferences; it challenges and opens me to the new; it transforms my self. For O'Leary (2009), who has a similar preoccupation, works of literature are capable of effecting transformation. He similarly recalls that until the nineteenth century, "experience" in English carried that dual connotation of both one's meeting with the world and an undertaking, a perilous or testing encounter. In an interview from 1978 Foucault says, "The idea of a limit-experience that wrenches the subject from itself is what was important to me in my reading of Nietzsche, Bataille, and Blanchot, and what explains the fact that however boring, however erudite my books may be, I've always conceived of them as direct experiences aimed at pulling myself free of myself, at preventing me from being the same" (Foucault [1978] 2000b, 241–42).

Oksala suggests that "it is possible to imagine limit-experiences that fall outside of what is constituted by discourse in the sense that these abject or transgressive experiences are rendered mute and unintelligible in our culture" (2004, 110). Not all limit-experiences are, of course, positive, and indeed Foucault's own formulation is entirely agnostic on the utilitarian consequences of being wrenched from himself, transformed. He is interestingly unusual in his juxtaposition of the knowledge of his own mortality—after being hit by that car, he tells Stephen Riggins in an interview, he related the proximity of death to the most intense kind of pleasure (Foucault [1982] 1997b, 129). While for many people near-death experiences are psychologically profound and transformative of one's experience of one's self, they are also, on some readings, definitive of "trauma" and often cause prolonged anxiety and fear.

This makes it hard to think through why a limit-experience is ethically significant, especially given Foucault's concomitant resistance to prescriptive ethics. To find value in experiences that are capable of effecting radical shifts in subjectivity might imply that there is something specifiably wrong with that subjectivity in the first place, but I don't think this is Foucault's intention. Rather, he is critical of certain social practices that constrain our possibilities at a metalevel by making it impossible to experience ourselves differently outside of a culturally defined range. The value of limit-experiences for the individual cannot lie in any specific expectation of transformation but can only lie in valuing the existential freedom that comes with more possibility for self-transgression. To call an ethics "aesthetic" is to ally ethical experience with the experience of art: we don't look at a sculpture or watch a dance performance with the expectation that a particular norm will be conveyed. Every artist knows that the reception of her work cannot be guaranteed. Her art provides a space for experience—or for an *experiment*—the shape of which will differ between different members of her audience. Aesthetic-ethical responses to novel experiences are both unpredictable and unintentional, and this is part of Foucault's point. To approach our unfolding experience as if it could teach us a predetermined lesson, or with a particular political objective in mind, is already paradoxically to have decided what one is ready to learn and how one's goals will be achieved.

This insight is developed in a literature in analytic philosophy in a different, and perhaps more commonsense, form. (These two conversations—the continental discussion of limit-experience, mostly via Foucault, and the analytic debate about transformative experience and imaginative projection in the context of thought experiments, never seem to touch each other, despite reaching rather similar conclusions in different philosophical vernaculars that could be mutually enriching). For example, L. A. Paul opens her book *Transformative Experience* with an improbable thought experiment: imagine that you have the opportunity to become a vampire (2014, 1–2; see also Mackenzie 2008). All of your friends have already seized the opportunity, and recommend it. Yet, Paul points out, there are still no foolproof criteria for making a rational choice: you can't know that you will enjoy being a vampire just because your friends do—not least because they are now vampires, with vampire-like preferences. You can't know what it's like to be a vampire until you are one, at which point you will be assessing what it's like from within your new vampire subjectivity. Thus, Paul concludes, there are no rational decision procedures to follow in this kind of case to enable you to decide what you should do. "This kind of case" is not only imaginary. Having one's first child—a paradigmatically life-changing decision that Paul assumes is carefully planned and agonized over, and normatively so (71)—is a major transformation of the same order as becoming a vampire (82). The aftermath of a dramatically personally transformative experience cannot be anticipated (although in Paul's selective examples the experience is prompted by a voluntary decision, and can be seen coming), and thus cannot be cognitively modeled in advance. Paul is left, then, with the question of how—indeed, why—one might ever elect to have a transformative experience. What could it offer to the kind of feminist philosophy of experience (and the ethics-as-aesthetics) I have been describing? Her response is to support sometimes having experiences for the sake of having them, in the necessarily uncertain hope that the "revelatory character" of a novel undergoing will offer a value that goes beyond utilitarian calculus (92–93). To the extent one can choose to have a transformative experience, that is, it cannot (rationally) be chosen "because you know what it will be like"; one can choose it only "in order to discover who you'll become" (119; emphasis in original). Paul continues to parse the rational consequences of seeking out revelation, but ultimately her argument comes down to this: "If you choose to undergo a transformative experience and its outcomes, you choose the experience for the sake of discovery itself, even if this entails a future that involves stress, suffering, or pain" (120). In the course of this experience, one of the things you will discover is the parameters of your previous self: while the future self who is a vampire/parent will be a different, unimaginable subject than her human/childless predecessor, she will be able to look *back* on her own past, and understand her prior self from a new vantage point. I don't believe either an ethics or a politics can be entirely based on unpredictability or lack of anticipated consequence, but this insight into the epistemology of transformative experience shows (as my own discussion of childbirth in chapter 5 of this book suggests) the limits of engaging Foucault's "anatamo-politics of the human body" as a site of power with yet another discourse of sovereignty and control. The attempt to predict and manage how our lives will unfold is not only a pragmatically futile endeavor in many respects but also one premised on a regulative ideal of agency with its own disciplinary effects.

Foucault doesn't give many explicit examples of limit-experiences, in part (presumably) because of his aversion to confessional writing, and his emphasis on becoming, making life into a work of art rather than being told how it should go. Pleasure—new kinds of pleasures, or perhaps extreme pleasure, including as it approaches pain—seem to be key to his account, especially of bodily experience. In a situation of passion, he says, "one is not oneself. One no longer has the sense of being oneself. One sees things otherwise . . . there is also a quality of suffering-pleasure [*souffrance-plaisir*]."[7] Foucault argues that the discourse of sexuality closes down to the tiniest window the possibility of an experience not already fully contained in the power/knowledge nexus he describes. So our ethical responsibility becomes the creation of spaces in which more possibility for self-transformation is opened, where the self can see itself exceeding the background experience of the cultural moment. If sexuality as represented in the first volume of Foucault's *History* is, as Lynne Huffer argues, this kind of account of the foreclosure of subject-centered experience by a totalizing discourse, then we have to look to some of Foucault's interviews for a more personal and positive story about sexuality as a source of limit-experiences. Gay men, he said in an interview in 1981, are "taking the pleasure of sexual relations away from the area of sexual norms and its categories, and in so doing making the pleasure the crystallizing point of a new culture—I think that's an interesting approach" ([1981] 1997e, 160). S&M, he says in 1982, is "the real creation of new possibilities of pleasure, which people had no idea about previously." It also breaks down the idea that sexual pleasure must ground all bodily pleasure: "If you look at the traditional construction of pleasure, you see that bodily pleasure, or pleasures of flesh, are always drinking, eating, and fucking. And that seems to be the limit of the understanding of our body, our pleasures" ([1982] 1997c, 165). Some drugs, he also says, "are the mediation to those incredibly intense joys that I am looking for, and that I am not able to experience, to afford by myself." "Those middle-range pleasures that make up everyday life," he avers, "are nothing for me" ([1982] 1997b, 129).

This last quote shows perhaps most clearly that for Foucault personally limit-experiences, although found in "souffrance-plaisir" of a particular kind, are not readily found in ordinary, daily life. Philosophically speaking, I can see why: given the complexity and grip of postdisciplinary power, it might take something dramatic to tear the subject away from their habitual mode of subjectivation. This is one of the reasons that radically transformative experience is valuable: it reveals post hoc the contours of a regime of power-knowledge for the subject. Practically speaking, however, as Huffer (Huffer and Wilson 2010, 335) and Oksala (2016, esp. 59–66) stress, the limit can also be encountered in petty everyday experience, in the gaps between experience as a product of the knowledge-power axes and the moments when these products fail to match the relation of self to self. The limit-experience as imagined in Foucault—and, perhaps more explicitly, in some of his influences and his interpreters—may seem heroic, even melodramatic, and thereby perhaps inaccessible. This impression, however, resides more in the popularized examples (from Foucault's own life) of sadomasochistic sex or a road trip to Death Valley on LSD (Miller 1993, esp. 87–89, 245–52; Wade and Dundas 2017), or (from a broader literature) extreme body modification practices, physical endurance challenges, or radical performance art, than it does in the epistemic qualities of the limit-experience itself. Part of my feminist philosophy of experience is to show that experiences that are frequently trivialized and stripped of their existential significance can be rethought as powerfully transformative. The temptation to render our most intimate bodily experiences as private and natural—and hence, rather paradoxically, as universally shared—too often makes them seem ethically irrelevant. As Foucault teaches us more than anyone, this is an epistemic temptation that is deeply embedded in the discourses of psychiatry and sexuality, and indeed by now is a generic part of our epistemic frame. We are endlessly willing to reify subjectivities (especially to make them biological) as a mode of knowing ourselves and speaking our truth. We don't need to give up talking about bodily experience, my work demonstrates, but we do need political language for doing so in a way that respects its discursive production as well as its lived experience.

In looking for the edges of experience, I've suggested we should understand how it is normed (and thus what lies outside those norms, as my description of anaesthetic time in chapter 4 demonstrates). While experience often builds on itself through these normative frames, iteratively laying down subjectivity, it also clearly sometimes has its abruptions and ruptures, as when we have a transformative experience that brings us up against the limit of our selves. This is the third "edge" of experience: a more radical aspect of its temporal interruption comes from breaks in the cogito—being unconscious being the most obvious case. ("The unconscious" as a psychoanalytic category also undercuts the idea that self-reflective awareness is a precondition of experience, although that is outside the scope of this book.) Can we have experience when we are asleep and not even dreaming, for example (de Warren 2010)? This is the most literal and generally accepted frame for thinking about "things that happen to us that are not part of our experience"—a shorthand I've often used in trying to describe this book's topic, and that is my starting point in what comes next. Thinking lived experience when it appears discontinuous is a philosophical challenge that the phenomenological tradition helps us meet, as I explore in the next chapter through a reading of "night" and anonymity in temporal and spatial experience. As ever, my engagement with the lived experience of unconsciousness is also ethical and political: the chapter offers a feminist reading of the harms of rape for unconscious victims. There is no prior feminist theoretical treatment of this question, not because it hasn't been politically salient until now—concern about women being sexually assaulted while anaesthetized was a public issue in the 1860s when ether and chloroform were first introduced. I could add that Thomas Laqueur famously opens his book *Making Sex* with the eighteenth-century recounting of the case of a peasant girl, believed to be dead, who is raped by the monk watching her body and who wakes as her coffin is lowered into the ground only to later find she is pregnant (Laqueur 1992, 3–4). As Laqueur notes, debates about (what we would now call) sexual violence against unconscious women, mostly in the context of the connection between women's sexual pleasure and conception, have a very long folkloric tradition (245n4). The neglect of the hugely widespread problem of sexual assault against unconscious women stems in part, I suggest, from the centrality of experience (understood only to include conscious experience) to knowledge in feminist theory (and elsewhere) and hence our difficulty in conceptualizing unconsciousness as being part of human life, and thus available for ethical thinking (Cole-Adams 2017).

In this chapter I have sketched the importance of the category of experience to feminist politics, and how the problem of the simultaneously discursive production of experience and its first-personal nature has been understood, especially in the feminist philosophical literature on Foucault. To think with Scott that any particular experience as well as the concept of experience itself has a genealogy is already to think that no individual's experience is simply given, or can function prima facie as a signpost to politics. Rather than repeat this by now familiar point, I show its consequences by showing where experience has its edges—and hence by implication what contours it has. Experience and "what is not experience" are disclosed most powerfully in loss of consciousness.

CHAPTER TWO

Dead to the World

RAPE, UNCONSCIOUSNESS, AND SOCIAL MEDIA

RECENT MEDIA ATTENTION to sexual violence against unconscious women has largely focused on a certain kind of victim, the photogenic high school student assaulted by her male peers at drunken parties. In North America the most widely publicized case was in Steubenville, Ohio, where several teenage boys sexually assaulted an unconscious girl whom they carried between locations, slung between them like a dead animal—as a notorious photo showed. There was also the case of Rehtaeh Parsons, the Canadian teen who committed suicide after being photographed being raped from behind by male peers while simultaneously vomiting out of a window.[1] Then there's Audrie Pott—a high school sophomore who got drunk at a party, fell asleep, and woke to find herself partially undressed with drawings on her body. Photos of Pott became the talk of the school, and she killed herself the following week.

The main journalistic angle on these cases has been "youth rape culture" and the role of social media.[2] In particular, reporting focuses on the paradox opened up by communications technology: cases that once would have been dismissed as unfortunate but unprosecutable now turn into crimes with evidence, but that very evidence is the medium of a new kind of pornographic violence against the person.[3] In the best-known cases the girls have had advocates—their families and friends, Anonymous, feminist bloggers, an outraged public—who have pressed cases forward (typically also using the internet and social media) that otherwise would have languished.[4] More critical media have addressed the way these crimes are nonetheless still not taken seriously. Commentators point to the reluctance to prosecute or otherwise punish offenders, as well as to ways the experience of the victims is downplayed and the consequences for the offenders exaggerated. The Parsons case, for example, was controversial because police and prosecutors initially decided there was not enough evidence to press any charges, and it took a petition signed by more than 450,000 people to initiate a review of police conduct and, eventually, charges of creating and distributing child pornography against two teen boys (Hess 2014). Ultimately, the most contentious aspect of the first legal judgment in Steubenville (short terms in juvenile detention for two of the attackers) was the subsequent media slant that the lives of star football players had been ruined.[5] When in 2015 Stanford student-athlete Brock Turner sexually assaulted Chanel Miller while she was unconscious behind a dumpster on campus, he was sentenced to six months in county jail—a sentence widely criticized as too lenient, especially in light of the victim's powerful statement about the damage the assault had done to her—yet which Turner's father wrote was "a steep price to pay" for "20 minutes of action" that had left him without the life "he dreamed about and worked so hard to achieve."[6]

A final feature of these cases is my focus in this chapter: the victims were sexually assaulted while unconscious or semiconscious. This is a long-standing feature of sexual assault, whether the victim is asleep, drunk, drugged, anaesthetized, asphyxiated, suffering from a head injury, or in a coma.[7] In her history of rape since 1860, for example, Joanna Bourke describes popular concern in Victorian England about cases of sexual coercion involving alcohol or "stupefying draughts" (Bourke 2007, 54), as well as alluding to worries that the new anaesthetic drugs chloroform and ether were being used by unscrupulous dentists and physicians to take advantage of their women patients (53–61). The temperance movements of the late 1800s and early 1900s were intimately tied to emerging feminist concerns about the sexual dangers posed to women by alcohol—most commonly the danger of violence from drunken husbands, but also the danger of getting drunk for women's vulnerability and moral reputation (see Masson 1997; MacLean 2002). In her discussion of the trial of the rape of Mary Burton in 1907, for example, Constance Backhouse describes how Burton was cross-examined at length on her alcohol consumption—on the day of the assault and in general—in order to make her out to be an "inebriate" lacking in respectability and hence credibility (2008, 27–28).

The dangers posed by loss of consciousness for women are a theme of public discussion of sexual assault through to the present day. For example, in September 2018 the actor and comedian Bill Cosby was finally sentenced to between three and ten years in prison for drugging and sexually assaulting Andrea Constand in 2004 while she was unconscious and then semiconscious. More than sixty women came forward to say they had been harassed or assaulted by Cosby over decades, with many identifying a pattern of being given pills and then sexually violated while they were incapacitated (Durkin 2018). In May 2014 a man in Indiana named David Wise was sentenced to twenty years (twelve suspended and eight under house arrest) for drugging and raping his unconscious wife over a period of several years and making videos of the assaults. (The case made headlines because Wise received an unusually light sentence and did not actually spend any time in prison, and the judge advised his now-ex-wife, Mandy Boardman, that she should forgive him [see Matt Pearce 2014].) In 2011 the Canadian Supreme Court heard the final stage of a case that had provoked a tremendous amount of jurisprudential and media attention: in *R. v. J. A.*, the accused was charged with sexual assault against his common-law wife. The background to the case is complex and involves a history of violence (including violence against his spouse) on the part of the respondent. In short, on the day in question J. A. choked his spouse into unconsciousness—at least overtly likely consensually, as part of a practice of erotic asphyxiation—and when she regained consciousness she found him penetrating her anus with a dildo (an act to which she initially said she had not previously consented). The court was then required to decide whether consent could be provided in advance of sexual activity anticipated to occur after someone is unconscious. Although *R. v. J. A.* was widely treated as unusual and titillating, it has become part of a long jurisprudential trail in Canada, with precedent indicating that sexual activity requires a kind of ongoing, active consent that unconsciousness precludes (for discussion of the case, see Benedet and Grant 2010; H. Young 2010; Gotell 2012).

I could continue to provide examples from the news media or the legal record, and indeed the single most common response I've received in discussions of the material in this chapter has been a first- or third-personal anecdote about being sexually assaulted while unconscious. The examples I've given so far, while not atypical in this broad sense, do not, however, capture all the specific vulnerabilities that place some women at higher risk of sexual assault while unconscious than others. Many cases do involve very young women (girls, really), who are certainly vulnerable to peer pressure and inexperienced with alcohol or drugs. In addition, however, women with addictions; homeless or underhoused women; and disabled, ill, and institutionalized women are all multiply vulnerable to sexual violence while unconscious. All of these categories are in turn overrepresented among certain racialized groups—especially Indigenous women in Canada and African American women in the United States—who are also typically stereotyped as sexually promiscuous and morally unreliable. Cases involving women from these groups are much less likely to make the press, or to be pursued by police, or to result in a conviction.[8] Given what we know about the low rates of follow-up for all sexual assaults, and the powerful discourse of victim blaming that attaches to women who are sexually assaulted while drunk or using illegal drugs, or who are raped by someone they know well, it also seems likely that there are many more cases that none of us have heard of or ever will.[9]

The question that came to preoccupy me after thinking about this litany of examples was: what is distinctively bad about the experience of being sexually assaulted—especially being raped—while unconscious, or semiconscious, or transitioning between states of consciousness? A certain thread in popular representations of these cases makes it seem as though being sexually assaulted while unconscious is less serious than under other circumstances—again, because the cases typically involve consenting consumption of alcohol and an offender known to the victim, which are generally the scenarios that receive the least public sympathy. There also seems to be a tacit belief, however, that being less aware of one's assault while it is happening makes it less damaging.[10] In this chapter I want to argue against this view by providing a phenomenological analysis of the harms of rape while unconscious. As I outlined at the beginning of this book, phenomenology's central method is to provide descriptions of lived experience from a first-personal perspective, attempting to bracket the subjective particulars in order to find some essentially shared qualities. This often apolitical and ahistorical project has been adapted in the feminist phenomenological literature, which takes methods and insights from phenomenology's canon while situating lived experience within temporal and cultural horizons. This chapter is part of that literature, but it faces a novel challenge: in the cases I am interested in, "lived experience" might seem notably lacking. In these cases, the sexual assault becomes known to the victim because she wakes up while it is happening (the most common situation, as far as I can tell) or because there is some post facto evidence of it—fragmented memories or periods of mysterious amnesia, inexplicable traumatic responses, symptoms of having consumed drugs involuntarily, photos or video, pain, injury, disturbed clothing, marks on her body, witnesses, gossip, pregnancy, or disease.[11] Sexual assault in these situations, I'll argue, exploits and reinforces a victim's lack of agency and exposes her body in ways that make it especially difficult for her to reconstitute herself as a subject. It damages both her ability to engage with the world in four dimensions (through a temporally persisting body schema) and her ability to retreat from it into anonymity. In this way, I argue implicitly, unconsciousness *is* part of lived experience.[12] Deviations and interruptions in the stream of sensory perception, and the anonymity unconsciousness (usually experienced as sleep) provides are just as important to subjectivity and to feminism as discussions of waking agency and the cultivation of individuality. Sexual assault while unconscious can make the restful anonymity of sleep impossible, leaving only the violent exposure of a two-dimensional life. There is a final temporal aspect here: the way the assault is played back to a victim after the fact can draw out the experience in a way that forecloses her future, and this is especially true given contemporary communications technologies. Of course, women do reassemble their lives and recover from the trauma of sexual assault, as, for example, Susan Brison (2002) and Karyn Freedman (2014) have described in their philosophical memoirs. With such courageous texts, I want to counteract contemporary attitudes of victim blaming, which I think is made possible in part through the erasure or trivialization of women's lived experience. Simultaneously, I hope to articulate an equally philosophically rich and explanatory language for the particular harms of rape while unconscious.

RAPE, AGENCY, AND EMBODIED SUBJECTIVITY

In her book *Rethinking Rape*, Ann Cahill argues that rape denies the intersubjectivity required to sustain self-identity. She maintains rape as a distinctive category of sexual assault, although she broadens it beyond the traditional definition of nonconsensual vaginal penetration by a penis to "the imposition of a sexually penetrating act on an unwilling person," which includes the penetration of any bodily orifice by any bodily part or nonbodily object (2001, 11). For Cahill, this subgroup of wrongs has special embodied significance, which emerges from the meanings attributed to sexual difference and the special damage to bodily integrity that comes from penetration of the body's depths. In all cases of rape, she argues, the agency of the victim—her capacity to develop her own desires, beliefs, or preferences, and to have those receive

uptake (even if she is disputed or refused)—is eclipsed by the rapist. In denying those expressions, he denies her the recognition that she is a subject, defined in those moments through complex and mutual negotiation with him
as a subject. Of course, this is a negotiation shaped from the beginning by a
history and political context, which includes norms about men's sexual rights
and women's sexual responsibilities to men, men's lack of sexual control and
women's role as sexual managers, and so on. During rape, in Cahill's analysis,
the victim ceases to exist as an agent—to the rapist and to herself. As Cahill
says,

> When one person rapes another, the assailant utilizes his power to affect,
> destructively, another person's being and experience—a power that is a
> necessary aspect of embodied intersubjectivity. At the same time, the as-
> sailant severely limits (and assuming he is successful, effectively albeit
> temporarily nullifies) the power of the victim to practice her intersubjec-
> tive agency. . . . Because that intersubjective agency is essential to embod-
> ied personhood, an act of rape is more than a temporary hindrance of one's
> bodily movement, more than a merely unpleasant sexual encounter. The
> actions of the rapist eclipse the victim's agency in a particularly sexual
> manner. (Cahill 2001, 132)

Cahill's analysis is not explicitly phenomenological, although it is clearly indebted to thinkers in that tradition. It is a basic claim of existential phenomenology after Merleau-Ponty that my subjectivity is necessarily embodied
and that this embodied self is the ground of any possible lived experience. My
body is not something "I" "have," but it is the condition of possibility of any
I. I always experience the world from my body, as a *here* in relation to which
everywhere else is *there*. This embodied self also necessarily relies on other
embodied selves to allow it to build an ontological and ethical world. A body
schema is for Merleau-Ponty the total of my prereflective experience of my
felt self (Merleau-Ponty [1945] 2002). It is the organization of my embodied
experience that makes it possible for me to walk casually down the street without thinking, "left leg, now right leg," or to know that I can squeeze through
that gap, or move to hug my crying child.

Other philosophers have explained and applied this model in the context
of feminist thought (I. M. Young [1980] 2005; Salamon 2010, 2018), so I'll just
make one, less obvious connection with Cahill: on this model, agency is not
(or not only) the capacity of an individual so much as an embodied possibility
that emerges from much larger social contexts. We all make those contexts,

usually in small ways, at the same time as we are constrained by them—a critique to which I return in a more pointed way in chapter 3. Rape massively emphasizes this latter moment, when an individual woman's choices have become narrowed to the point of (what Foucault calls) a situation of domination, in which dynamic power relations are completely frozen. That process of narrowing is shaped by individual decisions only in a very small way, although of course the way rape is talked about makes them seem huge: if only she hadn't gotten drunk, if only she hadn't gone to that party, if only she hadn't fallen asleep on that couch. The feminist counterclaim that "only rapists cause rape" is truer but also not the whole story. That whole story is complicated, and emerges from multiple connected actors who are making systems within which any identifiable decision (to defund women's emergency shelter services, to pass a law on consent, to institute a new sexual assault policy on campus, to move in with one's boyfriend, to drink, to go to sleep, to rape) is a part of that whole. Cahill's account also posits that agency isn't just intellectual, but also embodied. For example, to freeze and smile politely when a man pushes into your personal space is an embodied habit more than an intellectual decision. If I decide that habit of action is antithetical to my interests, I will probably need an embodied corrective. Cahill's analysis thus correctly emphasizes both embodiment and intersubjectivity, but it doesn't pursue the way we make the world together through our bodies as far as it might. Nor does Cahill consider cases of rape in which the victim is unconscious—cases that I think incorporate a denial of agency with specific significance.[13]

SLEEP, "NIGHT," AND ANONYMITY

Before I turn to sleep and rape, I need to address a prior philosophical question: what is significant about sleep to subjectivity in general? Some of the contemporary social preoccupation with managing and minimizing sleep views it as a necessary obstacle to productivity, a hindrance to all the things I might get done if only I were awake. In this view, sleep is both the absence of my agency and a block to its continuous exercise. For example, the US Army is apparently continuing research into drugs that will enable soldiers to stay awake for ever-longer periods while maintaining cognitive function (Crary 2013). When I ask students if they'd take such a drug—during exam period, say, or even as a long-term proposition—many of them say yes. Those who say no often find it difficult to articulate why sleep is important to them beyond its mere biological necessity. If we *could* function without sleep, why wouldn't we? There is a philosophical answer to this question that makes sleep necessary to my continuing coherent existence. Recall that existing as an embodied subject, for Merleau-Ponty, involves existing in relation to space: I gauge my own body schema by referencing objects as out there, apparently separate from me yet a part of my perceptual world, and the boundedness and determinacy of those objects shapes my self-perceptions. Further, it is not just a matter of looking out at those objects: I must be able to move among them, to touch them or engage with them through my senses, to realize their dimensions and interrelation, in order to form a body schema. Likewise, I need other embodied subjects to join me in this project, to confirm through their words and movements that our shared world is real.

If this is the basic lived experience of space, then is there an experience of unbounded or indeterminate space? The phenomenological psychologist Eugène Minkowski labels this experience of depth "dark space," or sometimes "night," and describes it not as a third spatial dimension so much as a mysterious and immediate apprehension of density and totality in which distance collapses and I cease to perceive myself as separate from objects ([1933] 1970, 405–33). This account of the (dis)orienting significance of "pure depth" is taken up by Merleau-Ponty in his *Phenomenology of Perception* ([1945] 2002, 330–47), and in turn by Lisa Guenther in her phenomenology of solitary confinement (2013, 161–94). "Night," in Guenther's words, is "the name for an experience of space unhinged from determinate objects and from the limits or outlines that distinguish self from nonself" (172).[14] "Night" is literally meant here, but not only so: it doesn't have to happen when the world is dark, although darkness presumably facilitates an experience of space as indeterminate, lacking in bounded objects. If I were to spend all my time in "night," I would lose the ability to locate myself and other objects in space; my body schema would start to disintegrate. In fact, Guenther makes precisely this claim about the experience of prisoners in solitary confinement, although ironically this happens in a situation in which cells are illuminated 24/7. Another example she gave me is of people who undertake long-term solo sailing voyages, and who for months see only a vast expanse of water stretching to the horizon uninterrupted by objects or people. Prisoners and sailors often develop perceptual hallucinations in which the edges of objects become wavy and blurred. They might start to stumble over their own feet, misjudge their reach, or walk into walls. In more extreme cases, the prisoner, at least, might become "unhinged" and pace compulsively (184), fling his fists into the walls

(181), or feel his body being catapulted around his cell (183). Night thus has the potential to destroy my ability to locate myself in space and thereby the coherence of my body schema.

For Merleau-Ponty, however, night is also necessary to my continued existence. It is, Guenther says, "fecund and generative" (172), offering both a respite and a contrast to the typical conscious experience of bounded and determinate space. As I mentioned in my introduction, for example, the immersion tank—a large enclosed vessel filled with salt-saturated water at body temperature—is a form of sensory deprivation that is commonly offered (for short periods) as a restful and healing experience. The person floating in the water loses their perception of their body's own boundaries, and some users report their minds eventually settling and expanding into a sense of enlarged and peaceful unity familiar from many meditation traditions. Night (as the experience of pure depth), then, can be, at its limits, deeply destructive of the capacity to orient oneself in the world, but restorative when contrasted with normal spatial and sensory experience. Sleep is, arguably, one way of encountering night. In Guenther's words, "Sleep is the escape that both reconnects me to the experience of primary spatiality—to the night—and also allows me to retain and even recover my sense of personal identity, my distinction from the night, the root of my own subjective existence. The temporal rhythm of alternating night and day, sleep and waking, release and return, sustains the fabric of embodied subjectivity in a world that is experienced in depth, somewhere between the extremes of pure depth and objective space" (173). This suggestion finds an echo in the intuitions of those students who say that there seems to be something important about the daily cycle of sleeping and waking, of engaging the world and retreating from it (see also Wortham 2013, 58–67).

This retreat might be described in another way, not just in relation to night. Sleep also gives us a different relation to agency: while asleep I may continue to have mental content (I may dream), but I don't direct this experience; it is both mine and not mine, and thus it offers an opportunity to continue existing while taking a break from being myself, exactly, for a while. Comparing a night's sleep to a hysterical fit, Merleau-Ponty writes that "any decision that interrupted them would come from a *lower* level than that of 'will'" ([1945] 2002, 189). And that

> loss of voice as a situation may be compared to sleep: I lie down in bed, on my left side, with my knees drawn up; I close my eyes and breathe slowly,

putting my plans out of my mind. But the power of my will or consciousness stops there. . . . There is a moment when sleep "comes," settling on this imitation of itself which I have been offering to it, and I succeed in becoming what I was trying to be: an unseeing and almost unthinking mass, riveted to a point in space and in the world henceforth only through the anonymous alertness of the senses. (189–90)

When I am deeply asleep and not dreaming, I enter a world in which I no longer exist at all to myself. One way of saying this is to say that sleep is a time of anonymity. In Merleau-Ponty's phenomenology, a capacity for anonymity is important to all subjectivity. I develop my self-identity not only by actively distinguishing myself as an individual but also in those moments when I retreat from my specificity and rest in a neutral space:

> Even when normal and even when involved in situations with other people, the subject, in so far as he has a body, retains every moment the power to withdraw from it. At the very moment when I live in the world, when I am given over to my plans, my occupations, my friends, my memories, I can close my eyes, lie down, listen to the blood pulsating in my ears, lose myself in some pleasure or pain, and shut myself up in this anonymous life which subtends my personal one. (191)

In her reading of this passage in Merleau-Ponty, Gayle Salamon (2006) argues that this capacity to withdraw into the anonymity of the body is the converse and twin of the ability to relate to others, to open out and create a world. She makes this point clearer—and more politically pressing—by arguing it in part through Frantz Fanon's *Black Skin, White Masks* (1952). Recall that in this analysis of the experience of colonialism, Fanon, a Black Martinican, a doctor (a psychiatrist), and an intellectual describes his arrival in Paris. He encounters the gaze of a little white girl on a train, who utters the famous line, "Look, a Negro!" Fanon describes the painful experience of his racialized body as the object of this racist gaze, which carries with it the weight of a white man's history.[15] Fanon's body is laid out, rendered hypervisible by his blackness under colonial racism: "My body was given back to me sprawled out, distorted, recolored, clad in mourning in that white winter day. The Negro is an animal, the Negro is bad, the Negro is mean, the Negro is ugly" (Fanon [1952] 1967, 113). He calls this "the racial-epidermal" schema—a negative self-consciousness that overtakes the tacit body schema (110). As Fanon repeats several times, all he wants (that is denied him) is to be "a man among other men" (112). He wants to disappear into the crowd sometimes (literally) and occupy the subject position of the neutral, generic citizen (metaphorically). This is a more tangible and vivid description of what it means to be permitted or denied the bodily anonymity that Merleau-Ponty thinks is central to effective intersubjectivity. Lacking anonymity, Fanon not only has no place of rest or neutrality, but his attempts to go out into the world and be open to others are contaminated by the same racist overdetermination. When he "moves toward the other" he finds that "I was responsible at the same time for my body, for my race, for my ancestors. I subjected myself to an objective examination, I discovered my blackness, my ethnic characteristics; and I was battered down by tom-toms, cannibalism, intellectual deficiency, fetishism, racial defects, slave-ships, and above all else, above all: 'Sho' good eatin'" (112). He can never exceed this racist inheritance, either in his explicit attempts at active intersubjectivity nor, in a way more chillingly, when he tries to retreat to "this anonymous life" of the body (see Salamon 2006, 107–10).

When Fanon says "I wanted to be a man, nothing but a man" ([1952] 1967, 113), his words tacitly indicate both a racial and gendered component to this possibility: the black man in Paris of the 1950s cannot be just a man (i.e., a white man), and indeed there is plenty of sexual imagery in the racism directed against and internalized by Black men that Fanon describes (e.g., 63–108). Women, however, experience their bodies "given back to them sprawled out, distorted" by a differently sexualized gaze. This sexualization is always already racialized, in ways Fanon himself touches on but doesn't fully understand as forms of abjection: if the white woman is idealized as pure and privileged, the better to humiliate and reduce through rape, the black woman is scarcely rapeable at all, especially by the white man—either because in his racist imaginary she is not worth the effort "rape" implies, or because she is already completely his property. Thus racism and sexism both, and in mutually constitutive ways, preclude the possibility of an anonymous lived experience of the body.[16] We all need the space of anonymity—including but not limited to sleep—but for those whose waking lives are marked by the kind of hypervisibility and forced relation to a stereotyped self that typify racism and sexism today, sleep brings a special kind of respite that goes beyond what I suggested was a necessary (if necessarily intermittent) part of any four-dimensional subjectivity. How does this account of body schema, "night," and anonymity relate to rape and unconsciousness?

RAPE WHILE UNCONSCIOUS

Turning back to rape, I want to expand Cahill's argument in a direction compatible with her existing emphasis on embodied subjectivity while incorporating these concepts of night and bodily anonymity. There are two components to my extension: first, a more deeply phenomenological understanding of the kind of agency rape nullifies by rendering the body all surface, a two-dimensional "dead" image; and, second, an analysis of the particular wrong of rape while unconscious in relation to our need for bodily anonymity. Although these two related arguments stand alone, the rendering of rape victims' bodies as superficial artifacts that are denied bodily anonymity is exacerbated by a frequent corollary of sexual assault while unconscious—the taking and distributing of photos or videos of the assault itself, or of the victim's body before or after. Sometimes rape of unconscious women occurs without such images, and sometimes those images are taken while victims are conscious, but often the two go together for an assortment of practical reasons—perhaps because perpetrators want to pore over their deeds or brag to their friends, because it's easy to frame your shots when your subject is lying still, or because it was a DFSA (drug-facilitated sexual assault) set up to create amateur rape porn.[17] There are reasons, however, that cases involving the post-rape circulation of images of the victim have seemed sufficiently horrible to merit special media debate. The same harms perpetrated by rape of unconscious victims, I suggest, are exaggerated and extended when that assault is recorded, and extended even further when a community of voyeurs is created around the images.

First, rape forcibly exposes the victim's most private body parts to others' intrusion, including her body's literal interior—her vagina, her rectum, her mouth and throat. This renders her bodily schema "all surface" in a much more extreme way than Fanon describes, leaving nothing for her to retreat to. All of her body is somewhere the violent and destructive Other has been and left his traces. Guenther makes a similar point in relation to strip-searching and body cavity searches in prison, which are, after all, forms of institutionally sanctioned sexual assault (2013, 189–91). Fanon's skin is given back to him "clad in mourning," but for the rape victim even her body's inside is taken over when the rapist uses her for his own embodied ends. This philosophical point has a psychological counterpart: it is expressed by victims in feelings of being intensely surveyed after a rape (that is, even more than women usually are), especially (but not only) if the rape becomes public knowledge. Women report feeling that others are staring at their bodies all the time, imagining what was done to them and how their bodies looked. This feeling of power-lessness in the face of the gaze is intensified for women whose rape has been photographed or videoed, as images of their violation are circulated in ways they cannot control, perpetuating a collective visual representation of their objectification and loss of self. This feeling is compounded when the rape victim has been unconscious or semiconscious during her rape.

Let me try to make this point about bodily exposure more vivid. In 2012 California teen Audrie Pott was partially stripped while drunk and asleep at a party, and woke to find pictures and words in marker on her skin indicating that she had been sexually assaulted.[18] She had no memory of the assault, but feared that boys at her school were sharing photos of the incident. As the ex-posé in *Rolling Stone* in 2013 describes it, "Audrie started her sophomore year at Saratoga High two days after the assault, with the knowledge that photos of her naked and luridly decorated body were circulating around school. . . . [Her friend] Amanda told her she had seen a group of boys huddled around Joe and his phone and assumed they were looking at pictures of Audrie on the night of the party" (Burleigh 2013, 3). Writing to "Joe" on Facebook, Aud-rie accused "him of sharing the photos. She wrote that the 'whole school knows. . . . Do you know how people view me now? I fucked up and I can't do anything to fix it. . . . One of my best friends hates me. And I now have a reputation I can never get rid of.' Writing to another boy on Facebook, she said, 'My life is over. . . . I ruined my life and I don't even remember how'" (2). Eight days after the assault, she killed herself.

The *Rolling Stone* headline is "Sexting, Shame, and Suicide: A Shocking Tale of Sexual Assault in the Digital Age," and indeed the number, speed, and ready-to-hand nature of smartphones with built-in cameras and video cameras, and the way many people are networked through social media and texting, are central to the outcomes of such cases. Note that in a stand-alone infographic ABC News reported that on the thirteen smartphones seized in the Steubenville investigation, 308,586 photos and 96,270 texts were re-viewed (the large majority, presumably, unrelated to the sexual assault).[19] That's an average of nearly 24,000 photos and about 7,400 texts per phone—noteworthy figures that ABC evidently believed were in themselves a com-mentary on contemporary communications. Less often pointed out is the *effect* of the rapid-fire and relentless circulation of two-dimensional images of a person in lieu of intersubjective embodied engagement. Audrie asked, "Do you know how people *view* me now?" Actually, she wasn't quite sure how

FIGURE 2.1 Photo collage accompanying Nina Burleigh, "Sexting, Shame, and Suicide: A Shocking Tale of Sexual Assault in the Digital Age," *Rolling Stone*, September 17, 2013. Photograph by Jesse Lenz.

people viewed her—her fellow students wouldn't talk to her, so even third-personal narrative perspectives on her experience were being withheld. The images showed her unconscious body, mostly exposed, after it had been treated as a public space for graffiti, a whiteboard on which others had literally inscribed their meanings, labeling her body parts almost as one would a diagram of a carcass.[20] "In interviews with police later, [the boys at the party] admitted, to varying degrees, coloring half of her face black, then pulling down her bra, taking off her shorts and drawing scribbles, lines and circles on her breasts and nipples. [One boy] wrote 'anal' above her ass with an arrow pointing down" (Burleigh 2013, 2). *Rolling Stone* heads its story with a staged photo capturing the imagined scene from a bird's-eye perspective (figure 2.1): a young white girl lies curled on her side on a large bed, naked and apparently unconscious, her face hidden, with a discarded red plastic party cup near her hand. Squiggly green lines are drawn on her legs, and a goofy face on her side, while two uncapped Sharpies lie near her. The room is dark, but she is illuminated by eerie greenish-white light coming from five devices held by fellow partygoers who surround the bed but are somewhat physically distant, typing or texting or taking photos (it is hard to tell). The only one who is not anonymous is a young man sprawled out next to her (but not touching her), himself fully dressed, who is looking at the back of her head, grinning and pointing at her as he apparently texts with his other hand, his own face illuminated by the light of his phone.

This image doesn't match the details in the story that accompanies it in a number of ways: it is not clear whether Audrie Pott was ever completely naked, and the writing on her body wasn't just squiggles. Three boys were eventually prosecuted for sexual assault—including digital penetration—and there were no other witnesses to their actions, although at least one other girl helped Audrie to the bed. Nonetheless, the picture can be read as an apt phenomenological commentary. It effectively captures the profound isolation of the girl and her subjective absence at the same time as it emphasizes the community of voyeurs that is formed not only through the shared act of looking at her while unconscious and naked but also by capturing her image and circulating it with unknown and distant others. This is not a Merleau-Pontian form of chiasmic intercorporeality, in which to see is always also to be seen. These voyeurs, in classic Sartrean style, have the privilege of seeing without themselves being seen (even by their victim in the moments of the assault), thus assuring a profound anonymity that is the converse of their victims' exposure. (I would add that public discomfort with punishing a certain kind of perpetrator—"those poor boys whose lives have been ruined"—is perhaps tacitly motivated by the breakdown of the assumed anonymity of privileged masculinity through the publicity that is involved in being prosecuted for sexual crimes.) In the way *Rolling Stone* tells the narrative, some of Audrie's friends (girls and boys) later avoided her at school; she became detached from the four dimensions that made her existence real and instead started to exist only in some abstracted way as the unconscious subject of some photos. The boys weren't talking to her. They weren't even *looking* at her. They remained "huddled around Joe and his phone," themselves creating their intercorporeal community through the medium of her erasure. Audrie is frozen in time and space in this sprawled-out state, unable to begin reconstructing her self after rape in the way that Susan Brison (2002) has so powerfully described.

At least some perpetrators of rape seem to know that they have denied an intercorporeal existence to their victims. Consider, for example, the way that

Trent Mays, convicted in Steubenville of rape for digitally penetrating an unconscious teenage girl's vagina and of distributing a nude photo of a minor, commented, "Yeah, dude, she was a deady. I just needed some sexual attention." In a video of boys joking later about the assault, high school student Michael Nodianos says, "'You don't need any foreplay with a dead girl.' . . . He is laughing uncontrollably, as are several other boys in the room. 'She's deader than O. J.'s wife. She's deader than Caylee Anthony' . . . Nodianos keeps on riffing, and his audience keeps on laughing, for more than twelve minutes" (Levy 2013, 3, 9). Although these remarks have been treated as shocking (and titillating), a necrophiliac aesthetic is commonplace in visual culture: it is a small step from Snow White in her glass coffin (figure 2.2) to the genre of fashion photography that Jacque Lynn Foltyn (2011) has labeled "corpse chic"—or, to the extent these images are sexualized, corpse porn. Numerous fashion houses have mounted controversial ad campaigns in which models appear passive, pale, and supine, possibly dead. For example, in 2007 *W* magazine ran a series of images of model Doutzen Kroes under the title "Into the Woods," in several of which she is featured lying on her back in deep autumnal leaves, her long, thin limbs awkwardly angled, partially dressed. These photos are among the most widely featured in online criticism of corpse chic (and are easily found by image searching). They seem to be messily trying to hit all the troubling notes: Kroes is wearing fur in all of the pictures, making her look even more like an animal corpse lying on the forest floor; in a couple of the conscious shots she also wears teddy-bear ears or a fur coat with its own floppy ears, conjuring a life-size stuffed toy; or she sports a giant bow in her hair, or a teddy bear lies alongside her, evoking her childlike youth; in the most controversial images, she lies on her back with her eyes closed and legs slightly parted, and a fur coat is flung open, revealing Kroes's pallid torso, as well as the only other visible clothing—a pair of oyster-colored high-waisted lace underwear. The pose prompts the question, not only, is she dead, but also, has she just been raped (and left for dead)? Another Mert and Marcus shoot from 2008 features an equally lanky, youthful white model reclined on a huge red bed: her eyes are blank, one arm is thrown up beside her head, and the other lies across the covers; her legs are open, and she wears a very short, frilly white lace dress. The image is shot dramatically foreshortened, from the foot of the bed, inviting the viewer's gaze into a shadowed space between the model's thighs in another subtly necrophiliac provocation. In Miley Cyrus's campaign for Marc Jacobs in 2014, she is sitting pouting and brooding on a dark beach, facing away from a young woman lying stiffly supine and inert, her tousled hair spreading over her face, eyes open, in the sand.[21] I could go on; the iconography of the female corpse waxes and wanes, but never quite goes away—my most recent example is from a Gucci Instagram post (figure 2.3) in December 2016. Sometimes the genre crosses from implied demise to overtly featuring the imagined manner of the model's death, as in this much-decried 2006 Jimmy Choo ad, in which a white woman's beautiful corpse is dangling out of a Lincoln trunk in the middle of the desert, while an ominously dressed African American man (Quincy Jones) takes a rest from digging a putative grave (figure 2.4). The TV show *America's Next Top Model* featured an episode in which contestants were made up and posed to look like murder victims—each killed by a different method (figures 2.5 and 2.6). Corpse chic then recirculates in our visual economy, informing norms of beauty, desirability, and sexual availability. Notice that the vulnerability of these various sleeping beauties is a part of their appeal; to be reclining and unconscious is to have expression wiped from your face—a kind of auto-Botoxing (Jones 2008, 129–49).

Consider and compare the last two images here (figures 2.5 and 2.6). At first glance they look very alike, perhaps because typical fashion models are extreme outliers in the range of human femaleness: the women who compete on TV for prize contracts are very young; unusually tall and exceptionally thin, lacking prominent musculature; and narrowly built with disproportionately long limbs. Because they are so uniformly unusual it is easy to see this last photo as very like the previous one, and of course they are posed within the same genre. This last woman is also beautifully lit, and implausibly reclined against a red and gold sofa. She is also the only one in the series of images who does not look white, but because of the standardized features of the photos this isn't particularly striking. Race is only a tacit feature of corpse chic, just as the purity of Sleeping Beauty or Snow White is only quietly represented by their alabaster skin.

These pictures may *evoke* violence against women, but they don't actually *look like* violence against women. Imagine what real crime scene photos look like: they are poorly composed, shot to capture information in harsh light. They mostly show ordinary people amid ordinary objects looking very ugly indeed. In *these* photos, disproportionately many of the victims are women of color. In the United States, for example, an African American woman is most likely to be murdered at age twenty-two (about the age of this model) and is more than four times more likely to be killed than her white counterpart.[22] Andrea Smith (2005) argues that systematic sexual violence, including

FIGURE 2.2 Snow White in her glass coffin. *Vogue*, 2006. Photograph by Eugenio Recuenco.

FIGURE 2.3 Model in pink slip dress lying in the grass with snake. Gucci Instagram post, December 29, 2016.

FIGURE 2.4 Murdered white woman in trunk with black assassin. Jimmy Choo ad, 2006.

FIGURE 2.5 "Model fell down stairs." Still image from *America's Next Top Model*, season 8, 2007.

sexual murder, was a key tool of cultural genocide during settler colonization and continues to be a part of state-sanctioned violence against Indigenous women. In Canada a systematic study in 2013 suggested that there are 824 First Nations, Inuit, or Métis women listed in public records as "missing or murdered" (Maryanne Pearce 2013), and the continuing national scandal of settler indifference to MMIWG (missing and murdered Indigenous women and girls) reflects now-classic arguments in Indigenous studies that settler colonialism is an ongoing structure rather than a time-limited event.[23] If we recall the political realities of groups who have seen massive, systemic sexual violence and murder as part of racist and colonial projects, corpse porn avoids overtly eroticizing racism only to the extent that the presentation of models can avoid specific visual reference to this history.

Thus, first, the act of rape (and its technological aftermath) renders the victim's body fully exposed, open to scrutiny, and lacking in subjectivity. If, during that aftermath, she moves out toward those who have witnessed some part of the scene, they all too often turn away—to look again at her exposed and unconscious body on their phones. She loses the capacity to be open to

FIGURE 2.6 "Model stabbed." Still image from *America's Next Top Model*, season 8, 2007.

the world, to put herself back together anew. Recall also that the flip side of this becoming-all-surface is the impossibility of anonymity. Fanon is laid out through the racial-epidermal schema and thereby loses the capacity to be a neutral citizen moving through the crowd, or even an embodied subjectivity, retreating into the sound of his own breath and blood.

Sleep is a state of distinctive defenselessness for all humans that requires us to trust in the surrounding world as we fall (and stay) asleep. Unconscious, we can enter a space of anonymity that makes intersubjectivity possible. For women in particular it can also be a state in which we are not self-conscious or surveilled, and in which we get a respite from the anxieties of bodily exposure. Second, therefore, I want to argue that the sexual assault of a *sleeping* woman threatens her most vulnerable state of anonymity, and her ability to retreat into night. To be roused by someone penetrating or attempting to penetrate your body—as a lot of victims in these cases are—is to have the deepest place of anonymity, the part of one's life when one's existence is most dangerously yet crucially suspended, erased. Again, there is a psychological counterpart: women who have been sexually assaulted while unconscious report that they become hypervigilant, unable to close their eyes for fear of losing control and becoming vulnerable again. The victims of Toronto doctor George Doodnaught, for example, orally raped by their anaesthetist while semiconscious, gave testimony about this anxiety, of struggling to let down their guard and trust another to witness and protect their vulnerability (CBC News 2013; Small 2013). (This is something we all implicitly do every time we fall asleep, but that is intensified when the rape occurs in the doubly vulnerable situation of surgery.) This victim struggles to feel safe lapsing into the one form of anonymity that is biologically and existentially necessary for human life, yet ultimately she will have no choice but to revisit this place over and over. All victims of sexual assault find it hard to reencounter the contexts of the event, and many will choose to avoid particularly triggering spaces or people if they can. But no one can avoid going to sleep for very long.

A NECESSARY ETHICS

If you are foolish enough to read the comments following blog posts and online news features about prominent sexual assault cases like those I have been discussing, you find a lot of garden-variety victim blaming. Many people seem quite comfortable saying that girls and women invite rape—by getting drunk or high, by going to sleep in this bed or passing out on that couch. Despite extensive research on the incredibly low rates of reporting and even lower rates of conviction for sexual assault in general, others are concerned that sexual assault is too harshly punished when it involves people who know each other, who have flirted with each other, who are dating or married, or when it fails to leave cuts and bruises. For others, what gets called sexual assault is merely sex that is being vindictively reinterpreted as nonconsensual after the fact— that's not "legitimate rape," as US senator Todd Akin famously pronounced. Still others fear that legislating on cases in which the victim is unconscious might make the man giving his sleeping wife "a loving peck on the lips" into "a sexual predator" (Prutschi 2011).[24]

I am no fan of the criminal justice system, so this chapter is not a tacit demand for more police or prisons. Instead it is a philosophical response to these different ways of trivializing a particular subcategory of sexual assaults and their potential aftereffects. I am trying to create a richer language for thinking about the harm involved here—a harm that has, after all, led a number of victims to suicide.

It might seem, conversely, as though I've exaggerated the personal destruction that rape while unconscious can wreak. I am *not* arguing that no women ever recover from this experience, and many do find the resources to reassemble their lives and relationships. By putting together cases that involve alcohol with those that involve drugs (illegal or prescription, voluntarily or involuntarily consumed), asphyxiation, anaesthesia, or ordinary sleep, however, I've tried to show that there really is no way of completely managing the risk of unconsciousness—and nor should women have to shoulder this responsibility. Agency is not just something exercised in a series of moments that happen in an open field of choice. My agency is also sustained or foreclosed by what other people say and do. The ethical challenge facing us all is to consider whether our words and actions contribute to a world where victims' subjectivity can be rebuilt, and not only destroyed; in which none of us see pleasure in sex with "a dead body," without the full presence of an Other's lived experience; and, finally, in which these forms of violence become awful to contemplate, rather than an image to gather around.

CHAPTER THREE

Down
and Out

TEMPORALITY
AFTER DISCIPLINE

To convince the proletariat that the ethics inoculated into it is wicked, that the unbridled work to which it has given itself up for the last hundred years is the most terrible scourge that has ever struck humanity, that work will become a mere condiment to the pleasures of idleness, a beneficial exercise to the human organism, a passion useful to the social organism only when wisely regulated and limited to a maximum of three hours a day; this is an arduous task beyond my strength.—Paul Lafargue, "The Right to be Lazy" (1883)

IN HIS ESSAY "Über Coca" (1884), Sigmund Freud recounts how cocaine—the alkaloid then only recently successfully extracted from coca leaves—makes it possible to focus and perform physical labor in otherwise impossible ways: "Long-lasting, intensive mental or physical work can be performed without fatigue; it is as though the need for food and sleep which otherwise makes itself felt peremptorily at certain times of the day were completely banished" (Freud 1884, 211). Freud admiringly recounts the auto-experimentation of a couple of medical colleagues who undertook prodigiously long walks on an empty stomach under the influence of cocaine, and also cites research showing it helped soldiers complete their "maneuvers and marches"—a concern of military drug research to the present day. As was the practice of his time, Freud also experimented with taking cocaine—"I have tested this effect of coca, which wards off hunger, sleep, and fatigue and steels one to intellectual effort, some dozen times on myself"—and parts of his essay are virtually a primer on how to get more done while under its influence (211). Freud seems to appreciate cocaine for this reason, and enthusiastically recommends it: "Coca is a far more potent and far less harmful stimulant than alcohol, and its widespread utilization is hindered at present only by its high cost" (212).

Because cocaine is now an illegal drug, used primarily for recreational purposes, it is difficult to find frank descriptions such as Freud's of its effects on ordinary activities such as a long hike or getting a writing project finished. We are left with a vernacular that mostly jokes about such pale shadows as strong coffee—although prescription drugs such as Ritalin and Vyvanse have emerged in the popular imagination as powerful focus enhancers, while the superpowered energy/caffeine drinks that have superseded Red Bull can keep people going for a long time until they drop. Amphetamines have long been nicknamed "speed" for their ability to enable users to sustain a frenetic pace, experiencing increased energy, focus, and enthusiasm without their usual need for sleep. A small ethnographic literature describes the experience of speed for people seeking to manage alertness: shift workers, students cramming for exams, or all-night partygoers. Stacey McKenna's (2013) study of meth users, for example, found that their addiction to amphetamines had functional meaning, allowing them to forgo sleep and stay vigilant in risky situations, especially those generated by insecure housing or homelessness. Taken together, these substances allow human beings to keep going when they would otherwise need to rest, which is hardly a new human concern. There is a certain provocative consistency to the nature of the imputed change, too: people in a variety of times and places have been equally convinced that they lived in the busiest time imaginable, or were required to work harder than any generation before them (Reiss 2017, e.g., 206). In this chapter I want to provide justification for the claim that increasing productivity, managing challenges of focus and distraction, and iteratively postponing adequate rest and leisure have a distinctive contemporary timbre. This work sets the stage for the next chapter, in which I describe the lived experience of anaesthetic time that serves as counterpoint to this contemporary existential situation. These two essays address *temporality*—that fundamental feature of our worlds that, together with spatiality and embodiment, provide the structuring features of lived experience within the phenomenological tradition. They also exemplify the method I am developing in which genealogy meets phenomenology.

DISCIPLINARY TIME

In his essay "Time, Work-Discipline, and Industrial Capitalism" (1967), the social historian E. P. Thompson famously argued that the move to a universal "clock-time" by the mid-nineteenth century in England is key to understanding the postindustrial management of labor. His erudite but necessarily vague analysis spans a huge gamut of historical sources and several centuries. Most centrally, he details the emerging technologies of timepieces as they relate to the expectations and imperatives of postindustrial employers. He reveals his Marxism by emphasizing the changes in the material conditions of agricultural and industrial production as they create a new need for what he calls *time-discipline*—simultaneously an inner experience of time, a way of talking about and understanding time, and a practice for managing time.

What *is* time-discipline? It contrasts with the "task-orientation" of preindustrial societies, he says, in three ways. First, task-oriented time is more humanly comprehensible (Thompson is reluctant to say "natural"), as it follows the rhythms of days and nights, the seasons, and the needs of other humans and animals: if the sheep are lambing in springtime, for example, you tend them at all hours. Postindustrial time, however, is clock time: we show up to work at 8.30 a.m. every Monday through Friday, vacations excepted. The vagaries of daylight hours, harvesttime, or a sick child are not worked into the schedule of most jobs. Second, task-oriented time mixes everyday social interaction and labor without making a clear distinction between "work" and "life." If your fellow villagers have not completed the harvesting of the hay, but you were planning to use it to thatch a roof, then you take a rest until it's ready. Clock-time, on the other hand, treats chatting with your coworkers about the game as slacking off, unless it's a prescribed break. Finally, task-oriented time appears (from the perspective of the time-disciplined) to be "wasteful and lacking in urgency." To the task-oriented, Thompson argues, time is not (yet) a currency—something to be spent or saved, wasted or used productively. If no task presents itself, you simply do what you feel like doing. The time-disciplined, on the other hand, are preoccupied with clocking in, overtime, or billable hours, as well as life hacks for time saving, avoiding wasted time, increasing productivity, and so on. In the unlikely event that we find ourselves with nothing pressing to do, we tend to run to the to-do list, think about what projects are on the back burner, and try to catch up with the task logjam.

Thompson's analysis is remarkably conceptually similar to Foucault's comments on the temporality of discipline. In *Discipline and Punish*, Foucault argues—in one of his more Marxian moments, in fact—that disciplinary power invents "a new way of administrating time and making it useful" (1977, 160). It yields "a new technique for taking charge of the time of individual existences; for regulating the relations of time, bodies and forces; for assuring an accumulation of duration; and for turning to ever-increased profit or use the movement of passing time" (157). Specifically, time is broken down into units, each of which is appointed a specific basic exercise, these exercises are cumulative and progressive, and the individual is examined on their aptitude at the end of a series before being permitted to advance. This mastery of duration, Foucault argues, allows that "power is articulated directly onto time; it assures its control and guarantees its use" (160). Typically, Foucault describes this new "linear," "evolutive" time in terms of the individuals it produces, rather than how those individuals perceive it.

Who are those individuals? As time-discipline is sedimented into the nineteenth century, Thompson argues, the view of time as a commodity with a use value and an exchange value acquires an increasingly moralistic patina. Not wasting time, in other words, is not just a desirable feature of a cost-efficient worker—it is a virtue. What Weber famously called the Protestant ethic was not just a contractual agreement but also a subjectivity. Kathi Weeks (2011, esp. 61–77) has more recently argued that this ethic has become even more powerful in neoliberal economies, where it serves two functions. First, it operates as a mechanism of discriminatory social control in employment-scarce markets, by representing certain marginal social groups (such as immigrants, mothers, the very poor) as not living up to norms of hard work and productivity, enabling dominant groups to hold on to employment, and driving wages down for employers willing to hire the less "ethical." Second, and more important for my argument, the new work ethic constitutes a carefully cultivated motivational nexus that focuses on "style, affect, and attitude" (73). The decline of industrial labor and the expansion of the service sector has placed more and more workers—and not coincidentally, more and more women—in jobs that require smart and attractive clothing, a nice smile, a solicitous approach to the customer, a caring attitude, or a deferential willingness to please (Hochschild 2012). In this recasting of subjectivity, behaviors previously cast as private or part of a person's "personal life" have become part of a working identity (Fleming 2009). "Working hard" and "being productive" is thus connected even more strongly to overcoming the danger of stereotypes, ironically through the performance of qualities that epitomize powerlessness. To the exhaustion of the basic time demands of neoliberal economies (Povinelli 2011), then, we can also add a layer of affective depletion that comes from pretending it isn't happening (or from being disciplined when this presentation fails).

If this is work, then what is leisure? By the early 1800s it was already hard to conceptualize leisure for working people; eventually, leisure came to be viewed through the medium of disciplinary time and its concomitant work ethic. Thompson quotes several Victorian bourgeois moralists who are exasperated by the tendency of the masses to pass the time without any structured tasks or goals—a sentiment not unfamiliar among conservative pundits today. The laborers who simply annihilate portions of time by sitting on a bench, or lying on a hillock, "yielded up to utter vacancy and torpor," are the objects of stern censure. For Thompson, these criticisms are ideological, since time-discipline is profoundly tied to exploitation and the commodification of human relationships. And they inspire him to conclude that, in a less objectified world that respected humanity, "unpurposive passing of time would be behaviour which the culture approved" (Thompson 1967, 96). Notice that this phrase doesn't only imply a need for "eight hours for what we will"—the tail end of the slogan popular among labor organizers from the late 1800s ("eight hours for work, eight hours for rest, eight hours for what we will"). In her book Weeks dwells on and tries to revive campaigns for a shorter working day in the context of today's extended working hours, the extension of working hours into the nonwork day (and night), and the overwhelm of the second shift for working mothers (2011, esp. 151–74). These are important demands, but they don't address the carryover of the lived experience of time from one context to another. If even leisure is colonized by disciplinary time, then "utter vacancy and torpor" cannot be justified—although, as I'll show, this is a way of experiencing time that exerts a siren call.

Thompson is especially interested in changes in "the inward notation of time." How does our *experience* of time change with changing material conditions? He doesn't actually describe this in detail, and nor does Foucault, precisely because they are both committed (in this work) to methods that take the historical *longue durée* as their frame. We can infer from both analyses, however, that the worker after discipline is harried, pressed for time, committed to measuring and subdividing and accounting for time, and committed to her own "productivity"—including her leisure productivity. This is an oxymoronic phrase but one that makes sense within disciplinary time: if all time gains its meaning and value from a close accounting in relation to its yields, then time spent doing nothing is wasted. *Leisure* may be antonymic to *work*, but it does not have to be outside disciplinary time.

Do women and men experience disciplinary time differently in these texts? Foucault says nothing about this, although all his examples are of men. Thompson makes only one quasifeminist aside. The hardest job of all, he remarks, was being the wife of a laborer in the nineteenth century. Not only were such women expected to do their share of agricultural labor during the workday, but they also worked a second shift in the evening and nights, preparing supper for their husbands, feeding and putting the children to bed, and tending to the children during the night—again, a perspective with clear contemporary resonance:

> Such hours were endurable only because one part of the work, with the children and in the home, disclosed itself as necessary and inevitable, rather than as an external imposition. This remains true to this day, and, despite school times and television times, the rhythms of women's work in the home are not wholly attuned to the measurement of the clock. The mother of young children has an imperfect sense of time and attends to other human tides. She has not yet altogether moved out of the conventions of "pre-industrial" society. (Thompson 1967, 79)

I hear a strange distorted premonition of Kristeva's (1981) germinal analysis of "women's time" here. Thompson is almost saying that women fail to offer a critical perspective on sexist labor expectations; that we are in both our undertakings and our attitudes "pre-modern." We *could* charitably interpret Thompson as saying that disciplinary time places even greater pressure on women's everyday lives precisely because of the impossibility of conforming human needs to its imperatives. The anxiety that emerges when children do not conform to disciplinary time but their mothers still must is extraordinary: how many of us have sat awake at 2 a.m. with a crying baby, thinking, "I'm going to be so incredibly tired in the morning, but I still have to be ready to go to work at 8 a.m."? The kids are hungry *now*, but you are still trying to deal with the back pain caused by working a long shift. Furthermore, mothers are typically charged with making their children's time productive too: from Baby Einstein to gymnastics, good use of time is a marker of class privilege and good parenting. More women than men work in the kind of administrative, pink-collar jobs that require strict punctuality, are charged with keeping their children on schedule, *and* work a double shift that continues to make time poverty so crushing. In the next chapter I examine some habitual forms of checking out that are responses to this kind of temporal environment.

NEOLIBERALISM AND POSTDISCIPLINARY TIME

Thompson and Foucault thus offer us a historical analysis of what Elizabeth Freeman (2010) has called *chrononormativity*: the use of time to organize human bodies toward greater productivity. Both set the scene for us in important ways, and their analyses continue to shape our twenty-first-century experience, including in the ways I've indicated. Nonetheless, these analyses are dated and don't directly engage the reshaping of postindustrial work time under so-called neoliberalism and within a radically different technological world. Indeed, this is a task that has already been taken on by a large preceding literature (Brown 2015; Dean 2009; Glennie and Thrift 1996; Povinelli 2011; Sharma 2013), and here my analysis is more local: I briefly sketch a picture of neoliberalism in relation to disciplinary time and women's work, before describing a *postdisciplinary time* with a distinctive attitude to task management, the relation of work and life, and its own affect. Taken together, I conclude, these features of postdisciplinary time undercut traditional concepts of agency in political theory.

Recall that one of Thompson's characterizations of time-discipline's early days is that it served to separate work and life. Early commentators on technological innovation, the growth of the middle class, and the consequences of capital accumulation (including, famously, John Maynard Keynes, and Thompson himself) thought (as recently as the early 1970s) that our future would be one of extensive leisure, with the proportion of our time spent on work steadily diminishing.[1] Things haven't exactly turned out this way. In 1967, however, toward the end of Fordism but before neoliberalism was truly in plain sight, it must have seemed as though the demands of industrial labor on the working man might finally be in remission. Technological development promised fewer hours and less physically challenging or repetitive work. More jobs were unionized, and the family wage was not yet dead. The defined-benefit pension plan was still available to significant numbers of middle-class workers, and a Keynesian welfare state model in which health, education, unemployment benefits, and basic income support might be provided by the state was still a realistic aspiration (if never quite a reality) in Western democracies. Thompson does imply, as I've shown, that the demands of time-discipline seep into "time off," but he didn't anticipate the reconflation of work and life that flexibilization and communications technology have wrought. As Paul Glennie and Nigel Thrift remark, in their 1996 reformulation of Thompson's influence, "In 1967 . . . the impending breakdown of some facets of modernity into the desynchronized society of postmodernity was presumably much less obvious than it appears in hindsight" (1996, 278). Similarly, in her 2003 critique of Foucault, Nancy Fraser suggests that "if we now see ourselves as standing on the brink of a new, postfordist epoch of globalization" then we need to reconsider his corpus (especially the middle works that have been most influential in political thought) as grasping the logic of social regulation—owl-of-Minerva-like—on the cusp of a major transformation in economic systems:

> From this perspective, it is significant that his great works of social analysis . . . were written in the 1960s and 1970s, just as the OECD countries abandoned Bretton Woods, the international financial framework that undergirded national Keynesianism and thus made possible the welfare state. In other words, Foucault mapped the contours of the disciplinary society just as the ground was being cut out from under it. And although it is only now with hindsight becoming clear, this was also the moment at which discipline's successor was struggling to be born. The irony is plain: whether we call it postindustrial society or neoliberal globalization, a new regime oriented to "deregulation" and "flexibilization" was about to take shape just as Foucault was conceptualizing disciplinary normalization. (Fraser 2003, 160)

It is ironic that a thinker as deeply committed to undoing our own presentism as Foucault should be vulnerable to this charge. Fraser is surely right that Foucault did not fully foresee the neoliberal turn of the 1980s nor imagine its long-term consequences. Nonetheless, his untimely death in 1984 hardly makes this a reasonable expectation. Further, Foucault did speak and write insightfully and at some length on postwar neoliberalism in his lecture course at the Collège de France in 1978–79, published as *La Naissance de la biopolitique* (*The Birth of Biopolitics*) in 2004 (2008 in English translation), which Fraser would not have read prior to making her critique. In this series Foucault has two focuses: first, on German postwar economic reconstruction, which he argues represents "a new programming of liberal governmentality," within which the market economy became the guide of governmental action: "The problem of neo-liberalism is . . . how the overall exercise of political power can be modeled on the principles of a market economy. So it is not a question of freeing an empty space, but of taking the formal principles of a market economy and referring and relating them to, of projecting them on to a general art of government" (Foucault [2004] 2008, 94, 131). His second focus is on the twentieth-century US neoliberalism of, most notably, Gary Becker. In Becker's work he identifies *homo oeconomicus*—the individual who is an entrepreneur of himself—and who has "human capital" through a series of investments made by himself and others (226; see also Brown 2015; Murphy 2017). Human flourishing, in this view, is best supported by creating an institutional context in which each individual can best exercise his entrepreneurial capacities and make his own unfettered, rational choices. This context includes minimally restricted markets, trade, and unconstrained rights to accumulate capital. While all these remain important features of contemporary political economy, in the past forty years neoliberalism has become more a set of anti-Keynesian political and economic practices that no longer require systematic empirical or conceptual defense. While the state plays a role in developing these practices, neoliberals typically view state intervention with suspicion (at least, as we've seen recently, state intervention on behalf of the poor or even the middle classes. In a paradoxical turn, state support for the very wealthy has been justified on grounds of economic sustainability). Increasingly, political economic institutions (e.g., central banks, regulatory overseers) have been moved by neoliberals outside the realm of state control. Critics of neoliberalism have pointed out that it creates a dwindling but ever more powerful economic elite, and an ever-larger economic underclass, both within nation-states and on a global level (Navarro 2007; Milanovic 2016).

Anna Yeatman (2014) articulates the significance of this economic transition for the inclusion of women in the labor economy. The extension of market logic to government more generally that Foucault alludes to as a relatively abstract phenomenon has more specific effects: all work that is not priced by the market, Yeatman suggests, has become less legitimate and valued, including direct service provision by the state, and unpaid work in all its forms (domestic, volunteer, affective). Concomitantly, human services have been commodified, and state service provision diminished in scope and value. Within this market logic, "employer prerogative" (the position that the hiring and firing, role definition, discipline, etc., of employees should be under the authority of the corporation, rather than defined through collective bargaining or law) has broadened, and an emphasis on measurable performance management has spread to more workplaces, including public institutions. The expansion of market logic comes with "the transformation of the political discourse of rights (freedom, equality, and political community), an inherently public discourse, into a narrow, legalistic, and private discourse of property right" and "a parallel derogation of all things public, especially of: the state's facilitation of an open and informed sphere of public conversation; the state's responsibility for public provision of services that enhance the well-being of all considered as subjects of this public jurisdiction; and the assumption of state responsibility for this political community, understood as a community of fate, past, present and future" (Yeatman 2014, 89–90).

For women, these structural trajectories further diminish the value and legitimacy of traditionally feminine work—caring, sex/affective, domestic, volunteer, state service provision (such as teaching, nursing, civil administration)—and, to the extent that women are overrepresented in the "flexible" and part-time workforce, make them especially vulnerable to the vicissitudes of labor market supply and demand. Put simply, the economic transition to neoliberalism has seen women's real incomes diminish and become less secure, while social support (in terms of public service provision, other people's time, and an ethic of shared social responsibility) for the caring labor that forms the "double shift" has also eroded. As the hours men spend working declined through the twentieth century without their participation in "home production" increasing at the same rate, so women massively *increased* their hours spent in paid employment *without* equivalent decrease in the time spent on housework and childcare. More women and especially mothers have less time for chosen activities they enjoy, given that for most such activities are *not* paid labor, including housework, commuting or traveling between jobs, and childcare that involves appointments or life-maintenance (taking one's child to the doctor, bathing one's child) (see Ramey and Francis 2009).

In Hartmut Rosa's lengthy and complex work on social acceleration, he identifies a "late modern" everyday temporality marked by flexibility and complexity. Articulating a number of methodological difficulties with measuring the pace of life, he ends up with the definition "the increase of episodes of action and/or experience per unit of time as a result of a scarcity of time resources" (2013, 121). This definition includes both subjective and objective components: how much and how many things people actually do in certain periods of time, and how they experience the speed of their own action. As he points out, there is plenty of evidence that people in the postindustrial world experience themselves as being harried, pressed for time, and increasingly rushed in their undertakings. This subjective aspect of social acceleration, however, has been perceived to be a feature of modernity and postmodernity, as my own earlier discussion of Buck-Morss on Benjamin pointed out, since long before the advent of neoliberal economics (Rosa 2003, 9). What is distinctive about the experience of time that accompanies the digital revolution in particular is the speed of potential communication (and expectations about how that speed will be deployed) combined with the possibility of multitasking. Rosa cites important empirical work by Karl Hörning, Daniela Ahrens, and Anette Gerhard, who argue that "linear time management and sequential time planning has become untenable and that the figure of the 'time manager' is gradually being supplanted by a new life-style: that of the 'time-juggling player.' The 'player' overcomes the linear, calculating, and planning time orientation of modernity and replaces it with a situationally open, 'event-oriented time praxis'" (Rosa 2013, 236). This neoliberal subject has four separable temporal tasks: to accelerate their action, to reduce idle time, to multitask, and to replace slow activities with faster ones (281–83).

In some ways this speeded-up and time-impoverished way of living represents an intensification of disciplinary time, in which more and more must be accomplished in the same 24/7. We can still see the contemporary legacy of disciplinary time in practices of "time management," for example, that are aimed at self-directed workers as well as their managers, and that recommend breaking time down into segments, during each of which a discrete task must be completed, with the goal of completing a larger project within a set period of time and overall increasing productivity. Such strategies are often experienced as tyrannical (including when they are self-imposed), and notoriously lead to failures of "attention management," such as procrastination, deviation from the assigned task, and daydreaming. Our increasingly desperate attempts to manage time go hand in hand with both passive resistance and iterative failure. In other ways, however, the emergence of neoliberalism as I have characterized it has made our temporality more truly "postdisciplinary." As Rosa and his interlocutors explain, multitasking is more a part of our experience than Foucault's descriptions of eighteenth-century military training allow, and it presses on the demand for effective use of time in contradictory ways. On the one hand, the multitasker is not a plodder (in the popular imagination), but rather someone deftly and seamlessly managing the myriad small yet differentiated tasks that characterize many jobs and lives. On the other hand, actually finding enough time and maintaining sufficient attention to bring any particular task to completion is ever more cognitively challenging or affectively demanding. Many difficult projects take a long time and many small, developmental steps to accomplish (as anyone who has ever written—or supervised—a dissertation can attest). The more traditional version of disciplinary time that both Thompson and Foucault describe is conducive to this kind of project, while the neoliberal speeded-up and multiply directed experience of postdisciplinary time shatters much of the focus disciplinary time cultivated. In postdisciplinary time, work and life are reconflated by virtue of work entering into all of life (lowendtheory 2012). In the collection of ghastly narratives by academic mothers in *Mama, PhD* (Evans and Grant 2008), for example, we hear story after story about women attempting to grade papers while breastfeeding, or cooking dinner with one hand and typing email to the department chair with the other. In these contexts, it is not so much that work is done in and through social life as that paid labor infiltrates almost every waking moment. (That qualifier— "waking"—is one of the reasons that I am interested in the politics and phenomenology of sleep, which may be the last frontier of productivity.) What remains with us is that increased sense of linear, protensive time urgency that discipline fostered, although our capacity to make good on its demands and be conclusively satisfied that we are not wasting time is constantly undercut by the postdisciplinary nature of the task environment.

If there is an increase in the number of experiences and actions the individual fits into a unit of time—what we might call an "accelerated present"— there is also, according to Rosa, a related structural reason that our present itself becomes shorter—a "contracted present." Citing the social philosophers Hermann Lübbe and Reinhart Koselleck, Rosa articulates the time of our lives as marked by rapid cultural and social innovation that, crucially, also shrinks our experience of the now: "For Lübbe, the *past* is defined as *that which no longer holds / is no longer valid while the future denotes that which does not yet hold / is not yet valid*. The present, then, is the time-span for which . . . the horizons of experience and expectation coincide. . . . *Social acceleration is defined by an increase in the decay-rates of the reliability of experiences and expectations and by the contraction of the time-spans definable as the 'present'*" (Rosa 2003, 7; emphasis in original).

In other words, the skills I learn quickly become outmoded or cease to be dependable; more existentially, I can no longer expect that my situation will endure and that my subjectivity will be matched to it. My sense of my very self as quickly receding into the past—which is also a part of all experience that also accelerates within the course of a human life (Beauvoir [1970] 1972, 373–76)—speeds up. This contraction of the present, of course, sometimes catalyzes nostalgia for a longer, slower past present. This is a place where a commonplace feature of the slower individual temporal past (recalling the long days of one's own childhood summers, for example) coincides with sociopolitical observation about postdisciplinary time (such as when people born before about 1980 recall when a written letter took days to reach its recipient and a week or two to elicit a reply). The contraction of the present, though, most forcefully orients our attention to the future: we fear that our experience will fall away more and more quickly as the future comes toward us with increasing rapidity and uncertain demands. We tend, I suggest, to experience anxiety about the contraction of the present because we routinely try (and often fail) to anticipate this pressing future, again often as a matter of individual responsibility. For example, many bureaucratized workplaces implement new technologies for routine transactions (such as expense claims or internal budget transfers) ever more frequently and in the context of less and less management support. A new employee learns the system in place when they are first hired, and then perhaps the first replacement, before realizing at some point that investment in a skill that will quickly and iteratively become redundant is a "waste of time," and tolerating their own low-level incompetence in the service of future impending imagined changes. That "incompetence," though, is represented by the company and imagined as just that—a personal failure to learn know-how (which it also is)—and comes with a knowledge that the future will only bring more opportunities to demonstrate one's own marginal ineptitude.

The individualization of temporal experience is reinforced by the larger political system that creates that experience. Note, for instance, Yeatman's phrasing as she theorizes the disappearance of a public sphere that supports all members of political community—"understood as a community of fate, past, present and future." The radical individualization and economization of the relationships she imagines not only erode political imagination about our shared fate; they also erase the very idea of a shared timeline leading from past through the present to the future. Time is less likely to be experienced collectively in terms of "our future" but rather as confined to the psychic life of the individual, and as a matter for self-government. Of course, we still sometimes think in terms of utopian or dystopian political worlds, but the growth of human capital discourse has tended to gradually narrow *our* concern with time to *my* time—my own efficiency, productivity, or time scarcity. The more individualized our experience of time, the easier it is, in turn, to dwell on the affects postdisciplinary temporality generates, as if these affects originated in the self and must be caused and managed by me alone.

Finally, the very discourse of speed itself conceals what Sarah Sharma (2013) calls, in her careful theoretical ethnography of work and temporality, "power-chronography": the multiple, related forms of temporality that different jobs demand and that must interface with each other. In some ways, she suggests, the worker who is most preoccupied with their speed and productivity, with eking out the very most from their precious moments and controlling and maintaining their workflow, is a privileged worker—her example is frequent business travelers who live in the spaces of airports, lounges, planes, and hotels (Sharma 2013, 28–54). To assume that a speeded-up world, or even the critiques of social acceleration that have permeated popular culture, is hustling us all along in the same way is to ignore the interwoven temporalities that reflect the relationships between different kinds of working subject: Focusing on the issue of fast or slow pace without a nuanced and complex conception of the temporal does an injustice to the multitude of time-based experiences specific to different populations that live, labor, and sleep under the auspices of global capital. The social fabric is composed of a chronography of power, where individuals' and social groups' senses of time and possibility are shaped by a differential economy, limited or expanded by the ways and means that they find themselves in and out of time. Contrasting with the elite business travelers, in some other service sectors "hurry up and wait" is part of power-chronography. For example, the taxi drivers Sharma interviewed described waiting at the rank for the next fare, or idling waiting for a customer to complete an appointment and then hustle them on to the next stop. They must interface with the time-pressed, rushing businesspeople who need to get to a meeting or to the airport, and their temporality is not so much either consistently fast or slow, as governed by the temporality of others. They work nights or other shifts, and are radically asynchronous with a more normative temporal world, managing their schedules to fit with the demand for taxi services (55–80). Sharma's analysis reveals that the normative tasks of neoliberal temporality that Rosa identifies (to accelerate one's action, to reduce idle time, to multitask, and to replace slow activities with faster ones) are still social imperatives, but that only certain subjects at certain times are fully engaged in them, while others exist to enable this temporality and mitigate its negative effects.

AFTER AGENCY

Through its transformation of temporal experience, finally, social acceleration implicates our self-understandings as *agents*—understood most simply as subjects capable of reflecting on our desires and values and acting in accordance with them. Think back to my discussion of Paul's work on transformative experience. When deciding whether or not to become a surgeon or have a child (her examples), we cannot make a straightforwardly rational decision—and thus be the kinds of agents "we" want to be—because we face a paradox of not knowing the preferences such a transformation will lead to. In chapter 1, I suggested that Paul's position leads her to defend the value of revelation for a self as-yet-unknown—a curiously Foucauldian moment in an otherwise resolutely rationalist text. To back up a step from this conclusion, Paul's highly abstracted account of such dilemmas is palpably informed by a desire to make decisions that will dictate the course of one's life, and the revelation that major transformations are not amenable to this kind of procedural management is presented as (and feels as though it is experienced by the author as) a blow to autonomy:

> As an authentic, rational agent, you are expected to take charge of your own destiny. You chart your future, deliberating and reflecting on who you really are and what you really want from life, and, once you've determined your preferences, you determine the right course and act accordingly. You live an authentic life by faithfully modeling your preferences, and you live a rational life by matching your choices to these preferences. Rational authenticity, then, is hewing as close as you can to the kind of life that best realizes your dreams, hopes, and aspirations. (Paul 2014, 105)

A footnote to this paragraph tells us that "this is a cultural notion prevalent in wealthy, Western societies." This is a somewhat partial situating: it is also a "cultural notion" especially prevalent in anglophone analytic philosophy (which, in circular fashion, is populated overwhelmingly by wealthy, western people), and is a mode of thought for those who have sufficient control over their lives to believe (whether or not it's true) that there could be any traceable consequence or even meaning at all to this kind of reflection and idealized decision-making. I happened to read this part of Paul's book on the same day as I was rereading parts of Elizabeth Povinelli's *Economies of Abandonment* (2011), and the stark contrast between the two texts provoked an extraordinary cognitive dissonance. Povinelli is certainly interested in the generic possibilities for lives that reflect our hopes, but she also grounds that interest in the stories of particular subjects: the protagonist in Charles Burnett's 1977 neorealist film *Killer of Sheep*—a (poor, Black) man trying to put together a functioning car when "nothing is ready to hand in the Heideggerian sense.

Nothing in [his] world simply works" (102); or a group of Indigenous Australians in a leaky boat on rough water trying to get to the beach where they hope to work on a digital storytelling project that will reanimate their local economy (111–12). The very specific subjects of late liberalism in Povinelli's book endure (or not), even as they are exhausted by the forms of biopower that constantly eat away at their attempts to create alternative worlds. For those whose experience is marked less by the work of effectually striving to create a self-determined life, and more by holding on, the conative work of enduring—continuing to exist, persisting despite slow death—Paul's fantasy of subjectivity risks being not just implausible, but actively demeaning. This is surely the kind of "literalizing logic of visible effectuality, bourgeois dramatics, and lifelong accumulation or fashioning" to which Berlant refers in the epigraph that opens this book, and a particularly reductive description of a regulative ideal of an agent, rather than of any situated person with an unconscious—much less those marginal subjects of late liberalism who are "the parts that have no part" in it (Povinelli 2011, 102).

My interest, then, is in what this kind of imagined agent elides. If we believe, as I do, that the self is historically and socially constituted in ways that any more sensitive account of agency must incorporate (Christman 2009), and temporality is key to subjectivity, then our historical and social experience of time will be central to agency. In a postdisciplinary world, for example, if my temporality is such that my own experience very rapidly recedes as "outdated" and I am required to learn new skills or practices, then I'm less likely to invest in cultivating or sedimenting that experience as an important epistemic resource, and more likely to dismiss the value (epistemic or political) of experience itself. The contraction of a present that falls away from under our feet is also the contraction of the temporally enduring subject—a concern that Beauvoir described already in 1970 (Beauvoir 1972, 380). If the future looms somehow closer, threatening the advent of the new, while the present as a space of predictability where one's subjectivity maps to its situation shrinks, then forms of agency that appeal to the endurance of one's knowledge, beliefs, and even values are likewise truncated. Acting with agency, in the increasingly self-referential political tradition of the liberal west, requires knowing who I am—where that "I" importantly includes a "temporally extended self-concept"—so that I can make "meaning of [my] ongoing experience and action" in the ways autonomy demands (Christman 2009, 9, 103). Where my own experience has decreasing reliability within a shrinking present, my self-rule is thereby undercut.

This schematic argument perhaps deserves a book of its own, and here my concluding goal is modest: in anticipation of my account of anaesthetic time in chapter 4, I offer a word of caution about celebrating *agency* (or its more philosophically robust sibling, *autonomy*) as a redemptive quality of political subjects, whether attributed or cultivated. The two-dimensional ideal of the agent in rational choice theory or libertarian-leaning liberalism can be pushed yet further away from caveats about material conditions. The growing disconnect between abstracted philosophical accounts of agency and the neoliberal narrowing of possibilities for individual or even collective action aimed at changing political life should be of profound concern for the way it mystifies limits on our capacity to act and enables blame and cruelty. For example, as I've argued elsewhere, agency is increasingly represented in contemporary popular culture through facile equivalences with "doing," in turn sometimes absurdly reduced to "working"—no matter how exploitative the working conditions might be (Heyes 2017). The complete fetishization of agency as a symbolic property only of the right kind of subject, rather than as a description of a real capacity that emerges (or not) from relations within shared political life, finds its apotheosis in the constant hollow vox pop of Trump supporters: "at least he's getting things done." This is what a powerful white baby-boomer tweeting through the night connotes; the refrain typically doesn't refer to any record of tangible policy successes that can reasonably be attributed to the strategic choices and leadership decisions of the US president (indeed, the man's own boast about his accomplishments provoked a round of incredulous laughter from the UN General Assembly) but rather, I suggest, attaches purely to the subject—this is what successful "doing" *looks* (and feels) like.

This analysis implicates *resistance* (as a particularly politically important form of agency), which, within a genre of Western feminism, is conversely understood as transgressing the norm in ways that are legible as politically successful within dominant systems of meaning. As other commentators have long suggested, the regulative fictions of self-rule in Western political thought are (among other things) symptomatic fantasies that entrench normative understandings of subjectivity as much as they sort through the conditions for freedom.[2] The temporal stresses I've described are part of a larger picture in which conventional views of agency—especially as a quality of individuals, and especially when understood through normatively legible action—are a part of the very discourses they are often deployed to challenge.

To make this case, consider two key texts. First, Saba Mahmood's 2005 theoretical anthropology of the Egyptian piety movement has by now become a touchstone text for a new generation of scholars attempting to decolonize feminist understandings of agency (Mahmood [2005] 2012).[3] *The Politics of Piety* details Mahmood's two years of ethnographic work with women in Cairo who were part of the mosque movement—an attempt to reintroduce Islamic values and practices to an increasingly secular society. As an American feminist anthropologist with poststructuralist leanings, her own ethics and politics are not aligned with the women who take up *da'wa* (the call to piety and its practice [57–58]); indeed, she understands her own research as necessarily engaging her "repugnance" at the way religious practice reinscribes women's subordination (37). Nonetheless, she writes,

> If the ability to effect change in the world and in oneself is historically and culturally specific . . . then the meaning and sense of agency cannot be fixed in advance, but must emerge through an analysis of the particular concepts that enable specific modes of being, responsibility, and effectivity. Viewed in this way, what may appear to be a case of deplorable passivity and docility from a progressivist point of view, may actually be a form of agency—but one that can be understood only from within the discourses and structures of subordination that create the conditions of its enactment. In this sense, agentival capacity is entailed not only in those acts that resist norms but also in the multiple ways in which one *inhabits* norms. (14–15; emphasis in original)

Key to following through on this insight is the acknowledgment that the exercise of agency—including by women against patriarchy—cannot be reduced to overt transgression, understood as the only meaningful form of political resistance. Mahmood therefore suggests that Judith Butler's assumption that resistance can only be understood agonistically as the refusal to iterate a norm fails to take seriously the culturally various ways in which norms can be engaged (17–22). This separation between agency and transgression opens up new possibilities for inquiry into different forms of subjectivity and the politics with which they are enmeshed (188).[4]

In one of her most challenging examples, Mahmood questions "how suffering and survival—two modalities of existence that are often considered to be the antithesis of agency—came to be articulated within the lives of women who live under the pressures of a patriarchal system that requires them to conform to the rigid demands of heterosexual monogamy" (167–68). Specifically, she discusses the contrast between two single women in Egypt who struggle with being unmarried and the stigma that carries. Iman—a single woman in her late twenties—is asked by an already-married colleague for her hand in marriage (i.e., to become his second wife, which is permissible under Islamic law). Iman's pious friend Nadia—who is the subject of most of Mahmood's discussion—gives Iman the surprising advice that she should allow the man to formally request her hand in marriage from her parents, and thus allow them to investigate his suitability. As Mahmood recounts their discussion, Nadia presents a clear (feminist) critique of the predicament of Egyptian women with regard to marriage, and the double standards for unmarried women and men. While an unmarried man has simply yet to choose his wife, an unmarried *woman* above a certain age is construed as defective and un-desirable, yet many husbands (in Egypt as elsewhere) are unloving, unkind, exploitative, or violent. Nonetheless, Nadia advocates cultivating the virtue of *sabr* (patience, endurance of hardship without complaint, steadfastness) in the face of God's will.

Sana, however, is a single professional in her midthirties, and a secular Muslim. When Mahmood explains Nadia's defense of the virtue of *sabr*, Sana finds it "such a passive way of dealing with this situation," a way of accepting one's lot, rather than working to improve one's situation. She prefers to cul-tivate self-confidence and self-esteem—ethical capacities that would enable her to shrug off the negative views of others on her unmarried status, and to focus on her professional achievements and talents (172). While Mahmood is clearly more closely identified with Sana than with Nadia, she tries to un-derstand the latter's perspective as grounded in "a notion of human agency, defined in terms of individual responsibility, that is bounded by both an es-chatological structure *and* a social one" (173). The political theoretical lesson that Mahmood draws from this anthropological moment is as follows:

> It is clear that certain virtues (such as humility, modesty, and shyness) have lost their value in the liberal imagination and are considered em-blematic of passivity and inaction, especially if they don't uphold the au-tonomy of the individual: *sabr* may, in this view, mark an inadequacy of action, a failure to act under the inertia of tradition. But *sabr* in the sense described by Nadia and others does not mark a reluctance to act. Rather, it is integral to a constructive project: it is a site of considerable investment, struggle, and achievement. What Nadia's and Sana's discussions reveal are two different modes of engaging with social injustice, one grounded in a

tradition that we have come to value, and another in a nonliberal tradition that is being resuscitated by the movement I worked with. (174)

Mahmood is right that feminist disdain is often directed toward any perceived failure to resist patriarchy that looks like passivity or docility within its local context, and also that what is construed as such failure deserves closer scrutiny. She makes her critique in part because she wants to show how liberal traditions continue to make assumptions about nonliberal cultures that occlude and devalue indigenous modes of self-understanding and action. The decolonization of feminist theory in this sense, however, extends not only to non-Western contexts. Rather, the theoretical gestures Mahmood makes can be reworked back into the fractured contexts of the very liberal Western cultures that for her are the origin of a parochial approach to agency.

Consider as a second exemplary text that makes this last point Alisa Bierria's insightful analysis of Black women's agency (2014). Bierria argues that agency is not simply a feature of the mode of practical reasoning exercised by an individual but is rather distorted or legitimated by larger processes of social authoring that lend meaning to acts. She focuses on cases involving the systematically racist representation of African Americans' actions: when two white-skinned people are pictured in a news report after Hurricane Katrina, for example, they are described as wading through chest-deep water after "finding" food and drink at a grocery store, while an almost identical picture of a black man describes his actions as "looting." The infamous "finding/looting" distinction, then, captures different social attributions of meaning to the same ostensible act (129–30). Bierria wants to argue that the meaning of acts does not reside solely in actors, while resisting the inference that oppressed people are distinctively lacking in agency because structures of power overwrite their intentions (see also Scales-Trent 1999). Taking this analysis a step further, she proposes a "heterogeneous model" of agency, and asks how we can interpret the actions of oppressed people—Black women in the United States in particular—as intentional and strategic (as exhibiting agency) in ways that dominant models fail to recognize. "Transformative," "alien," or "insurgent" forms of agency, Bierria suggests, are all active within resistant moments in forms of political life structured by anti-Black racism. Citing Maria Lugones, she concludes that "a coherent theory of oppression must be able to hold the following contradiction: oppression, in its full force, is inescapable, and the possibility of liberation must be affirmed. This is the field of contradiction in which I argue human agency and oppression must be theorized. Perhaps instead of asking 'if' or 'whether' people can be agents within the contradiction of ongoing oppression and resistance, we might ask 'how?'" (Bierria 2014, 141).

That "how?" is one of the things that lies behind my curiosity about not only action and agency but also, to take Bierria's project in a direction she may not have intended, failing to act and refusing agency. The suggestion that "passivity"—that most stereotypical quality of abject femininity—might embody a form of agency is anathema to many feminists. Saidiya Hartman points out that such unrecognizably agential forms of expression and resistance—like some of Bierria's examples—are often barred from "the political" entirely (1997, 61). My suggestion is that "passivity" and "passive resistance" ought to be rethought as the forms that agency sometimes takes not just under slavery or within a patriarchal form of religious life but also under the neoliberal economic conditions that shape contemporary work in the West. Indeed, under such conditions, our attachments to pain and pleasure and our commitment to work—including working on ourselves, and including political work—are used as very effective points of manipulation. Thinking back to Foucault's aesthetics of existence, what is it like to be this critical, questioning, laboring subject, and how could that labor be separated from the enterprising self-making that neoliberal economies cultivate as means to increase consumption, devolve social responsibility, and diminish civil society?

In a book that is more a provocation than an argument, Jack Halberstam proposes that "feminists refuse the choices as offered—freedom in liberal terms or death—in order to think about a shadow archive of resistance, one that does not speak in the language of action and momentum but instead articulates itself in terms of evacuation, refusal, passivity, unbecoming, unbeing" (2011, 129). Even the countercultural forms of work that are epitomized in Foucault's notion of "working on oneself" and in what we understand political resistance to be might be tied up with a simultaneously entrepreneurial and docile subject (Dilts 2011; McNay 2009). My own project has talked me out of contrasting passivity with feminism or with resistance. Indeed, I no longer even know what actions or failures to act might properly be described as "passive," or what a feminist politics of passivity would look like, Halberstam's enthusiasm notwithstanding. I am interested, however, in less-well-explored qualities of the good agent: her ongoing attention to the production and transformation of her self—her vigilance, if you like, about her own aesthetics of existence, and (a related quality) her productivity, and in particular her productive use of time. In this light, recall Ferrari's love of anaesthesia, which points toward a deeper philosophical challenge than her embodied aesthetic: far from being vigilant, she withdrew from a particular economy of time that keeps postdisciplinary society functioning. In this most literal and extreme example of the *an*aesthetics of existence, I show how a philosophical reading of losing consciousness might be one part of a new feminist ethos more attuned to the exigencies of contemporary living.

CHAPTER FOUR

Anaesthetic Time

Time you enjoy wasting is not wasted time.—misattributed to Bertrand Russell

WHAT IS A DRUG? Opinions vary, but we might say that a drug is a chemical substance that, when ingested, changes one's physiology—whether for the purposes of overcoming disease or changing one's state of mind. With this definition in mind, think about some everyday drugs: alcohol, cannabis, and benzos (sedative antianxiety drugs such as Valium or Ativan). Here I bracket together a collection of somatic substances that can take a while to consume, or have slow, drawn-out, and relatively mild effects on one's sensorium, and provide a way of gently checking out of any metaconsciousness of time's passing moments. After taking these drugs—and maybe *while* taking them—time drifts. Instead of the linearity of a punctuated time, a time divided into ever-smaller units, each of which must be productively used, they induce a relative indifference to time passing and to the sensory demands that render our typical temporality so exhausting. Anxiety subsides. Eating junk food, for example, Lauren Berlant argues, "can make interruptive episodes happen in which suspending the desire to be building toward the good life in rational ways involves cultivating a feeling of well-being that spreads out for a moment, not as a projection toward a future" (2010, 35). These everyday substances can be used in other ways, of course—perhaps in a big binge to mitigate an emotional crisis, or more benignly in a social situation to make us feel more open to others, or maybe just to satisfy hunger. I want to suggest, however, that they share a common but underdescribed use as informal anaesthetics, in contrast to coffee, Red Bull, Ritalin, cocaine—the antithetical substances that we take to speed ourselves up, power through a long night, keep focused. A good dose of any of the anaesthetic drugs—or a mixture—generates a different lived experience of time. It moves on without our noticing—whether because we are sitting in a haze, numb, or because, more literally, we're unconscious (blacked out, sedated, asleep). The sociologist Ben Highmore describes one of the more harmless instances: "I tell myself that I will use my time more productively, that I will start a new fitness routine, I will use my evenings to pursue new hobbies, but old routines hang on insistently and I find myself slumped in front of the TV, glass in hand, relaxed, happy and slightly ashamed. Everyday life often drifts, sometimes in fits and starts. Distraction and inattention often characterizes a routine consciousness that might be described as diffuse" (2004, 311).

This is an everyday experience of time that barely edges into our cultural consciousness *as* an experience. Highmore describes himself as "happy," but this kind of temporality, I'll argue, typically doesn't make it over this bar: it serves to give us time out of time, a few moments in which the future fades and consciousness contracts (or is extinguished). It is, ironically, a way of being in the moment. Why is Highmore "slightly ashamed"? He implies it's because his plans for the effective use of time, directed toward self-improvement, have come to naught. His willpower has failed him, and habit has reasserted itself. It is an "interruptive episode" in which the demands of postdisciplinary time are briefly set aside in favor of a dispersed consciousness that doesn't recognize any grand future (Baraitser 2009, 66–89).

Within the phenomenological tradition, the lived experience of time is a key structuring category of human consciousness. As David Couzens Hoy (2012) points out, following Heidegger, possible versions of lived time are different from those of "objective time" and can stand in many different relations—"the time of our lives" as contrasted with "the time of the universe," as he puts it.[1] E. P. Thompson and Foucault don't clearly distinguish these two forms, although they seem to be talking more about the latter as it is socially constituted in particular historical periods, and, as I showed, they eschew the first-personal. If chapter 3 emphasized the genealogical, this chapter focuses on the phenomenological: like Hoy, my focus is on lived experience of time, on *temporality*. Rather than delving into the conditions of possibility of temporality, I want to step back from one local, commonplace experience and try to gain some perspective on its contingency. This is tricky, because it hardly seems to count as experience at all. In the next chapter I talk about the normative experience of childbirth represented in mainstream media and medicine; in *this* context, we have an anticipated experience and a framework for interpretation, even if what we actually undergo evades capture within this proffered cultural narrative. Highmore's "syncope," however, seems to include no experience to represent—just a blank. This erasure is made possible because the advance of time—our movement toward the future—requires, in our cultural imaginary, "activity." Only certain undertakings count as activity (and drinking on the couch is certainly not one of them), yet we must be doing things for our temporality to be linearly protensive. This is such an engrained assumption—yet such a profoundly political one—that it can scarcely appear as a belief about the world, and hence absent experiences are removed from politics.

In this chapter I call this experience "anaesthetic time," and I provide a local, first-personal account of it that parallels and complements my account of postdisciplinary time. Anaesthetic time, I argue, is part and parcel of postdisciplinary temporality—it is a logical response to it and a way of surviving in an economy of temporality that is relentlessly depleting. I show how anaesthetic time has a gendered aspect, and point out that it is subtly marketed to more privileged women as a respectable and politically unthreatening exit from the demands of the double shift, at the same time as it is constructed as a dangerous and irresponsible practice for scapegoated groups—especially the racialized poor. Passing out is the logical limit of anaesthetic time, I suggest, and provides (however tacitly) a thoroughgoing way of checking out from postdisciplinary temporality and the fantasies of autonomy it offers that can be so exhausting and deceptive.[2]

TEMPORALITY IN PHENOMENOLOGICAL PSYCHOPATHOLOGY

The work of describing "pathological" temporalities has been undertaken by phenomenological psychologists who are relatively unstudied by feminist philosophers, even as time itself is an important feminist theme, including within the feminist phenomenological literature (e.g., Schües, Olkowski, and Fielding 2011). Following in the tradition of Husserl and Heidegger, a number of late nineteenth- and early twentieth-century thinkers with interest in psychology and psychiatry—most famously Eugène Minkowski ([1933] 1970) and Ludwig Binswanger (1960)—attempted to understand psychopathology through its existential and phenomenological manifestations, rather than through psychoanalytic or biological origin stories. For later thinkers, such as Maurice Merleau-Ponty and Frantz Fanon (as well as, in a different way, Foucault), the so-called abnormal individual continued to provide insight into structures of human consciousness in general, as well as its sociopolitical contexts. Focusing on phenomenology's organizing concepts of spatiality, intersubjectivity, embodiment, and temporality, phenomenological psychology has often understood disturbances of the latter to be central to psychopathology, and especially to the conditions now known as schizophrenia and depression. Of course, to say that a mental disorder has temporal disturbances as its symptoms is already to presume something about the *normal* lived experience of time. Here I want to start from just one set of generalizations about normal and pathological temporality appearing in recent philosophical psychopathology to show how even self-consciously phenomenological work can be incomplete in its own bracketing, introducing cultural and political assumptions that would be better made explicit.

First, to have experience is to be in time. That is, to be aware of oneself as a subject moving through the world, whether as generated by one's own actions or undergone as a bystander, is necessarily to move through time. This deceptively simple claim can be unpacked in a lot of different ways: most obviously, my experience of myself as a coherent being is made possible by events organized into a self-narrative. In order to put my autobiography together I need a sense of myself as persisting—as having a past and existing now. This is so no matter how skeptical we might be about the subject being the origin of experience rather than its effect. I may or may not literally imagine my future, but any structuring of past and present invites a through line to what comes next, even as it resists forecasting. In this way, second, our normal experience of time is future-oriented, as Minkowski notes ([1933] 1970, 80). A commonsense phenomenology of time characterizes the past and the future as asymmetrical, in the most tautological (if not entirely uncontroversial) sense because the past has happened while the future is yet to occur. The past is done, while the future is something that needs to be anticipated or prepared for. We might say that the past is known, organized, and interpreted while the future is unknown, open, and ripe with possibility. Yet the rewriting of history, the destruction of evidence, the unreliability of memory inflects this claim: the past may be radically open to question and available for creative reworking with a variety of psychic or political motivations (Hoy 2012, esp. 98–116). Similarly, failures of imagination, lack of hope, assessment of political constraint, and so on, may make the future look curtailed, repetitive, or predictable.

North American mainstream popular cultures are shot through with normative judgments about the proper experience of time that deeply shape what is (or even can be) experienced. We are supposed to be optimistic, to orient ourselves to an imagined trajectory both personal and societal in which our lives, the economy, living up to enlightenment values, or just things in general "get better." When recently making some financial investments, I found myself in a futile discussion with an adviser who was willing to debate the merits of particular stocks—although debating the ethics of investing in fossil fuels was clearly a bit outside his comfort zone—but who was not able to talk about the general prospects for capital accumulation at the end of the world. "The markets always go up," he kept saying, adding, when pressed, "in the long term." "*In the long run* we are all dead," I said, quoting Keynes's most famous remark, but that went over his head; it was seemingly impossible (as well as impolitic) for him to countenance a financial future that was not rosier than the present, once (as Keynes continued) the storm is past and the ocean is flat again (Keynes 1923, 80). Keynes's meteorological analogy can be thought more literally, as climate change offers us ever-more crises that run into each other and jibe with scientific analysis to throw into question the idea that the world can be recovered. Negative predictions, personal pessimism, or larger-scale dystopian thinking are often seen as "depressing," as anyone who has ever tried to teach environmental politics to undergraduates can attest. These judgments are of course local, too. They might be connected to a political story about the place of Canada (in my experience) in the larger political world—as a force for good, a site of ever-increasing human rights, or a progressive country. One's personal story needs to be a piece of this larger historical narrative, as we are urged to tell ourselves through tropes (touted with special urgency to immigrants) such as "pursuing one's dream," "beating the odds," "building a life," "making it," and so on. Beneath this normative temporal imagination lie a number of exclusions: while dystopian thinking can be strange and alarming to white bourgeois Canadians, Indigenous people on Turtle Island are already living in a "postapocalyptic" world (Whyte 2017). The normative account of time as moving forward not only literally but also politically is a key part of "settler time," which, Audra Simpson (2017) argues, must continually put the colonial liberal state's unjust treatment of

Indigenous people into "history," urging them to reconcile rather than re-fuse its legitimacy—even when, paradoxically, those injustices happened only yesterday, or are happening today, or will happen tomorrow. With this ma-nipulation of temporality even the modest promise of liberal democracy to self-correct its own immanent exclusions can be sustained alongside ongoing injustice of genocidal proportions. Finally, in resisting Dan Savage's siren call to gay youth that "it gets better," through which he implies that the homo-phobic taunts of the schoolyard will be replaced with DINK (double income no kids) urban metrosexuality in an able-bodied prime of life, Halberstam (2011) defines failure as a "queer art." Thus to speak at the phenomenological level of the time of our lives is always to risk erasing the cultural contexts that also structure these lived experiences.

Third, the embodied subject is both spatial and temporal, in linked ways: our eyes look forward, and we habitually walk and run ahead of ourselves. Walking or running backward is possible, of course, but as anyone who's ever trained to play soccer knows, it is a learned skill rather than an extrapolation from baby's first steps. This is an embodied and temporal orientation that is in some minimal sense essential to human beings (no human has eyes in the back of their head), yet clearly both technologies and cultural attitudes make this phenomenological commonplace equally contextual. Take yoga's warrior pose, for example—a standing lunge with arms outstretched. Many Western students of yoga habitually and unintentionally thrust their bodies forward in poses modeled or taught as symmetrical. They also allow a back arm or leg to be limp, unengaged. The back body is out of sight, and out of mind. In Drew Leder's (1990) terms, it is a "corporeal absence." Many of us (especially intellectual laborers) move from our upper body, with head advanced. Our awareness is high in the body, and oriented to its frontal plane and the space ahead of us. Look around any university campus and you'll see this embodied pattern much in evidence. We are projecting ourselves forward in space to reach our goal. Accompanying this general spatial orientation is also a chron-ological attitude: what's next? This is a temporality that is produced in the individual by a larger environment, just as Iris Young ([1980] 2005) argued the discontinuity of phenomenal space is produced for women by a sexist situation. Thus while the anticipation of the future might be in some sense a "normal" temporal orientation, it is also a culturally specific and embodied practice and an attitude toward the world.

Our lived experience of time has meaning, finally, because lived time is synchronized with others in a shared world. Merleau-Ponty argues that "my living present opens upon a past which I nevertheless am no longer living through [no-more], and on a future which I do not yet live [not-yet], and perhaps never shall, it can also open on to temporalities outside my living experience and acquire a social horizon, with the result that my world is expanded to the dimensions of that collective history which my private existence takes up and carries forward" ([1945] 2002, 433).

While different people can live most any schedule, to the extent that this timing fails to jibe with the shared temporal world they inhabit, it will be experienced as jarring or difficult, rather than easeful (Minkowski [1933] 1970, 65; see also Sharma 2013). When I get up each morning at 7 a.m. and put my child on the school bus, greeting neighbors as we walk along the block, watching the rush hour traffic build, feeling the crisp morning air, I am in tune with the city I live in. I drive myself to work along with thousands of others; I work in my office, teach a class, attend a meeting, and talk with a student until 5 p.m., when I drive across the busy city to collect my son from after-school care. When I was a graduate student, however, I rarely followed this kind of schedule. I rose late, to attend a midmorning class, but then went to the library before running into a friend and having coffee for two hours. I would start writing, and work late, walking home in the dark long after the campus had quietened. I remember a short period of reading and writing until 4 a.m., and sleeping until noon. Like the shift worker, I missed the bustle of the normal morning (in theory), and felt myself deeply alone during the long night—not spent in a noisy bar or club with other night owls but working by lamplight. My experience of time, in other words, is deeply shaped by how those around me live temporal existence.

In his "Lived Time and Psychopathology" (2005), Martin Wyllie focuses on melancholic states (known within contemporary psychiatry as "depressive disorders," where "major depressive disorder" in particular is connected to melancholy) as defined by a particular temporality.[3] For the melancholic, time becomes slow and stagnant. The future is foreclosed, and the past limited, understood as a repetitive collection of negative experiences.[4] Depression, then, is often understood as the foreclosure of a future, the impossibility that the yet-to-come might hold out anything new or positive: "I know that I can never be happy." Matthew Ratcliffe, in his phenomenology of depression, makes a similar point about temporality: "In depression, experience retains a coherent structure, but an aspect of that structure is missing. Loss of practical significance also amounts to a profound change in temporal experience. Without any sense that things could ever be significantly different, a kind of anticipation that more usually permeates the present is lost. So the experience of significant possibilities being actualized, which characterizes the transition from future to present to past, is lost too" (Ratcliffe 2015, 180). For the depressive, the present stretches endlessly—the eternal return of the same. There is no future that is not simply another iteration of the suffering present; the depressive is hopeless. She might think of suicide simply because she cannot bear to continue in this agonizing stasis.

This phenomenology is not novel, yet embedded in the way Wyllie presents melancholic temporality are a number of assumptions about time and experience. The stagnation of temporality, according to him, is fundamentally caused by ceasing to act: "Without activity, temporality stops because it is activity that produces lived time. . . . Ordinarily, experience is directed by the coming and going of events in the world" (2005, 180). He doesn't define "activity," and the concept of temporality "stopping" is unclear, but the underlying intuition is something like: I must be acting, initiating these events, in order for time to move toward the future. If I am "passive," time slows and eventually stops: "Lived time is our experience of things happening and this correlates lived time with the activity of the embodied human subject which in turn results in a bias toward the future. . . . Generally, one observes that passivity slows the course of lived time. In eliminating activity temporality is also eliminated and the experience of 'stagnation' occurs" (175). It's possible that by "activity" Wyllie simply means continuing to exist (even to eat, to sleep, to breathe is to "do something," after all), in which case without activity lived time tautologically stops—because you die—but given how meaningless this claim is, he must have something more substantive in mind. More probably he intends a Heideggerian understanding of intentionality, in which human beings engage the world primarily practically, expressing our concern about Being through ordinary undertakings and tasks (rather than through pure reflection). I find myself thrown into the world but can engage it through my projects in ways that require some initiative or orientation to that world. This is confirmed when Wyllie says, "In the suspension of activity or radical passivity, lived time is reversed because the future comes toward the inactive individual who simply waits for the future to become present" (178). In this account, then, there is a commitment to intentional activity—to projects—as the necessary marker of living in time. If I refuse all projects, and allow the world to eddy around me, then time for me will run slowly or stop. Wyllie describes this (non)experience as the central feature of melancholia, and although he does not infer the converse—that all people who have this orientation to the world are depressed—he does say that "phenomenological disturbances of sensed time, although not always of great importance to the human being, are an indicator that something is going wrong" (181).

Recall my reading of Saba Mahmood and Alisa Bierria from the last chapter. Wyllie's position—and the phenomenological tradition from which it derives—may thus undertheorize "activity" and agency, at the same time failing to make connections with political philosophy in which the subject's capacity to freely engage the world is a central concern.[5] Yet again, what we understand as mental illness finds itself on a continuum with all human life, both of which are part of a cultural zeitgeist in a way that phenomenology cannot ignore. The understanding of anaesthetic time I want to articulate sits uneasily in the space between addiction and the everyday. In this context, describing chocolate bars and Chardonnay as "drugs" is immediately tendentious; they are not the kinds of substances, in our cultural consciousness, that are administered by people in white coats or bought on the sly on street corners (Lenson 1995). Nonetheless, I want to argue, there is a category of substances that can induce a very particular temporality— some of which are tightly legally controlled, while others are freely available. To approach the experience of anaesthetic time in its everyday banality is philosophically challenging: it is so boring, so subtle, so routine, and so socially accepted that it barely stands out as an experience at all, just as Wyllie implies that the melancholic's stagnant time prevents experience. In this way, anaesthetic time is connected to boredom (in German, *Langeweile*, or "a long while"), which is an affect distinguished by a particular relation to time, and which, Heidegger famously argues, can, in its most profound form, depersonalize me and make the world seem entirely undifferentiated and irrelevant. Nonetheless, boredom of this deepest kind for Heidegger enables a kind of existential understanding; it is revelatory (if still unpleasant).[6] Anaesthetic time may work to disclose to us the reality of postdisciplinary time by virtue of their contrast, but it adds nothing to the project of temporally extending our self-concept to facilitate an account of agency built on sedimented experience. Indeed, its function is tacitly to refuse this task; it provides a respite from time rather than offering up deeper existential truths. As everyday anaesthetic time becomes addiction, which, if it goes far enough in a particular direction and in a particular context, becomes the permanent organization of life around one's habit in a holding pattern without trajectory, it stops time in a more holistic way. I therefore turn first to a small literature on the phenomenology of addiction and the temporality of psychopathology, which is supplemented by a larger oeuvre of fiction and memoir approaching addiction first-personally.[7]

DEAD TIME, JUNK TIME, ANAESTHETIC TIME

In writing on addiction, temporality is a consistent theme. For individuals more seriously or self-consciously addicted, time hesitates while the addiction reiterates. A hit takes one out of the synchronized, shared temporal world, and into a personal, amorphous zone, where time runs unaccounted for—either absurdly fast, or absurdly slow, it's impossible to tell. For example, in his book about hallucinations, Oliver Sacks describes his first (and last) experience of recreational intravenous morphine. Combining some historical reading with gazing at the sleeve of a decorated robe hanging on the door, he hallucinates the Battle of Agincourt for over twelve hours, a period he initially believes to be barely thirty minutes. "This shocked and sobered me, and made me realize that one could spend entire days, nights, weeks, even years of one's life in an opium stupor" (2012, 114–15). This is what William Burroughs called "junk time" (1977, 87), and it permeates narratives about addiction to opiates and alcohol: "When you look back over a year on the junk, it seems like no time at all. Only the periods when you were sick stand out. You remember the first few shots of a habit and the shots when you were really sick" (123).

What is phenomenologically distinctive about junk time? The two features I want to pull out are the loss of the long-term or organized future in favor of a frozen present, and the loss of temporal synchrony with the world (and in these ways it can be understood as connected to melancholia). Gerda Reith's (1999) analysis of thirty-eight Glaswegian addicts' experience of recovery set out to explore the life narratives of its subjects but uncovered a different, unexpected theme: "These narratives of addiction were mediated by a particular experience of temporality." "Over and over again," Reith writes, "the state of addiction was described, essentially, as a period of lost time, an extended present in which time seemed to freeze and the individual found it impossible to contemplate the future" (101). Because the present self is normally constituted by a relationship between its tacitly recollected past and an anticipation of its future, the addict's experience in the moments of the highs becomes very truncated. They retreat from the world, with its travails and pain, into an oneiric state defined primarily by the physical experience of the high but subsequently also by the search for the next hit. In more recent research, Ryan Kemp makes very similar observations: "The addict is not futureless but has a very limited future, a future that terminates in the appropriation and consumption of the addictive thing. They feel 'the now' will linger, in fact will endure forever. This 'now that lingers' is not just the being 'high' or 'winning elation' or post-sexual 'bliss' of the satiated addict. These states are prototypical, and the 'now that lingers' extends into the entire existence of the addict. It becomes their temporal way of being" (2009, 6).

Because the drugs consumed by these users were often illegal, dangerous to obtain, expensive, potentially highly addictive, and had serious health consequences and dramatic effects, their continued use turned into an all-consuming way of life, and the temporality induced by the drugs took over the subjects' entire lived experience. After scoring and using, Kemp notes, the addict sinks into long periods of "passive inaction"—his example is of his patient Chris, who spends his mornings raising the cash to get his next hit of heroin, before lapsing into a haze spent in front of daytime TV. He has lost his job because he cannot keep time, and becomes increasingly (like most addicts, Kemp says) unable to maintain a "normal" sleep routine. The addict becomes disconnected from social time—the rhythms of days spent hustling to get up and get to work, rush hour, dropping the kids off, picking them up, getting to the next meeting, making dinner, getting to bed. It is a commonplace of working with addicts, both Reith and Kemp observe, that they are always at least late, typically cannot keep appointments at all, and lead chaotic lives in which relationships are transient—often broken off or ignored entirely.

For both interpreters there is a consonance between the distress addiction causes to people other than the addict (the client who is so horribly unreliable, the man who wakes up from years of addiction to find himself with a wife and child he doesn't know) and its subjective distress (from Chris bored in front of the TV to the more intense forms of melancholic suffering, unwellness, guilt, and alienation Kemp describes through the lens of temporal asynchrony). Reith likewise describes what she considers an awful temporal experience, a tremendous loss (including the "peculiar horror" [1999, 114] of the very loss of self), and a way of living that has painful consequences for those who are close to addicts as well as larger social costs. Quitting, for these addicts within this framework, is positive, albeit incredibly difficult—"a process of awakening, as if from a long sleep" (109), or "re-animation of life in terms of an ability to envisage the future and act in a positive manner towards that vision" (107). It is perhaps this experience of time that leads to the recovery platitude that everything stops at the time an addiction begins, with no further personal growth or maturing being possible. Quitting takes one back to that point, experientially and emotionally.

I am not suggesting that the lived experience of this kind of intense addiction is in any way to be recommended, but I do find two things of interest in the phenomenological approach. First, moments in the addict's temporality are a much more extreme version of the temporality many ordinary people experience with everyday anaesthetics. The extreme version is easier to capture in a phenomenological analysis, more obviously damaging (to the addict and to others), and difficult to sustain. It irrupts into everyday life and breaks it down, in part through the addict's asynchrony with normal temporal rhythms. The individuals who invite (or offer) this kind of analysis are invariably addicted to opiates or alcohol—the agents I've described as anaesthetics—and normative temporality has ended for them in a global way.[8] But the lived experience this literature sketches is also reminiscent of the kind of evening lapse that Highmore lightly describes. This is so not only because the high addict—or the guy with a glass of wine on the sofa—lives in a now in which the past and future temporarily disappear. The addict is relatively unconcerned, Reith claims, about risk behaviors, as they fail to map out a future in which undesirable events must be avoided. Anxiety about the long-term future is mitigated by addiction; although the search for a drug supply can be consuming for impoverished addicts, the moments of the high obliterate concern about where the next hit will come from. This short-termism, Reith and Kemp both point out, pervades the entire experience of time in an existentially profound way. At the extreme, the addict is unmoved by the prospect of death, the universal limit against which Heidegger defines the lived experience of time. With its cultivation of anxiety and downloading of risk management onto individuals, much in the experience of postdisciplinary time I described in the last chapter makes addiction into a meaningful response to a cultural temporal condition. For some people at the edge of addictive collapse, shooting up while watching their friends die with relative indifference may represent a kind of existential boundary—although even under the direst of circumstances, care for others is not completely extinguished (Bourgois and Schonberg 2009, esp. 102–42). Even among those for whom the world of unlimited addiction is entirely foreign, many are eager to be momentarily relieved of the psychic tasks of future planning, imagining or managing lives that increasingly feel simultaneously highly future-oriented and without future.

The first postphenomenological question I want to ask about anaesthetic time goes beyond whether it is part of generic changes in social time: is it gendered? I'm sure that everyone drops into it at some point. There is a case, however, that the gendering of postdisciplinary time I described finds a corollary in anaesthetic time. From laudanum and patent medicines to Valium and Prozac, "feminine" drugs relieve anxiety, depression, disappointment, frustration, anger, and psychic exhaustion. They have long been prescribed to women in disproportion to men (see, e.g., Metzl 2003; Boyd 2004, esp. 59–60; Tone 2009, esp. ch. 8). The archetypical benzo addict is a woman who uses "little pills" supplemented with a couple of glasses of wine to get through an ordinary day. There is now an extensive marketing framework around this reality (at least for legal substances, with different inflections for prescription and retail varieties).

As a case study, I want to look at low-end, sweeter wines marketed to women, especially to mothers. Although it has a relatively long history as a class-aspirational and respectable form of alcoholic drink, the feminization of wine is a more recent, postwar phenomenon. Treating wine as a recreational anaesthetic for harried mothers, in ways that downplay or simply ignore the personal and political struggles that precipitate drinking (as well as the scarier consequences of addiction) has come to be a familiar part of the cultural landscape across wine marketing, mommy blogs, "women's" popular media, and self-help literatures.[9]

Take, for example, the complexly named Mad Housewife brand, which proclaims, "Above all else, wine should be fun, relaxing, and something you can afford to look forward to at the end of each and every day. This is your time. Time to enjoy a moment to yourself. A moment without the madness" (figure 4.1).[10] "Mommy's Time Out" wines speak for themselves. Notice that the Mad Housewife tagline, like many other marketing strategies, exploits the psychological demands of the daily cycle of work and life. All working people are expected to be able to switch personalities: from the productive, disciplined persona of the formal working day to the consuming, untrammeled persona of the leisured evening: "Tuck your kids into bed, sit down and have a glass of Mommy Juice—because you deserve it!" reads the promo for one disturbingly named wine, now defunct (figure 4.2). Here, the familiar interpellations of caring for small children ("Mommy, juice!") is carried over to mommy's own experience: now that the kids are fed and watered

FIGURE 4.1 Mad Housewife wines, website screenshot.

FIGURE 4.2
Mommy Juice
white wine,
online and
print ad.

and asleep, like them, mommy needs a drink and a rest. It's deeply condescending and infantilizing, but functions to take the sting out of drinking alcohol alone as a reward for the difficult work of caring for small children. Increasingly, of course, this polarized existence doesn't come in two discrete periods: we are expected to switch back and forth more and more rapidly and often, as work and life blur. Nonetheless, most anaesthetic time for most working people occurs in the late evenings. For many women, of course, the need for this period of anaesthetic time is intensified by the second shift of domestic work—a hard day at work can be compounded by a hard evening of housework and childcare. Hence the commercial exploitation of women's greater cognitive and affective need for end-of-day "time out."

The "Mad Housewife" model sports a retro pink cap-sleeve blouse, cat-eye glasses, and coiffed hair, all straight out of an episode of Mad Men—the cult TV show about midcentury misogyny to which the wine's name tacitly alludes. The cellar's website is styled to evoke both domesticity and fashion poise—baking in a floral apron before kicking off one's heels with a drink in hand (see figure 4.1)—in a series of parodic (if also tacit) references to Betty Friedan's postwar "problem that has no name." This wine, however, like its counterparts, is being sold to white middle-class women of the twenty-first century; the oblique visual allusions to their tormented forebears are softened by a retro chic look, a light-hearted postfeminist chortle at the idea that being something as old-fashioned and luxurious as a "housewife" is what drives contemporary women mad. This woman is "mad" in both senses— angry at her woman's lot, but also living in the fun zone of psychological distress where a glass of wine "takes the edge off" in a way we can all laugh about but that allegedly has nothing to do with "real" mental illness. Because white femininity has such a contradictory relationship to stereotypes of passivity, on the one hand, and to norms of upward mobility at work, on the other, white women are an ideologically available audience. As I mentioned in chapter 2, there is a long history of European bourgeois femininity being idealized through passivity—especially but not only sexual passivity—in which feminine withdrawal from a world of agency and action serves as a backdrop and enabling condition of men's control of time. This is the stereotype that critics say Lolo Ferrari confirms with her love of anaesthesia. Increasingly, however, it is as dated as a stereotype as it has always been as a description: the modern white woman is, in reality and expectation, busy, multitasking, working the double shift. A more contemporary image used by wine marketers is of a cartoon woman with multiple arms, managing the demands of middle-class

FIGURE 4.3 "Moms Who Need Wine," online logo.

work, home, and children. This is postdisciplinary time. She juggles a lap-
top, a family house, a soccer ball, a grocery bag full of vegetables—all indi-
rect markers of her class status (see figures 4.2 and 4.3). She is a striver but is
encouraged to have a cool, ironic attitude to her own striving through her
consumption of mommy-branded wine. This consumption isn't risky in this
tacit narrative. Instead, remarkably, it signals her knowingness, her ability
to take care of herself (however superficially) and relax into a form of life at
high speed.

We know that race and class intersect to reinforce labor market exploitation, especially in the United States, and so more women of color work shifts,
irregular hours, and multiple jobs, and are hence less likely to fit this daily
cycle of work and rest. If these mothers are juggling a frying pan or vacuum
cleaner, it could be a tool of paid work rather than of their own housekeeping,
and shift work makes it hard to put your kids in soccer. A more powerful
and dangerous set of norms, however, structure the lives of poor women
(especially if they are also racialized), who are commonly represented as more
likely to use drugs irresponsibly while pregnant or charged with the care of
their children (Pollitt 1998; Boyd 2004, esp. chs. 2 and 3). For example, in a
content analysis study of *New York Times* representations of pregnant women
who used either alcohol, tobacco, or crack cocaine, Kristin Springer (2010)
found that, despite the greater negative health consequences for a fetus of
maternal alcohol consumption compared with crack, articles about crack
users consistently framed them as bad mothers who are responsible for social

problems. The driver of negative representations of mothers or mothers-to-be, Springer argues, is not the actual risk posed to existing children or a fetus by the drug use of their mother but a prior commitment to representing poor and minority women as unfit and socially irresponsible. Springer cites other research showing that poor minority (especially African American) women are disproportionately targeted by law enforcement agencies for drug use while pregnant—for example, by enforcing compulsory drug testing of patients only at hospitals serving such populations (483).[11] Knowing that your class or race makes you vulnerable to social services or police intervention if you are labeled as a drinker or drug abuser changes your relationship to anaesthetic time. The ubiquity of whiteness attached to such a bourgeois drug as wine, then, softens and ironizes the social reality of anaesthetic time in much the same way as I argued in chapter 2 that the aesthetic representation of death evades racist violence.

In their rich and sympathetic photoethnography *Righteous Dopefiend* (2009), Philippe Bourgois and Jeff Schonberg examine the lives of chronically addicted homeless people in a San Francisco locale over a period of a dozen years. They weave close attention to the experience of drug use together with social analysis—here, most often, analysis of the failings of public health strategies in the United States due to punitive antidrug policy making combined with lack of accessible health care. The authors are in no doubt about the cultural conditions of addiction; their goal, they say toward the beginning of the book, is to "clarify the relationships between large-scale power forces and intimate ways of being in order to explain why the United States, the wealthiest nation in the world, has emerged as a pressure cooker for producing destitute addicts embroiled in everyday violence" (Bourgois and Schonberg 2009, 19). The book shows more than anything the impossibly high bar of escaping the life of street involvement and long-term addiction to heroin and crack. The paths that lead to street addiction are systemic and hence multiple, but there are no paths out. This population has its gendered and racial politics: of all the marginal ways of living, being a woman living full-time on the street is among the most dangerous due to the risk of violence and sexual exploitation. Bourgois and Schonberg also describe a complex "intimate apartheid" contained within "the ethnic components to habitus" (62)—manifested in racial dynamics of association and avoidance, different understandings of family relationships and loyalties, racist beliefs and actions, and drug-taking practices themselves. Although not an explicit ethnographic frame in the text, temporality matters for these addicts: the often frenetic and necessarily limited time of fundraising for the next hits, the agonizingly protracted time of "dopesickness" (withdrawal), the uncomfortable and interrupted time of sleeping on a damp mattress below an underpass, the busy but unstructured time of panhandling or looking for opportunities for petty theft or scrambling to get odd jobs, and of course the profound anaesthetic time after a hit. For these serious addicts, drug use is, as Kemp and Reith describe of different populations, an end in itself rather than a means to any particular subjectivity, disciplined or postdisciplinary. If anaesthetic time can sometimes be part of an inadvertent project of the self, these are *postdisciplinary postsubjects*—a population produced by late capitalism but without purpose for it, a biopolitical residue.[12] They can scarcely be put to any organized use but must nonetheless be managed by the institutions they encounter—especially the police, courts, paramedics and hospitals, and what public health services there are (such as needle exchanges or detox programs).

My dwelling in this chapter and the last on the afterlives of disciplinary power is unusual in the contemporary world of Foucauldian politics, where, as Mathew Coleman and Kathryn Yusoff ask rhetorically in their recent interview with Elizabeth Povinelli, "Who doesn't do biopolitics these days?" (Povinelli, Coleman, and Yusoff 2017, 169).[13] When giving a paper titled "Moms Who Need Wine" I intended it as an analysis of one twisted moment in the popular culture of white femininity in North America—indeed, as a rather acerbic critique of how structural injustice is obscured but also leveraged and made palatable when it is represented through privileges of race and class. These are among the most favored of anaesthetic subjects, but their example opens up larger questions about the role of anaesthetic time not just in managing the individual effects of postdisciplinary temporality for subjects pressed toward productivity, but how it is a part of lived experience among members of populations marked as expendable, socially remaindered, or marking time until their deaths. For all those individuals who use anaesthetic time as a respite from the labor of communicative capitalism, there are also those who are thrown out by systems of labor as surplus and who are anaesthetized as a way of managing or simply subduing them. These populations include psychiatric patients, prisoners, and elderly and disabled people in residential care. For example, Anthony Hatch and Kym Bradley show how psychotropic drugs are used in "technocorrections": "the strategic use of biotechnologies to manage prisoner's bodies and to facilitate unjust policies that reproduce mass incarceration" (2016, 225). Such "chemical restraints" are used in a context in which the distinction between therapeutic drug use for the mentally ill, and politically motivated silencing of prisoners' voices is entirely elided (231); the practices of imprisonment are a kind of destruction of subjectivity (as Guenther's [2013] work on solitary confinement shows), as well as leading, directly or indirectly, to mass death. The "war on drugs" that started in the United States in the 1980s, alongside the rise of neoliberal economic policy, funnels poor and racialized people (disproportionately women) into the prison-industrial complex through punitive and discriminatory antidrug (particularly anticrack) laws, tracing another path along which an individual experience of anaesthetic time emerges from one political world and leads to becoming part of an anaesthetically controlled population (McTighe 2012). This is not only a biopolitics—the power to manage life—but also a necropolitics—the capacity to effect the mass destruction of human bodies (Mbembe 2003), often along racialized lines (Dillon 2018, 84-118), including by drugging them, one way or another, to death.

PASSING OUT

In anaesthetic time my consciousness is altered and my temporality shifts, from the slight blur induced by that glass of wine on the couch to "nodding"— the moments not long after injected heroin reaches the bloodstream when the hit is strongest, and the addict's eyes close and their chin drops to their chest and then lifts as they enter a liminal state of blissful semiconsciousness (Bourgois and Schonberg 2009, 17). As chapter 2 showed, however, there are edges to experience not only as lived time shifts the subject's relation to normativity but also as consciousness fades away entirely. Unconsciousness is perhaps the limit of anaesthetic time. Consume enough anaesthetic agents and you will eventually get there. The cases of sexual violence I thought through earlier mostly involved women who were drunk or drugged, but part of my point was that we all move along the spectrum of consciousness and unconsciousness all the time, if only because we sleep and wake. Sleep has thus been of enduring concern to phenomenologists because of its various challenges to philosophical understandings of consciousness, intentionality, will, and agency. As Nicolas de Warren interprets Husserl,

> In sleep, consciousness abstains from its own interests, and, in this sense, consciousness has retired from itself while also retiring from the world. . . . Falling asleep is allowing the world and myself to slip away and come to a rest. Bit by bit, particular interests and activities are let go, until . . . the

entire "life of the will" has been let go. This "letting go" or "sinking away" ("Sinken-Lassens") is a mode of my entire life of consciousness. In other words, when I am fatigued, and falling asleep, or losing my gumption, my ego is still affected by things around me, yet the force of these affections slackens, and I no longer give myself over to these affections. I sink into an indifference in having relinquished any investment in the world. In a sense, I allow myself to become inert. (de Warren 2010, 291)

Sleep—whether drug-induced or not—can be very literally anaesthetic, as when someone who is depressed or traumatized does nothing but sleep. More generally, sleep is antithetical (and antidotal) to disciplinary and postdisciplinary time. It follows that it is often read as unproductive, "a waste of time," or even as equivalent to death. "Sleep, those little slices of death. Oh! How I loathe them," Edgar Allan Poe is supposed to have said. Alternatively, sleep might be understood as an annoying biological necessity that must be correctly managed in order to assure productivity during waking hours (Crary 2013). Many people are chronically deprived of sleep precisely because of our cultural commitment to postdisciplinary time, and need anaesthetic agents to get to sleep (or drugs of a different sort to stay awake). Our work routines increasingly intrude on our sleep—both because for many people the raw hours we must commit to working have increased, and because technologies make us newly available to work in the hours we would otherwise sleep. Postdisciplinary time ensures that we typically wake with the alarm, while postponing the hour of going to sleep to move along our task accomplishment.

Sleep is necessary to life, but somehow not a part of "lived experience." The interruption of self that sleep offers makes it hard to theorize; we tend to focus on the surrounding frame in which sleep occurs and treat actually being asleep as a philosophical blank space. This is in part because sleep so fully evades the ways we have of talking about subjectivity, including being imagined as a period of existence without agency, and (hence) outside of any kind of time. In chapter 2 I suggested that sleep provides us with an experience of "night"—in the phenomenological sense of indeterminate and unbounded space—as well as of anonymity (a condition as central to subjectivity as individuality).

Sleep, unconsciousness, and associated liminal states thus offer an opportunity for description that might enrich my analysis of anaesthetic time, and illuminate its connection to experience and to agency. Take *falling* asleep. Even someone who's very tired will have a short "hypnogogic" period between wakefulness and sleep, during which breathing becomes slower and more regular, mental experience becomes lighter and less self-directed, and the muscles relax, before imperceptibly one "drifts off." To fall into sleep is to give oneself over to a netherworld in which one ceases to act; to do so almost always requires an initial decision, a practice of letting go that has to be learned and can be resisted—deliberately or unconsciously. A baby might need a lullaby, rocking; most adults have their bedtime rituals that they need to go to sleep: a bath, a few minutes of reading, or narcotics. In his beautiful essay *The Fall of Sleep*, Jean-Luc Nancy writes, "Whoever relinquishes vigilance relinquishes attention and intention, every kind of tension and anticipation; he enters into the unraveling of plans and aims, of expectations and calculations. It is this loosening that gathers together—actually or symbolically—the fall into sleep" (2009, 3).

Part of what's important in Nancy's description is his suggestion, echoing Merleau-Ponty, that falling asleep represents a surrender not only of consciousness but also of agency, as I described in chapter 2. Recall that, in fact, in Merleau-Ponty's language it requires a choice to lie down to sleep, and (he says optimistically) stop mentally organizing one's future, but that is as far as the will goes. At some indefinable moment, sleep arrives, turning the mimicry of sleep into a reality, "and I succeed in becoming what I was trying to be: an unseeing and almost unthinking mass, riveted to a point in space and in the world henceforth only through the anonymous alertness of the senses" (Merleau-Ponty [1945] 2002, 189–90). In chapter 2 I used this quote to move into the discussion of the value of night and anonymity, but we could equally tie it to the discussion of agency in chapter 3. Falling asleep and being asleep are only two of the states in which our lived experience fails to line up with the qualities of an autonomous subject—indeed, this is one of the reasons that the ubiquitous experience of sleep has been so challenging for accounts of the subject committed to self-sovereignty (Goldberg-Hiller 2019).

I was recently interviewed by Bec Fary, a quietly wonderful young Australian who produces a podcast on sleep, and who was less interested in my philosophical insights than in provoking me to talk first-personally and specifically about my sleep experience.[14] I was recalled to the time after my son's birth—described in chapter 5—when he was breastfeeding every two to three hours and needed to sleep next to me, within smelling distance of my milk-soaked chest, to fall asleep, which he would do after he had fed copiously, often with my nipple still in his mouth. His sleep schedule seemed to be working fine for *him*: when he was awake he was a delightful, alert, responsive baby. I, on the other hand, was profoundly exhausted. I had certainly been chronically tired at times in my life up to that point, most notably in my teens when I went to a boarding school that operated on an absurdly Faucherian timetable, and I shared a small room with three other girls, and a house with forty-seven other young people who lived according to a wide variety of temporalities. But after having a baby I found that the constant interruption of my sleep and the exhaustion, and the cognitive states generated by that exhaustion, reached a new and intolerable level. I could see why sleep deprivation is such an effective form of torture, and at this point, some years later, the most positive thing to say about it perhaps is that my memory of that period of my life is notably patchy. (Sleep deprivation destroys recall.)

When you are desperately sleep-deprived, falling asleep assumes a different quality. It is more like passing out. The hypnogogic phase is radically shortened, and (at least in my case) the hamster-wheel quality of an anxious brain lasts a couple of minutes before the hamster simply keels over. The reverie that Nancy and Merleau-Ponty both describe, the period in which all the qualities of the self can be noted and abandoned, felt to me more like a short spell of more-or-less random mental firings, before night fell as it does close to the equator—more like someone switching off the lights than the slow dimming of the day we experience in northern summers. Weirdly, waking up was similarly shortened, rather than slowed. It's a cliché of novelistic descriptions of sleep that waking up is like being under water and swimming to the surface. My son's mild squeaks (presaging a full-bodied hunger cry) would wake me up in the small hours, but that waking was more like desperately trying to get to the air with bursting lungs after a near-drowning, knowing I had only a few seconds before I would be forced to inhale. I can hardly describe the sinking feeling that accompanied that upward dive; I just couldn't stop this other person needing me to wake up and serve. To a lover who routinely woke me in the night, I might say, unsympathetically, "Just go back to sleep," passively listening to their pillow talk or petty anxieties without anything more being required of me. Even with solitary insomnia (which has its own kinds of built-in torture), I ruminate on my failure to sleep and all the other disappointments of my subjectivity (even as that which I direct my will toward—going back to sleep—fails me). With a baby, however, there was a task at hand: minimally, half-sitting to lift a small body toward me, fumbling to get a latch, the intense sensation of milk letting down, the baby's mewing turning to grunts of satisfaction as he sucked, a period of waiting (often holding an uncomfortable position I dared not change), sometimes getting up and stumbling to a nearby table to change a diaper if he felt wet, before snuggling back with him near me, praying he would sleep quickly and not fuss. My nights became an unending experience of just getting him to sleep and getting to sleep myself before, it felt like, he woke up again.

"The anonymous alertness of the senses" defines sleep, says Merleau-Ponty. Being deeply asleep involves a strange doubled unconsciousness: on the one hand, I am indifferent to the world, removed from its life. Most of us can recall an experience of waking up to find we did something while we were asleep of which we have no memory: perhaps as trivial as shifting position in the bed, or maybe something as dramatic as the somnambulist antics of those who commit violent crimes. From the perspective of the awake, most of us have also had the experience of trying to rouse someone very deeply asleep and being surprised (or exasperated) by their unresponsiveness to what is happening to their body—the shaking of a shoulder, or exclaiming their name. However, being asleep normally includes that element of passive "alertness": if a door slams, I may suddenly startle awake, or if my radio alarm comes on I might bubble up through a hypnopompic phase in which my dream and the news combine in a surreal story. The external world is not entirely dead to me. Being the primary caregiver of a new baby sits on the hinge between these two states: when I would drop into exhausted sleep, I was (I'm told) oblivious to noise or adult presence. If my son moaned, however, I was instantly awake (I think). Of course, these claims are epistemically uncertain, given that I didn't have an independent observer consistently recording my sleep environment and reflexes, but many parents I've talked to concur that the experience of sleeping with kids around—especially babies—is an experience of sleeping "with one ear open." (For people sleeping in dangerous or insecure environments—in a homeless shelter, at a refugee camp, in a shared cell, on a park bench, or in a psych ward—there is a similar ambivalence, with different sets of risks.)

Marie-Eve Morin helpfully described Nancy's *The Fall of Sleep* to me as providing a phenomenology of losing consciousness, but actually it represents only one way of going under. We often misdescribe general anaesthesia as "going to sleep," which is the linguistic elision that allows Meredith Jones to describe Lolo Ferrari as being transformed by her cosmetic surgeon while she is in "enchanted sleep." In Jones's analysis, Ferrari provides a literal, living example of the fairy-tale heroine whose consciousness is suspended only for her to wake up after a difficult transition (for Sleeping Beauty, the transition from princess-girl to marriageable young woman; for Ferrari, the surgical transition from before to after). When each wakes up, it is as if no time has passed, yet each is transformed. Neither the rhetorically powerful "enchanted sleep" nor a general anaesthetic is like actually going to sleep, however, whether mythically, phenomenologically, or medically speaking (Cole-Adams 2017). General anaesthesia is astonishingly complete and abrupt. The only time I had a general anaesthetic—for twenty minutes, in a dentist's office, for the particularly difficult extraction of an impacted wisdom tooth—I heard the anaesthetist say, after putting the needle in my arm, "Here we go." Then, "You might get a metallic taste in your mouth." It was the middle of the day; I was flooded with adrenaline and completely wide-awake. I remember noting the time on a wall clock directly in my field of vision. I tasted metal, and said, "Oh yeah, there it is." Then a complete veil of unconsciousness descended instantly; there was no transition time at all between full alertness and nothingness. Under anaesthesia there is no dreaming. No matter how loudly the operating staff talk, or how much clatter of instrument noise or buzzing of the drill there is, I won't regain consciousness until the anaesthesiologist decides to change the drug infusion.[15] Coming around was less dramatic than going under, but still nothing like waking up from sleep. I was suddenly aware that I was conscious, and that the operation must be over, but it felt as though nothing had happened, and no time had passed. I was lying on a gurney, with partition curtains on either side of me, in a completely unfamiliar room; coincidentally, a different wall clock in my sight line showed me that it was exactly twenty minutes later than when I had had the metallic taste. Only the light throbbing and the wad of cotton in my mouth indicated that I had been operated on.

This may be the black hole that Ferrari loved: the immediate and utterly involuntary relinquishing of vigilance; the extinguishing of self; the dramatic suspension of existence; the total respite from postdisciplinary time. Early opponents of anaesthesia were philosophically motivated: physical pain (a sensation human beings had never previously been able consistently to avoid) was understood to be part of the vital spirit that makes us human and keeps us alive, including by helping us survive the shock of surgery (Snow 2006, 23). Asleep, we dream; we trust—perhaps—that, should disaster arrive, we can rouse ourselves. But anaesthetized I am completely dependent on another to bring me round. I am absolutely vulnerable. Ferrari was unusual in loving this dependence; since anaesthesia's earliest days, prospective patients have been deeply afraid of involuntary unconsciousness. Given that being unconscious carries the risk of sexual assault, the experience is riskier for women than for men, as chapter 2 showed. Whatever the pains, pleasures, or risks, this sensory oblivion isn't something to be recommended or rejected. Instead, it represents a limit, an experiential encounter with complete withdrawal from the exhaustion of contemporary fantasies of autonomy. What I have called anaesthetic time is a much milder version of Ferrari's eccentric preferences, but its motivations may not be completely different. The pressures of self-making generate their own demand for respite, for a retreat to a space undefined by working on the self.

Falling asleep, being asleep, and waking up are thus three states that challenge normative and singular understandings of will, agency, and temporality. Of course, no defender of even the most demanding account of autonomy would have reason to think that a 24/7 vigilance was required to secure it, yet stories about knowing ourselves and making rational choices imply that my autonomy is put on hold when I'm not fully compos mentis. The liminal states I've been describing, however, are not irrationalities or windows of insanity (which are also philosophically interesting); they are necessary states that are part of the human condition. They are also states in which insights or even epiphanies happen. Many of us have had the experience of a dream resolving some emotional or practical difficulty, or of having terrific ideas while falling asleep or waking up. "Sleep on it" is not just advice about allowing time to pass before making an important decision. It also suggests that sleep itself can work its magic on cognitive processes and affective states, smoothing out temporary excesses and refining our judgment. I must, at times, relinquish whatever I call my sovereign self, cease to exercise my will, become anonymous, and step out of the spatial and temporal dimensions that normatively structure subjectivity, and this can be crucial to self-understanding.

My sleep stories make a second point: sleep is a state of tremendous vulnerability that reveals our necessary interdependence. Finding a safe place to sleep is sometimes represented as a concern only for our prehistoric ancestors or an anthropological curiosity, but it remains a challenge for many contemporary people in the overdeveloped West—from the homeless or underhoused to those fearing domestic violence (Lowe, Humphreys, and Williams 2007). Sexual violence by an anaesthetist against his patients—as in the case of George Doodnaught I cited at the end of chapter 2—is especially horrifying because it exploits the entirely involuntary vulnerability of a powerfully drugged state to which one has voluntarily submitted. Further, the absolute dependence of a newborn on a particular person reveals another commonplace structuring feature of our capacity to act according to our own plans: other people redirect us in ways we cannot but heed. Recall the discussion of Bierria's work on Black women's autonomy: others author our intentions, and the worlds in which we act are deeply structured by asymmetries that limit not only what we can achieve but also what our actions can mean. In the dark nights of sleep deprivation with a new baby, the task is to endure, even in the face of cognitive collapse that results from exhaustion.

Jones's Ferrari is princess-like and playful, but Ferrari's own words are harder. She implied in interviews that her everyday life felt intolerable to her, and her anaesthetic practices seem concomitantly dramatic: "All this stuff [the cosmetic surgeries] . . . has been because I can't stand life. But it hasn't changed anything. There are moments when I disconnect totally from reality. Then I can do anything, absolutely anything. I swallow pills. I throw myself out of windows. Dying seems very easy then." Ferrari probably was psychologically destroyed by an abusive family—she said as much.[16] There's nothing prescriptive in her story, and it is shocking that a woman would see anaesthesia as a respite from her life, and troubling to note how easily Ferrari's actions can be understood through stereotypes about white women's essential passivity and masochism. Jones shows us, however, that her exemplary, paradoxical life can also teach us something about unconsciousness as an experience with epistemic and ethical implications, and about how we derive pleasure from refusals of agency as well as from its exercise. As Berlant says, "the body and a life are not only projects but also sites of episodic intermission from personality, of inhabiting agency differently in small vacations from the will itself. . . . These pleasures can be seen as interrupting the liberal and capitalist subject called to consciousness, intentionality, and effective will" (2007, 780).

BEYOND ANAESTHETIC TIME

Straight talk about willpower and positive thinking claims that agency is just a matter of getting on track, as if all the messy business of real selves could be left behind like a bad habit or a hangover. But things are always backfiring. Self-making projects proliferate at exactly the same rate as the epidemics of addictions and the self-help shelves at the bookstore.—Kathleen Stewart, *Ordinary Affects* (2007, 59)

There is no pleasure in having nothing to do; the fun is having lots to do and not doing it.—Andrew Jackson

The juxtaposition of postdisciplinary and anaesthetic time together form a time economy that is experienced psychosomatically, and has psychosomatic consequences for its subjects. Postdisciplinary time cultivates attention deficit, sleep disorders, anxiety, and "stress." All are complex constellations of psychopathological and physical symptoms, which emerge as entities, are exacerbated, or become more common because of the organization and experience of time. All are mostly "chronic"—that fascinating word that signals both a specific relation to time and an endurable level of suffering. Postdisciplinary time pulls us away from the present moment: it is forward-looking, connecting the now to a future reward, achievement-oriented, and prone to disappointment. It imagines time as a commodity that is, as Zeno famously imagined, infinitely divisible—and thus infinitely exploitable. Like every good Foucault scholar, however, I recognize that discipline is both constraining and enabling. Old-fashioned disciplinary time, for many of us, spurs and structures our class prep, our thesis completion, our workouts, or timely progress through a tedious meeting.

Anaesthetic time, by contrast, clearly depends on the ritualized, habitual consumption of addictive substances that provide neurochemical pleasures without requiring any particular intentionality. The lived experience of anaesthetic time owes a great deal to the interactive chemistry of substances and human bodies, which is why the popular blog "Moms Who Need Wine" sends a complicated message with its disclaimer: "We encourage our Moms to always use good judgement and drink only in moderation. We firmly believe that it's all about the release, and not about the drink. A piece of chocolate, a cafe latte, or a good chick flick can be just as effective" (see figure 4.3).[17] It *is* about the release, but it's *also* about the drink.

I'm not suggesting that all eating, drinking, or drug taking has the goal of bringing its subject into this "anaesthetic time," nor that individuals did not have a troubled or politically charged relation to anaesthetic agents available prior to modernity. Nonetheless, many of the habitual, emotional uses of substances that change sensory experience are, I am arguing, a tacit response to postdisciplinary time—among other stressors. During anaesthetic time my intentionality slackens and shifts: I no longer have a clear object of experience, or, perhaps, my object narrows to the consumption of my favored drug and the sensations it generates. Any larger sense of myself as an agent diminishes. Both this slackening of intentionality and the changing perception of time find a limit in unconsciousness, which marks the ultimate suspension of time, and the ultimate reprieve from discipline. Nonetheless, Lolo Ferrari is no role model, and anaesthetic time is not something I'm recommending. Anaesthetic time is risky and filled with suffering. It is a loss, and a form of escape. It is more an absence or an evasion than a way of being present. I am not suggesting that we should all go to sleep in lieu of feminist revolution.

These two chapters have brought together vastly different registers: as we analyze the forms of subjectivity into which postdisciplinary postmodernity interpellates us, we also need, I have suggested, to keep an eye on the lived experience of that interpellation. The defense of any form of subjectivity as part of "an aesthetics of existence" needs to consider how that subjectivity will reinforce or undermine the forms that power assumes today. Foucault's self-described "ethics of discomfort" needs to be read not as an abstract relation of the self to self but rather as a potential practice that runs into existing lived experience, including sensory experience. An ethics describing a mode of subjectivation either unattainable or in conformity with a politically damaging historical moment is no ethics at all. The historical and cultural intensification of the economy of time I've described is wrapped up with our exploitation as workers and how we are managed within biopolitical regimes, especially as norms of agency are linked to a contemporary work ethic. Political resistance has been undermined by time poverty and the expansion of the subjectivity of the good worker, while personal resistance lives, in part, in the ambivalent, diffuse moments of anaesthetic time. I have shown something of how agency can feel as it is tied to the political task (or maybe fantasy) of the cumulative transformation of a self through time—a project held out as the epochal critical task of modernity. Foucault once said of Merleau-Ponty that his "essential philosophical task" was "never to consent to being completely comfortable with one's own presuppositions. Never to let them fall peacefully asleep" ([1979] 2000a, 448). Perhaps our discomfort is such, however, that anaesthetized peace may sometimes be a necessary solace and counterpoint to the subjectivity of an aesthetics of existence.

CHAPTER FIVE

Child,
Birth

AN AESTHETIC

We have entered a time . . . that confronts us with a radically new threat. It is a time when, outside and inside the specialized language of medicine, pain threatens to become entirely meaningless.—David B. Morris, *The Culture of Pain* (1991, 77)

Pain's resistance to language is not simply one of its incidental or accidental attributes but is essential to what it is.—Elaine Scarry, *The Body in Pain* (1985, 5)

GIVING BIRTH IS BOTH EVERYDAY AND EXTRAORDINARY. As I write, people all over the world are having babies. In Canada over a thousand are born every day. Midwives, doulas, nurses, and obstetricians who work in labor and delivery witness many births every month. Every human being on the planet—the 7.7 billion of us here in fall 2019—was created in and by the body of another person, and then, one way or another, born of that body. Being born is, in this very general sense, a universal human experience, and yet it is also profoundly unpredictable. Hannah Arendt famously remarks at the beginning of *The Human Condition* that natality may be the central category of political thought, since the constant birth of human beings introduces a ceaseless novelty, and hence plurality, to the world. "The new beginning inherent in birth," she writes, "can make itself felt in the world only because the newcomer possesses the capacity of beginning something anew, that is, of acting"

([1958] 1998, 9). Arendt contrasts "natality" with the actual work of reproduction, thereby contributing to the tradition in which philosophers appropriate talk of birth, sexual difference, or maternity while typically managing to disregard the lived experience of women who gestate, labor, and deliver babies (see Guenther 2006, 29–47). Birth thus plays a curious role in philosophy: it is central to understanding "the human condition," but, as one of very few philosophically important activities that only the female-bodied can undertake, its intellectual and political significance tends to be abstracted and rendered metaphorical.

Part of this abstraction entails focusing on the child—who after all might be male, and even, one day, become a philosopher—rather than on the person giving birth. Feminist orthodoxy describes how the history of obstetrics and "maternity care" has been, at least in industrialized countries, one of a gradual erosion of women's agency (as both midwives and mothers) in favor of a technoscientific birthing process in which male obstetricians hold epistemic power (e.g., Brodsky 2008; Ehrenreich and English [1973] 2010; McIntosh 2012). The rhetoric of the welfare of the infant tends to predominate over the welfare of the mother—especially her psychosocial welfare. This transition is evident at the institutional level (as personnel authorized to manage a birth or locations considered suitable to give birth transform, for example) and at the phenomenal level (as the lived birthing body's sensations and affects are superseded by medical measurement of its objective status) (Kukla 2005, esp. 106–20). If philosophy's engagement with natality has tended to be metaphorical, in other words, medicine's engagement with birth has become differently abstracted—from the experience of delivering a baby as epistemically and ethically important. It's all very well to know all this, and probably it would be politic if more people intending to participate in birth did know it. I can personally attest, however, that the knowing of it is a poor substitute for knowing what it feels like to give birth, an epistemic unknown faced by all first-timers. Look for stories about childbirth, as surely all pregnant persons in the age of the internet do, and the first and really the only *aesthetic* theme to turn up is pain.[1]

My son was born at home in the middle of a frigid February night, exactly as we had planned. Whatever the pros and cons, a home birth guarantees one thing: no pharmaceuticals. I confess to having taken a kind of pride in my intention to deliver with nothing but a hot bath and gumption, but I do understand that it's not for everyone. Proximity to people wearing scrubs makes many women feel more secure, and if lady luck doesn't smile on your labor, then at a certain point it ceases to matter what you intended. Because the pain of childbirth is not necessarily an indicator of damage but rather a typical part of a predictable physiological process, and because it's not inflicted by anyone else (unless you count the baby, which seems both anatomically incorrect and unfair), for me it invited a certain kind of attention. What would it mean to watch this pain, to be with it, to witness sensation of the most extreme and urgent kind without indulging my aversion? Could something be learned from a nasty, brutish, and likely not short enough event that I had determined to endure? Now, reflecting much later, I wonder, how could by far the most excruciating experience of my life also be the most joyful, profound, and spiritually transformative?

The more I know about giving birth, the more I realize that any meaning I attribute to my pain is much less my own than I like to think: it is hugely dependent on my historical moment, national context, class, and relationship to Western medicine (Bourke 2014; Wolf 2009). The more I try to *write* about giving birth, the more I also realize that my pain is mute, elusive, liable to evade representation. These factors mitigate against a good birth story: historians mostly concur that our contemporary culture has an unusually narrow repertoire of aversive, negative meanings for pain (Glucklich 2003), while philosophers have argued that pain is notoriously hard to convey in language (Scarry 1985; Moscoso 2012; Vetlesen 2009). When the pain concerned is childbirth, telling one's story is even harder: this is a political battleground, with all manner of actors vying to make sense of someone else's experience for their own ends. Perhaps I should stop writing now, but I won't. The discursive space carved out for the meaning of pain in childbirth is my first theme, but my second remains that experience it fails to ask after.

CHILDBIRTH: REPRESENTATION AND EXPERIENCE

Representations of actual childbirth in Western countries are a world away from such profound ethical conclusions. They tend to render it ordinary in a different way, well documented by feminists over the past fifty years: fictional and documentary narratives are unrelentingly trivializing and objectifying. Supine women in flimsy hospital gowns puff and scream, while scrubbed doctors peer between their spread legs and make flippant and demeaning comments (in comedies); issue urgent, authoritarian orders (in drama); or both (in real life). Birth attendants—almost always male putative fathers-to-be—panic or reassure. There is a repertoire of standard lines: a shrewish woman shrieks, "This is all your fault!" to a rueful man; a nurse shouts, "Push! Push!" to a flagging woman (or "Don't push!" to a woman giving birth inconveniently quickly); if a birthing woman speaks at all, it is typically to deny her capacities—"I can't do it!" or "Give me the epidural NOW!" "Good girl!" exclaims the patronizing doctor. Birth is typically represented as by definition a dangerous process requiring medical intervention and management, and always as an emergency. Another slew of feminist research documents—and resists—this particular intersection of knowledge and power (for examples, see Elson 2009; Morris and McInerney 2010; Oliver 2012).

This general picture can be thought of as our background experience of childbirth, in the same sense that Timothy O'Leary says there is a classical experience of madness in Foucault. It is those "forms of consciousness, sensibility, practical engagement and scientific knowledge which take 'madness' [or childbirth] as their object" (O'Leary 2009, 80). I find it useful to think of medicalized birth as part of "experience"—including the experience of people who've never given birth—as it reflects the fact that our subjectivity is never fully outside this discourse. It represents the historical conditions of possibility for any individual experience, and individual experience of childbirth *can* be fully contained within it. For many women, birth just *is* a medical situation, an emergency, a state of affairs requiring their objectification that will be beyond their capacities to endure or to manage in any way. For others—and maybe even most—however, the individual experience of giving birth reveals the gaps between discourse and our own sensations, capacities, possibilities, limits. Medical knowledge runs up against bodies: that position for laboring is intensely uncomfortable; that light too bright; those voices too loud; cervical dilation doesn't follow the hospital's schedule for good progress, or (less often) the baby comes too fast; that keening sound cannot be stopped.

Because most of us—unlike many of our predecessors—have no direct encounters with childbirth beyond the birth of any children we may have ourselves, we are deeply beholden to these representations. If we *have* given birth in this kind of context, we are also wrapped up in this medical model even though we have a more personal relation to it. As a consequence, birth is viewed with tremendous fear by many: research indicates that even as we in the overdeveloped West now live in statistically the safest moment in human history to give birth (in terms of mortality), women are getting more frightened of giving birth (Walsh 2009; Hinsliff 2018). This fear in turn reinforces the medicalization of birth, as women see labor and delivery as something unknown and unmanageable that requires expert supervision. This discourse produces us as birthing women (whether or not "women" is what we want to be), and we ourselves reproduce its relations of knowledge/power.

That fear, however, is not entirely irrational. For most of us, childbirth will be the most painful experience of our lives, and (unlike a broken leg or an infected appendix), we can fully anticipate this. Yet the lived experience of this pain is elusive. It is a cliché of advice to pregnant people that although the pain is awful, you'll forget. The only good thing to say about the hideous experience awaiting you, unhelpful friends like to say, is that it will soon become an abstraction, a nostalgic simulacrum of pain rather than pain itself, about which you may eventually tell yourself convenient lies: "It wasn't that bad." How else, after all, does anyone ever have more than one child? This lacuna sits uncomfortably next to the proliferating genre of the "birth story": a first-personal, vernacular, and often overplotted account of late pregnancy, labor, and delivery that has found its own niche in parenting magazines, midwifery websites, and birthing books. I suspect that most women write these narratives a considerable time after their child's birth, because they are, generally speaking, pleasantly vague, and colored mainly by the primary emotion left long after the fact, which is typically either regret that such a dreadful trial was not handled better by someone or other, or rose-tinted relief that the whole ordeal is well in the past. Try looking for close descriptions of the physical experience of giving birth and you will mainly find medical sources that elucidate the analgesic options available to those giving birth in hospitals. The experience is pain, and the pain is terrible, goes the refrain, but nowadays we can make it go away. This promise of absence doesn't leave much incentive for imaginative projection or psychological preparedness. It only encourages knowing the quickest route to the labor ward. The top demand on your birth plan, a woman in the gym locker room told me in an urgent tone when I was thirty-five weeks pregnant, should be that they have to do the epidural first thing when you get to the hospital. Don't take no for an answer. I admired this unequivocal approach: going in with an ambivalent attitude to the offerings of Western medicine is likely to result in confusion all around. Better to seize the rare opportunity for powerful drugs on the government's dime and make the whole experience as painless as possible.

ON PAIN IN CHILDBIRTH

Narrating a positive relation to one's own experience of pain in childbirth carries political risks. Surely it is a part of women's liberation to be free from

Eve's curse? A British midwife—a male one, if it is not mean-spirited to point that out—generated controversy by suggesting that labor pain is a "rite of passage" that prepares one for the challenges of caring for a newborn (Campbell 2009).[2] This claim provoked women with all manner of childbirth experiences to object: Should we not then torture any prospective father to better galvanize his parenting instincts? Or perhaps stick pins into that one-in-a-thousand woman who finds childbirth less than agonizing? Despite the wisdom of some of his views on contemporary medical practice, Denis Walsh was apparently insensitive to two aspects of the history that precedes, and, arguably, informs his remarks. First, with the mid-nineteenth-century invention of anaesthetic agents (ether and chloroform), the necessity of pain in childbirth was defended by religious misogynists who declared it God's will (and punishment) for women. Genesis 3:16 famously reads, "To the woman he said, 'I will greatly multiply your sorrow in childbearing; in sorrow you shall bring forth children, yet your desire shall be for your husband, and he shall rule over you.'" The precise connection between labor pain and patriarchy deserves perhaps greater elaboration, but nonetheless this verse and the sentiments it evokes informed historical opposition to the use of anaesthesia in childbirth. Early defenders were compelled to engage in biblical exegesis in order to show that pain per se could not be divinely ordained (J. Y. Simpson [1849] 1995, 400).

These debates had their secular elements: on the one hand, it seems as though some male commentators wanted to trivialize women's experience of pain in childbirth, plausibly motivated by an epistemic discounting of women's testimony about more or less everything.[3] On the other hand, clergymen and physicians alike insisted that women were intended by God and nature to suffer in childbirth—and indeed that such suffering has positive consequences. In his *Treatise on Etherization in Childbirth* (1849), American midwife Walter Channing reports that he wrote to a "medical friend" asking for data on his use of ether and chloroform, and reprints the anonymized but much-quoted reply: "The very suffering which a woman undergoes in labor is one of the strongest elements in the love she bears for her offspring. I have fears for the moral effect of this discovery, both on the patient and on the physician."[4]

The second reason that Walsh should have hesitated has everything to do with the later, psychoanalytic habit of associating femininity with masochism. Following and reworking Freud, for example, Hélène Deutsch argues that the conflation of pleasure and pain is a necessary—even biologically inspired—part of the feminine psychic economy, due in part to the discomforts associated with defloration and childbirth. Even Deutsch, however, in lamenting the mastery of medical science over "normal physiologic processes," stresses that drugs do not only relieve pain but also diminish "woman's active part in the delivery process, her lasting pride in her accomplishment, the possibility of rapid reunion with her child," as well as, more controversially, depriving her of the opportunity to gratify her masochistic desires (Deutsch 1945, 247). To laud pain, again, plays into this tradition, which risks attributing unconscious attachments to painful experience to women at the expense of examining how suffering is forced upon us.[5]

The development of the continuous epidural block in obstetrics in the late 1940s changed some of the philosophical aspects of the debates about pain: women requiring pain relief no longer needed to be semiconscious or unconscious during labor but rather could have only a local loss of sensation. By the 1980s, the epidural was commonplace in North America (Wolf 2009, 168–96). Nineteenth-century physicians had worried about everything from the possibilities for sexual arousal under the influence of chloroform to the extinguishing of the "vital spirit" that characterized human agency (Snow 2006, 23). These concerns had largely fallen away by the twentieth century, replaced, as historian Ariel Glucklich (2003) contends, by a medical model that understands pain as a neurological indicator of tissue damage with no redemptive qualities for the patient. As more and more women gave birth in hospitals, and the medical technologies surrounding birth became more complex yet more routine, perinatal health care became, as many feminist commentators have described, increasingly overseen by (male) physicians rather than (female) midwives. If in the nineteenth century male physicians were suspicious of ether, in the later twentieth century the epidural was one of the technologies that guaranteed obstetric dominance over midwifery, and it is more likely to be midwives who suggest that even now, when a woman can give birth fully conscious but without significant physical pain, analgesia diminishes the experience of birth.[6] This history frames the horns of my dilemma: in the twenty-first century a pregnant woman in Canada can give herself over to medical birth and risk the objectification and even violence it too often entails (Cohen 2016, 2017; WHO 2015) while gaining access (in theory) to hard-won technologies of pain relief, or she can opt for a midwife-attended birth at home (or, if she's lucky enough to live near one, in a birthing center) without the possibility of pharmaceuticals.

To opt for the latter, then, is often as much a negative choice as a positive one: it is not necessary to have read Foucault to have a sense of the risks of entering a total institution where management of one's body-as-object is of paramount importance. Pain in this context can be understood as the price you pay for being allowed to bloody your own sheets in peace, and, given how incredibly painful childbirth is, that is a costly right. However, it is different than the lesser pains of an acute kidney infection or a broken arm, both of which have had me hustling to the emergency room for the blandishments of Western medicine. The pain of childbirth has a purpose, and is a predictable part of the process of delivery. It also has a guaranteed end in the not-too-distant future—although just *how* distant becomes a pressing concern when you actually get to it.

In other ways, though, labor is like all pain. It struggles to find a way into language. While physicians learning to diagnose used to be advised to ask their patients to select adjectives to describe their sensations—burning, stabbing, dull, aching, cramping, and so on—in the face of agony these words fall away, and there is only the demand of the body for an ending.[7] Linguistic communication approaches zero. In her brilliant book *The Body in Pain*, Elaine Scarry argues that, unlike other states of consciousness—love, fear, hunger—pain "has no referential content. It is not *of* or *for* anything" (1985, 5). Putting it another way, Ludwig Wittgenstein famously argued that pain illustrates a different way of using words than our ostensive process of definition: I can point to my cat and say "cat," in a way that my child will eventually grasp, for example, but I can't point to my pain to show what that word means (1953, §293). I can exaggerate my pain, or minimize it, but it's terribly hard for someone else to say what criteria they could use to know that I'm doing so—as insurance adjusters and parents faced with a sick child well know. I can't in any literal way make my pain into an object for you to see, but the worse it gets (ironically), the less able I become to tell you about it either. It disrupts my usual intentions and capacities and turns my attention inward, summoning me to the here of my body and the now of its sensation, while taking me away from intersubjective life, "the body's commerce with the world" (Leder 1990, 74). In extremis, we lose our words, which are all we have.

As Scarry points out, for the sufferer the reality of pain is the epitome of certainty, while for the witness to pain, its existence is always opaque, in doubt. Because pain lacks an object, she suggests, even when expressed it is always vulnerable to appropriation by this skeptical onlooker, its characteristics made into fodder for some cultural project that exceeds the representation of sensation. Scarry uses this fact about pain to build a political case against torture, which is often misrepresented as an information-seeking exercise; but pain's resistance to expression and its corollary availability for cultural repurposing also explain why birth stories are so empty of specifics and so narratively predictable.

Putting life into language is one way of remembering, so perhaps I've also explained why pain is liable to forgetting. Jesus himself is quoted as saying that "a woman giving birth to a child has pain because her time has come; but when her baby is born she forgets the anguish because of her joy that a child is born into the world" (John 16:21). It's true that sometimes the thrill of the baby takes over from other physical sensations, and there may be a physiology peculiar to childbirth that makes its intensity disappear from memory with alacrity. Try precisely to recall the discomfort of stubbing your toe, however, and you'll find your mental content also vague and allegorical. So the articulation of pain in general is ontologically frustrated, while contemporary medical models insist on pain's literal and hermeneutic erasure.

This erasure has a political timbre: we used to believe that infants cannot feel pain (thus was circumcision of male babies justified), and many people still use the claim that a very young child will not consciously remember painful incidents as a rationale for not trying too hard to avoid hurting her; likewise, another pernicious and largely discredited belief for which Descartes is often blamed is that animals are incapable of feeling pain. Children, animals, women: the triumvirate of the insensate or behaviorally unreliable. Of course, the cow may bellow and twitch in the slaughterhouse, and the baby might scream at the scalpel's cut, but these pieces of evidence cannot prove pain, any more than the laboring woman's wails should provoke more than wry smiles and a rush to strap on the fetal monitor. Childbirth happens in the interstices of these realities, which, taken together, work against the conscious, autonomous remembering of birth and its pains. Articulating the lived experience of the pain of childbirth thus goes straight from ontological challenge to epistemic irrelevance.

Philosophically speaking, therefore, everything is stacked against successful literary expression of pain, and accordingly there is very little of it. When I think of evocative first-personal representations of extreme physical torment—from Fanny Burney's ([1812] 1995) epistolary description of her agonizing mastectomy to James Frey's (2003) controversial account of unmedicated root canals—I see capable writers with the benefit of leisure and hindsight struggling to capture experiences that take their meaning from local worlds, and yet must be painstakingly translated for their intended readers.[8] A part of our modern context is that agony is often avoidable, and fewer and fewer people have had any experience at all of the kind of life-shattering pain that must have been ubiquitous among our ancestors. Combine this larger ignorance with the more local politics of medicine's indifference to women's voices, and it becomes almost impossible to carve out a space for writing.

It gets worse. Even as I don't know what I can possibly say about giving birth, I also doubt my right to say it: my experience is no more representative than anyone else's, my story no less liable to reflect only adaptation to the existing cultural script. Here I run into the more prosaic shortcomings of the personal as political: when each of us moves through the world from the null point that is one's self, it is constantly tempting to generalize one's own undergoings as part of the human and underestimate the sheer variety of other people's experience. This is a particular risk, I think, when one has an especially dramatic or life-changing experience. If it feels personally deeply meaningful, we often assume that others would find it that way too. Existential phenomenology post–Merleau-Ponty offers a method for incorporating lived experience while circumventing this epistemic risk. Although, as I've described, within analytic philosophy and extraphilosophical traditions, "phenomenology" is a term sometimes used to capture methods that approach intelligent storytelling, it in fact asks us to render our experience strange such so that we are no longer immersed in it without critical reflection, and can trace its conditions of possibility. In the politically attuned variants of phenomenology I have been working with in this book, we understand our experience as emerging from structures of space, time, and embodiment; and always at the same time from contingent social and political structures that also constitute it. Birth is, as feminist thinkers have long argued, a biopolitical event in Western cultures, which insist on managing it through medical systems that already claim control over sexed bodies in highly stratified ways.[9] For example, which mothers will be numbed and denied their birthing experience while high-tech medical intervention is piled upon them and their very important babies, versus those whose obstetric health is of little concern and who will deliver without basic care and with discriminatory disregard for sequelae is an important distinction—and one that receives extensive attention in the literature on the politics of maternal health care.[10]

These reflections, however, recommend only a better method with greater epistemic and political humility, not abandoning the project. I put it this way only because I'm a philosopher, but when I was pregnant I longed to read a birth story written by a feminist phenomenologist. *What is it like?* My expectation was not that there would be a singular answer to that question, a definitive description that would enable me to predict my own future. I did hope, however, for a richer, more evocative language to capture the lived experience of childbirth—one that managed to be self-conscious of its own historicity and politics, while not only telling a historical or political story; one that used the conceptual tools feminist phenomenologists have developed without denying the specificity of the body. Communicating the experience of pain is an art as much as a logical impossibility, and as art it doesn't aspire to mirror nature. So my own comments are offered in the spirit of responding to a philosophical challenge of representation both individual and political, rather than staking a claim to truth.

LIMIT-EXPERIENCE

Labor usually starts off as something most women have experienced. The uterine muscles begin to contract just as they do to cause menstrual cramps. Except that they just keep on contracting, harder and harder, and because my full-term pregnant uterus was the size of a basketball, while before I was pregnant it was the size of my closed fist, the sensations were exponentially more intense. Still, at lunchtime on a Sunday my partner and I were strolling around the neighborhood on a path we came to call "the labor loop," and I made it back up the steepish hill where we lived without feeling put upon. As afternoon turned into evening, when the waves of pain were more discrete and identifiable, we started to watch the Oscars. I managed to remark wittily (I thought) that Hugh Jackman's song and dance routine was more excruciating than labor.

Then, abruptly, just as Jack Black was announcing the award for best animated short, the tempo changed. My attention became entirely focused on my body, and I lost the capacity to speak in sentences. I had to stalk up and down the landing to deal with the pain, clenching my fists and yowling with each new wave of shooting, burning tightness. This entirely novel sound: where did it come from? It's a kind of low keening in the back of the throat, a groan or a moan, as primeval as a rainforest fern. Scarry writes that "physical pain does not simply resist language but actively destroys it, bringing about an immediate reversion to a state anterior to language, to the sounds and cries a human being makes before language is learned" (1985, 4). In having a baby, in other words, one recalls, just briefly, the state of preverbal infancy.

This might seem infantilizing, but an existential tradition sees it otherwise: freedom can be known only by finding the limits of our human subjectivity. As I suggested earlier, limit-experience describes a physical event that, by virtue of its very intensity, fractures the self's understanding and bursts the bounds of its hitherto imagined possibilities. Because a limit-experience is grounded in one's body and evades capture by processes of subjectivation, it cannot be conveyed in language. Rather it can be represented only in outline, by describing the techniques that circumscribe it. That's why it's important to have the experience, rather than reading about other people having it. In his irritatingly sensational biography of Foucault, James Miller writes that "through intoxication, reverie, the Dionysian abandon of the artist, the most punishing of ascetic practices, and an uninhibited exploration of sado-masochistic eroticism, it seemed possible to breach, however briefly, the boundaries separating the conscious and unconscious, reason and unreason, pleasure and pain—and, at the ultimate limit, life and death" (1993, 30). This sounds to me in many ways like giving birth—which was obviously, for Foucault, not an option. I am living birth after the fact through its narration, as a possibility fully contained in language and thus bearing its own relation to the tropes of history and culture, but I lived it first as a limit-experience that suspended my selfhood and my capacity to speak.

One feminist response to the medicalization of birth has been to try and reclaim women's choice, control, and autonomy from an institutionalized experience that can treat birthing women only as objects. Some feminists seem to believe that if one just makes the right birth plan, insists aggressively enough on one's own choices, and exercises one's sovereignty over one's body, then almost every birth can be a seamless experience of self-mastery. This attitude is troubling to many advocates of woman-centered birth, including me. Foucault's account of experience may help to give philosophical substance to this anxiety. Rebuilding the sovereign subject around feminist norms refuses to recognize the reality and the value of limit-experience. Birth often is a tearing away of the self from its mode of subjectivation, a temporary destruction of habitual subjectivity, a glimpse of the limit. Therefore demanding— even in a countercultural voice—a return to a disciplined subjectivity during birth itself is likely to be useless (birthing women can't do it) and represents a foreclosure of self-transformation. Even in the twenty-first-century West, birth requires a radical openness to what might be—to one's own possible death, to the possible death of one's child, to emergency surgery, to loss of control, to disappointment, to illness, to pain, as well as to euphoria, intense pleasure, entirely new physiological sensations, an encounter with subjectivity that is neither split nor self-identical. It is a profound unknowing, a surrender. That not every birthing woman encounters these possibilities in the same way is just to say that everyone has her own experience, in which her body encounters what (recall) O'Leary calls "the background." Nor does this analysis preclude working to change the background, as feminists do daily, so that (among other goals) limit-experience is more available and the experimental attitude it demands can be assumed without the risk of annihilating objectification. Many of the practices of childbirth we have inherited mitigate against transformative limit-experience, just as Foucault argues that the discourse of sexuality closes down to the tiniest window the possibility of an experience not already fully contained in the power/knowledge nexus he describes. So our ethical responsibility becomes the creation of spaces where more possibility for self-transformation is opened, where the self can see itself exceeding the background experience of the cultural moment.

Before long, as my contractions seemed to press upon each other in waves of burning intensity that suffused my entire lower body. I gasped out that I couldn't do it, couldn't take any more, and wanted to know how many more I would have to endure. Our doula took a Zen approach: "You've got through this one. Rest. Don't think about the next one, or how many more." This philosophy is utterly familiar to me from years of meditation practice: once you start wondering when the bell is going to ring, you've lost it. Be with the experience of sitting. Be in the moment—even if this moment is the worst of your life. This kind of in-the-moment focus cannot be bought; it can only be approximated after years of grinding practice, wearing away the habits of mind that make us flit from thought to thought, recoiling from our aversions and indulging our attachments. The pain was worst when I ditched the meditation practice, and just howled my way through a contraction, clenching every muscle and pushing myself off my seat as if upward momentum could take me away from the source of the agony. It was no less exquisite but easier to bear when I dove into it, finding its burning center, observing it.[11] But just as I can sit only for thirty minutes or so before I give up much pretense of trying, so I could maintain a positive attitude only for so long. Scarry remarks that in the depths of pain, the claims of the body utterly nullify the claims of the world; we are left with "an increasingly palpable body and an increasingly substanceless world" (1985, 34). My awareness turned inward, not toward calm but toward the mess of sensation and the steely panic of my body's life.

Interoception—our sense of the inside of our bodies—is notoriously patchy. This is just as well: if I were constantly and simultaneously aware of my blood circulating, my kidneys excreting, my gut digesting, and so on, there would be little room left in my consciousness for anything else, including the more important information coming from my five senses. If I start to jog, I can soon tally my heartbeat, however, and a sharp new pain deep in my abdomen might signal an infected appendix; interoceptive awareness emerges most often when the homeostatic balance shifts. It can also be developed with practice, as when yoga teachers instruct, "Turn into the pose. Feel the head of the femur twist in the socket." For years, those words are just words accompanied by an unconnected movement, then incrementally, perception creeps up to the edge of consciousness. Now I can feel those bones.

My labor was a colossal interoceptive experience—a host of body parts that had lain mostly dormant to perception were suddenly present in blooming, buzzing confusion. While he was still confined in my womb, seconds before each contraction began, my baby would burrow his head downward and simultaneously kick off with his feet under my ribs, like a foolhardy spelunker trying to pass through a tight squeeze. That wriggling feeling signaled the imminence of another wave of hurt, and each time it happened I could feel myself gasp, tightening and trying not to tighten, knowing that my resistance only exacerbated my suffering yet failing in the face of such mammoth sensation.

A lot of people say that the end of the first stage of labor—"transition," when the cervix reaches its maximum dilation—is the hardest. Let me concur. There is a peculiarly psychological quality to the pain, which is not only magnified in quantity but also altered in kind. I read somewhere that one of the symptoms of transition is "despair." Despair, an unbearable existential awareness of the enormity of the undertaking, the inexorable turn of the screw—say what you like. It's awful. I was in our walk-in shower cubicle, alone, with hot water futilely spraying against my lower back, when it happened. There was a shift: a contraction hit that included not only a final escalation of the agony that preceded it but also a nerve-jangling, teeth-on-edge feeling. Imagine a whole room full of students simultaneously drawing sharp nails down a blackboard. That sensation of the tight squeeze, of an anonymous body part that had been a strait for thirty-eight years opening to an estuary, all the while screaming its reluctance, became intolerable. Then, almost immediately, came another contraction. And, with no effort of will on my part, the potholer was wriggling his way to freedom as mystery muscles in my lower body began the greatest peristaltic act of their career. It was still agony, but also a tremendous relief to feel the physical and energetic release of a horribly large object moving inexorably down and out.

BIRTH, AND AFTER

I recommend stepping into a pool of warm water two minutes before you give birth. It can distract you from a host of nasty burning, stretching sensations and focus the mind wonderfully. Reaching down, I felt a large, firm object between my legs. It was wrinkled and slightly furry to the touch, like a catkin or the scalp of a bloodhound. Relentlessly pushing outward, it expanded and grew into a knobbly ball under my hands. Instantly, in a moment of epiphany, my entire consciousness changed. From the head-nodding coma of an endorphin-soaked dream, I woke up, into the fullest and most alive state of alert presence. My eyes felt bright, and I was aware of every detail of the drama unfolding as my body split in two. The midwife was vigilant, reaching into the murky water and feeling that the baby's head was halfway out. "Give a little push," she said.

That final gush of liquid and flesh is literally ecstatic: *ek*, out or away from, *stasis*, the place it stands. Moving apart from me, blissfully. Suddenly there is something there, something huge, and, more to the point, that object is no longer compressed into my body's cavities, confined and hidden. My body is light and limitless space, and my child is coming up through the water—gray, vernix-coated, slippery, and contorted. He's beautiful and screaming in my arms, and I do forget my anguish. This moment is profoundly ethical. We were one, perhaps, and now maybe are two, but in our doubling is the first instant of recognition. It's an ethics that is an aesthetic: the coming-into-existence for my son was also the moment of my own destruction and re-creation. For a minute or two, I am completely in the present moment. It's a tiny, precious slice of enlightenment, at the point of maximum intensity and impossibility. It's the death of the subject. But also a birth.

CODA

AS OF FALL 2018, there is a new edition of the tedious ludic exercise in capital accumulation known as *Monopoly*. "Monopoly for Millennials" features the harsh tagline, "Forget real estate. You can't afford it anyway," instead inviting players to collect Experiences. As the flavor text puts it, "Money doesn't always buy a great time, but experiences, whether they're good—or weird—last forever. The Monopoly for Millennials game celebrates just that. Instead of collecting as much cash as possible, players are challenged to rack up the most Experiences to win." The game is blatant (not to mention condescending) in its deployment of human capital discourse as a (dare I say, recalling Joan Scott's productive mishearing of fin de siècle) "fantasy echo" of actual wealth, suggesting that, just as one might buy Knightsbridge and Mayfair and charge rent, one might visit a friend's couch, vegan bistro, or meditation retreat and accumulate long-lasting individual value.

This is a particularly egregious example of the discourse of curating one's self through the accumulation of special experiences read as a form of human capital that I referred to at the beginning of this book. It is a cautionary tale that makes Scott's (1991) point that what will count as experience is always contested, and that a genealogy of the concept as well as genealogies of particular experiences will be necessary parts of any feminist politics. Still, just because a behemoth toy company has designed a patronizing game or float tanks are all the rage need not mean we have to give up on a radical politics and dwell solely on the vacuity and petty disappointments of bourgeois life in theorizing experience. In chapter 1 I cut through long-standing debates about Foucault's account of experience, about the feminist politics of experience, and about how these two conversations intersect, to suggest that experience is always already both genealogical product and individually irreducible. That chiasmic folding of subjectivity as constituted and constituting makes experience part of both a historical and a cultural trajectory, and of my personal life—to undergo without reflection, to interpret reiteratively within an existing background, or to critically engage as part of a subjugated knowledge. This account, I suggested, opens the door to case studies that deepen any existing theory of the role of experience in politics. The question of how sexual violence against unconscious victims is a specific harm, of how the biopolitics of drug use erases time in different ways for different populations, or of how obstetric objectification creates an overwhelming background against which any individual birth struggles toward *ecstasis*—these are all big questions for thinking race, class, and gender. If experience is one epistemic ingredient in the feminist recipe for politics, others are clearly institutions and histories. The method for cooking them up into an edible strategy, I have demonstrated throughout this book, is a tense balancing of a phenomenology that includes social and political structures as always constituting lived experience, with a genealogy that traces the larger trajectories of those structures. More than telling you about my method, I've tried to show how it can be implemented to think about particular problems in which the personal meets the political in particularly abrupt ways that are too rarely theorized as parts of a whole. These disparate case studies throw the category of "experience" into question, revealing its edges and hence its tacit form in three modes: interruption, normative temporality, and the limits of subjectivity.

The title of this book, *Anaesthetics of Existence*, speaks to the fundamentally sensory nature of experience and hence of building a self. Rather ambivalently pushing against the aesthetic project of self-making, it points out that although in Foucault's rendering a life and its author are in theory immanent to each other, this position quickly gets lost in discussions of agency, which inflate self-sovereignty and overstate the scope and value of choice, action, and (for feminists especially) transgression. Even for those privileged people who can find the most immediate meaning in the idea that life should be a work of art, the undertaking cannot avoid being implicated in stories about the self that deplete as well as accumulate our capacities. It is far away from

Foucault's frame, but the rationalist account of the agent who assembles her values and preferences and then attempts to bring herself and the world into line seems, against the postdisciplinary and neoliberal backdrop I've described, laughably dated as a mode of understanding both human psychological depth and the political landscape within which any of us act. But what is the alternative—not just in theory but also in practice? I haven't attempted a systematic answer to that question in this book (although I have posed it from several different angles intended to give some idea where I'm headed). Foucault's work, although positing experience both as a product of discourse and as a driver of critique, still treats freedom as a property of subjects. As I argue elsewhere, if we accept the Cartesian claim that the limits of my will—of those aspects of human life I as an individual can influence—are the limits of freedom, we inscribe tacit limits on what freedom can be that obscure alternative frames. What if freedom can live in necessity, sometimes accepting the imperatives of embodied experience and the impossibility of individual overcoming (Heyes 2018)? What if the locus of freedom is not (or not only) the subject but is also found in worldly practices (Zerilli 2005)?

This book has tacitly suggested that the "anaesthetic" techniques of everyday life, whether they are universal (like sleep) or parochial (like drinking wine), are not only part of everyone's life in some way but also part of the psychic landscape that structures agency and engagement with the world. Some anaesthetic experiences are grand epiphanies, while others pave a path to death—literal or social. In some moments these are the same experiences: getting drunk might help someone escape temporal overwhelm, but passing out at the end of the evening is an opportunity for the rapist to destroy one's capacity to sink safely into night. The agony of childbirth can complete a descent into profound obstetric objectification or be a part of an ecstatic break with the confines of the self. It thus feels premature to me to be offering criteria by which to decide when an experience at the edge is liberatory or oppressive. Neither phenomenology nor genealogy is a values-driven method, although (as I hope I've shown) both can be directed toward political and ethical projects. I nonetheless clearly make a number of value judgments in this book, but I've found it more politically useful to richly describe and recontextualize marginal experiences in order to shift our ways of thinking about them, than to stipulate what they should mean. The epistemic nature of experience is such that it cannot be guaranteed repeatable, so to recommend this or that experience as a normative ground seems like a category mistake. For example, in my discussion of birth, I suggested that we should change the background against which individual birthing experience is denied, in ways that feminist commentators have long recommended through critiques of so-called expert knowledge, obstetric objectification and violence, or the technologization of normal birth. It would make no sense, however, to say that any unique birth *should* be experienced in any particular way (indeed, this is a familiar enough way of adding another layer of guilt or shame to the birth trauma of those who didn't have the experience they hoped for); the political work is to open up a relatively closed field of institutionalized meaning to create a different range of conditions of possibility, from which irreducibly plural events will continue to emerge. If that's too meek a point, my analysis is also tied (in ways I have scarcely explored) to the politics of passive resistance, to antiwork and postwork politics, to Slow movements, and to, in the most general sense, a politics of refusal.[1]

I have tried to excavate some of the complexities of subjectivity, and especially the limits on self-sovereignty, in order to write about experience in a way that goes deeply into the structuring assumptions of a lot of philosophies of action and agency. In his prescient essay "In the Absence of Practice," Paul Harrison points out that across the human sciences, "doings, actions, and practices are *the* source and locus of signification" (2009, 987). What could happen, he asks, in the absence of practice? This is, from a slightly different angle, also my question. I affirm Harrison's identification of underexamined and undertheorized beliefs in much social theory, namely, action is the origin of signification, whereas inaction lacks signification; to be passive is to be weak and apolitical, whereas to be active is to be powerful and transformative; action is productive, and to be productive is to be ethically valuable (even to be human), whereas inaction is unproductive, and to be unproductive is to be unethical or lacking in value (even to lack humanity); and, perhaps the most deceptively straightforward, acting is better than not acting. What if these assumptions were revealed as such and their consequences for political theory unpacked?

I've been joking with colleagues that this book is a prequel. Over the past few years, as I juggled an administrative appointment, a demanding teaching load in a new discipline, an elementary school–aged child, and a separation, I found myself thinking a lot about sleep. There is plenty about sleep in *Anaesthetics of Existence*, but it never quite takes center stage. In my parallel and successor project, a feminist philosophy of sleep, I hope to remedy that. It is proving much easier to work on a theme than on a philosophically challenging method loosely applied to a set of disparate moments in the political life of experience, which is how *Anaesthetics* has mostly felt. In his doctoral defense, the candidate, my outstanding student Joshua St. Pierre, described coming to write his dissertation in philosophy of communicative disability as an exercise in remainders (St. Pierre 2018). All those questions left over from the more conventional lines of inquiry he had pursued in various side projects, as well as all the problems bracketed by those conventions, were gathered together in his thesis. That description struck a chord with me: this book is in many ways organized around things that could not be easily managed within the political and philosophical languages I knew best. In writing it, I pushed at the edges of my own existing expertise and knowledge, as well as at what I was capable of thinking and imagining. As solo writing inevitably is, it has been (recall the two epigrams that opened this book) both a way of working on "the beauty of my own life," and at the same time a wearying monadic melodrama. The experience of writing a book, as Foucault commented, transforms the author. Philosophically it constitutes an engagement outward with global political and economic life, as well as a reverse journey into the ways we interpret our selves. It would be easier not to try and hold these things together, but, to return to a very well-worn feminist phrase, if the personal is political (and vice versa), then we need methods for explaining the equivalence. As I developed one such method, I tried to draw back in to feminist philosophy some questions we have bracketed or even failed to notice: yes, rape is awful, but how to think about the particular wrong of violating someone who is unconscious? Yes, time is political, but how to make sense of time drifting away, passing unmarked? Yes, medical practice has misogynist inheritances, but how can we tell evocative first-personal birth stories that are neither reducible to those inheritances nor simply a reverse discourse against it? In trying to answer these questions, I am asking how the economic and political forms we live through deal with what they throw away (whether the living or the nonliving), as well as how social and political theory addresses all those things that are at—or beyond—the edge of signification.

NOTES

INTRODUCTION

1 Thanks to Gayle Salamon for reminding me of Joan Scott's "Fantasy Echo: History and the Construction of Identity" (2001), the title of which comes from an exam script that tried to render in writing a nonnative English-speaking graduate student's interpretation of an unfamiliar term ("fin de siècle") he had heard in a lecture.

2 Buck-Morss is using the term "shock" in its psychological context, rather than a medical one. That is, she appears to mean by "shock" the hyperstimulation of the sensory world as it overwhelmingly imposes itself on the human organism, rather than an organic condition in which blood flow to crucial organs is dangerously reduced.

3 These and related objections that Foucault recommends a kind of "dandyism" or is capitulating to a narcissistic "Californian cult of the self" have a long history. For Foucault's own comments on this risk in his work, see Foucault (1997a, 271) and Foucault (2005, 12–13). For the criticisms, see, e.g., Hadot 1992; Thacker 1993; Wolin 1994. For more recent sympathetic readings of Foucault against this charge, see Heyes 2007, ch. 5; O'Leary 2002; D. Smith 2015; Vintges 2001.

4 Foucault himself was ambivalent about the relationship between his own experience and his work: while he said that all his work was inspired by personal experience (Foucault [1978] 2000b, 244), he also evaded discussion of his personal life on the grounds that it would appear prescriptive and reinstall the author-function of which he had been so philosophically and politically critical

(see Foucault [1983] 1997d, 154). This ambivalence has been fueled by a secondary literature of philosophical biography: see especially James Miller's *The Passion of Michel Foucault* (1993), which agonizes over the relation between Foucault's sexuality and his philosophy and has in turn provoked charges of sensationalism and homophobia (see, e.g., Halperin 1995, 143–52).

5　"Slow Death," the article from which this quote is taken, has been very controversial (especially among scholars of fatness) for its association of obesity with certain patterns of behavior and in turn with certain political contexts (e.g., Crawford 2017; Kirkland 2011). I concur with much of this critique, and it was palpable when I heard Berlant present an early version of the essay. Nonetheless, the basic argument of the piece, on my reading, concerns how certain kinds of everyday, banal, or ostensibly extrapolitical activities are tacitly used to manage the demands of political life. This important argument should never have been yoked to claims about body size.

6　Quote is from Jones (2005, 198). The same point is paraphrased in *Skintight* (Jones 2008, 132).

7　ORLAN always capitalizes her own name—a practice I follow except when quoting.

8　Rachel Hurst and Luna Dolezal (2018), for example, contrast ORLAN's broadsides against medical orthodoxy and her willingness to live in the space between the "before" and the surgical "after" with the ambivalently conformist moments in performance artist(s) Breyer P-Orridge's *Pandrogyny* project.

9　Thanks to an anonymous reviewer for clarification here, and for putting this point in this way.

10　On Foucault's intellectual relationship to Sartre, see Flynn 2004a and Flynn 2000b. In an interview with Hubert Dreyfus and Paul Rabinow, Foucault says that while "Sartre avoids the idea of the self as something that is given to us," he nonetheless returns to the "moral notion of authenticity" and "the idea that we have to be ourselves—to be truly our true self." It's a confusing aside that doesn't especially capture Sartre's views, nor does it readily contrast with Foucault's description of his own project as creating ourselves as a work of art (Foucault [1983] 1997a, 262). On Foucault and Fanon, see Taylor 2010; on Foucault and Beauvoir, see Vintges 2001; on Foucault and Merleau-Ponty, see Sabot 2013.

11　These are the authors who most influenced me in writing this book, but the field of phenomenologists writing with a political cast about embodied life is far larger. See also, for example, Fielding and Olkowski 2017; Fisher and Embree 2000; Lee 2014; Neimanis 2017; Ortega 2016; Rodemeyer 2017, 2018; Schües, Olkowski, and Fielding 2011; Shabot and Landry 2018; Käll and Zeiler 2014; Weiss 1999, 2008.

12　Again, I'm grateful to a careful reviewer who helped me clarify this distinction.

13　Here and later in the book I sometimes refer to the victims of sexual violence while unconscious as "women." In researching chapter 2, I reviewed a large corpus of legal cases, news media stories, rape memoir, legal and social history, and psychological literature, and as I presented the work publicly and discussed it with students and colleagues, I was told plenty more personal anecdotes about sexual violation. Of this body of examples, just one of these latter anecdotes involved a male victim—a student who said that he had once woken during a train journey undertaken as a solo teen to find an older man sitting next to him and attempting to fondle his genitals. All of the other cases involve victims who identify themselves or are identified as girls or women, and in 100 percent of the cases the perpetrator is identified as a man (although as I note in my discussion of the Steubenville case in particular, girls and women are often complicit with sexual violence against unconscious victims, or subsequently participate in covering it up). My analysis addresses discourses of racialized femininity in ways that make some sense of this gendered phenomenon, but it is not my intention to deny the significance of sexual violence against male or genderqueer victims in the contexts I describe.

ONE Foucault's Limits

1   In his lecture course, Foucault footnotes the contemporary case report on which he bases his account as "H. Bonnet et J. Bulard, *Rapport médico-légal sur l'état mental de Charles-Joseph Jouy, inculpé d'attentats aux moeurs*, 4 janvier 1868" [Medical-legal report on the mental state of Charles-Joseph Jouy, accused of offenses against public decency, January 4, 1868] (Foucault [1999] 2003, 319). Bonnet and Bulard were head doctors at the asylum at Maréville where Jouy was detained. This report is reproduced in French with the author's English translation as two appendices in Taylor 2018.

2   Linda Alcoff's essay on this case, discussed in this chapter, is titled "Dangerous Pleasures: Foucault and the Politics of Pedophilia" (1996). Although Alcoff never directly says that Jouy is a (proto)pedophile, this is the implication of her essays on the case from 1996 and 2000. For a critique of the description "pedophile" that is both historical and conceptual, see Tremain 2017, 146–49.

3   A later essay titled "Phenomenology, Post-Structuralism, and Feminist Theory on the Concept of Experience" (Alcoff 2000) includes much of the same material as the paper from 1996, with slightly more elaboration of Alcoff's phenomenological perspective. In what follows, I quote from both essays to represent Alcoff's early position.

4   The feminist critique of the Jouy case that Alcoff mobilizes is part of a larger intellectual context in which Foucault's remarks on sexual freedom, sexual violence, and (to a lesser extent) gender politics have been both taken to task and recuperated. In an article written in 1978, Monique Plaza notoriously challenged his remark in 1977 that rape is only a crime of violence rather than a distinctive sexual harm (Plaza 1978, 97), and Foucault's defense of decriminalizing all consensual sex, including between adults and youth, in a radio interview from 1978 features in feminist charges that he trivializes child sexual abuse (including in Alcoff 1996, 101–6). Foucault was not unsympathetic to feminist and lesbian politics, however, and never said that rape should be unpunished or that sexual violence was politically unimportant, situating his comments instead in the

context of his critique of the psy disciplines and the legal regulation of sexuality. For a summary of this larger background debate and for citations of the literature between 1978 and 2013, see Heyes 2013, and for a more recent recuperation of Foucault, see Tremain 2013, 2017, esp. 153–54.

5 In the notes to the lecture of March 19, Foucault cites only the Bonnet and Bulard report of 1868 as a source on the Jouy/Adam case, although he also cites a number of contemporaneous psychiatric texts in the later part of the lecture that support his broader account of the emergence of racism against the abnormal individual (Foucault [1999] 2003, 319–21nn1–40).

6 This point is reinforced by Alcoff's book *Rape and Resistance* (2018), which was published just after I completed this manuscript.

7 My translation of "on n'est pas soi-même. Ça n'a plus de sens d'être soi-même. On voit les choses autrement. // Dans la passion, il y a aussi une qualité de souffrance-plaisir" (Foucault [1981] 1982, para. 4).

TWO Dead to the World

This chapter, "Dead to the World: Rape, Unconsciousness, and Social Media," was first published in *Signs: A Journal of Women in Culture and Society* 41, no. 2 (January 2016): 361–83.

1 The Parsons case drew public attention because of the lack of adequate response from police, Crown prosecution, and the schools involved. There was a campaign for an investigation and an intervention by Anonymous; eventually external inquiries into both the prosecution service and the school system found systemic lapses. It was only several years later that two young men were charged with making or distributing child pornography and conditionally discharged and put on probation (for discussion of the immediate aftermath of the case, see Hess 2014). Parsons became a target of relentless online bullying and moved schools several times before she killed herself. A law against cyberbullying in Nova Scotia that referenced Parsons was eventually passed in 2018.

2 For media analysis of prominent cases involving youth and social media in the United States, see Friedman 2013. On Steubenville in particular, see Levy 2013. On the Audrie Pott case, see Burleigh 2013. A similar case of a fourteen-year-old girl allegedly raped while very drunk by a seventeen-year-old football player occurred in Maryville, Kansas (Arnett 2013; Bazelon 2013). See Oliver 2016 for further analyses of this type of case.

3 There is now a large literature on (and extensive campaigning against) sexual violence as a digital or digitally facilitated phenomenon, including not only the circulation of images or video or text discussion of acts of sexual assault, but also the circulation (or threat of circulation) of explicit images (sometimes originally taken consensually) for revenge or blackmail, online harassment or threats of sexual violence, the circulation of simulated pornography, the malicious circulation of personal information (doxing) attached to bogus advertising for sex work

or with calls to sexually harass or assault a particular individual, or the resurrection of old legal cases of sexual assault for the purposes of harassing former victims. For an overview, see Powell and Henry 2017.

4 The activist hacker group Anonymous famously pushed the Steubenville case forward and has been involved in others.

5 As epitomized by the remarks of CNN reporter Poppy Harlow, covering the verdict (TheSublimeDegree 2013, at 1:22–2:30). There have been subsequent grand jury indictments in Steubenville, brought against the director of technology for schools and his adult daughter, the school superintendent, a teacher, and two sports coaches.

6 As quoted in Samuels 2016. Turner served just three months of this sentence but also appealed for a new trial and lost his appeal in August 2018. As this book was going to press in fall 2019, the victim in the Stanford case, Chanel Miller (previously known as Emily Doe), released her memoir, *Know My Name*.

7 These forms of cognitive absence involve different brain states, and it is technically inaccurate to call them all "unconsciousness"—neither sleep nor the semiconsciousness followed by amnesia that is the typical effect of consuming certain drugs (including alcohol) is "unconsciousness." Nonetheless here I sometimes use "unconsciousness" as a shorthand that captures the lived experience of one's subjectivity being interrupted.

8 On cases involving Canadian Indigenous women and alcohol, see Lindberg, Campeau, and Campbell 2011, 99–103; and Vandervort 2011. For further general comments on the role of racism in prosecuting sexual assaults, see Benedet 2010, 457–59; and Sheehy 2011a, 486–88. On sexual assault and mentally disabled women, see Benedet and Grant 2007, especially the discussion of *R. v. Harper* at 263–65. On violence against homeless women, including rape, see the United States–based study of Meinbresse et al. 2014.

9 For some data on double standards with regard to gender, alcohol, and attribution of responsibility for sexual assault, see Finch and Munro 2007. For a popular discussion of the issue, see Yoffe 2013 and the reply by Antony 2013.

10 This view is challenged in a more clinical vein by Jeremy Gauntlett-Gilbert, Anna Keegan, and Jenny Petrak 2004, who describe both the specific harms of drug-facilitated sexual assault (DFSA) and their own cognitive therapeutic approach to treating survivors; see also Padmanabhanunni and Edwards 2013.

11 It is probably very rare for someone to be sexually assaulted while unconscious and retain no memory of the experience and encounter no post facto evidence. (There is no way of being more specific than this, clearly, since in the absence of third parties or a visual record the only conscious witness is the rapist, and the extent of the crime is almost impossible to assess.) Nonetheless, this is the scenario that always gets raised by interlocutors: What if she doesn't even know? What if she *never* knows? Is it still bad? That anyone could think nonconsensual penetration of someone else's body in a way fraught with risk and abuse of power is wrong only "if something bad happens" is an absurd consequentialism that

in my mind reveals the extent to which women's bodies are understood instrumentally. Put in more clinical terms, there is evidence that, as Gauntlett-Gilbert, Keegan, and Petrak 2004 report, "full DSM-IV criteria for PTSD [posttraumatic stress disorder] can be fulfilled even when a survivor is entirely amnesic for the trauma; criterion A only requires that an individual should experience intense fear, helplessness or horror when 'confronted' with a traumatic event, even if they did not experience or witness it. Thus, it is both clinically and medico-legally essential to recognize that the PTSD caused by DFSA is not necessarily less severe when a dampened peritraumatic emotional response or fragmented trauma memory are present. This has already been recognized in the head-injury literature, where it is accepted that PTSD can exist where a person has complete post-traumatic amnesia for the event that caused the injury" (217). There are real cases: for example, in 2014 Corporal Derrick Gallagher was charged with multiple counts of sexual assault and voyeurism against women in Quebec and Ontario, some of which involved drugging his victims. Given the extent of his alleged assaults, Canadian police asked women who had been in contact with Gallagher to come forward, saying they might not know that he had sexually assaulted them (CBC News 2014).

12 Although this is a controversial claim, it is not a new one even in the more traditional parts of the phenomenological canon, from Edmund Husserl's remarks on time-consciousness to Jean-Luc Nancy's (2009) book on falling asleep. See de Warren 2010 for a discussion of the phenomenology of sleep that draws on these sources.

13 In Cahill's second book on objectification, she does very briefly consider cases of sexual violence in which the victim is unconscious (see Cahill 2012, 135).

14 I am grateful to Lisa Guenther for introducing me to this concept and talking me through some of its implications.

15 It is fascinating and troubling that Fanon's leitmotif in this famous chapter of *Black Skin, White Masks* is uttered by a female child (to her mother) and not by the "white man" whose culture Fanon theorizes.

16 In her book *The Life and Death of Latisha King* (2018), Gayle Salamon shows how this works in the case of a mixed-race trans teen, Latisha King, murdered in 2008 in her California classroom by Brandon McInerney, a white male classmate. Salamon attended the murder trial and offers a careful, compelling phenomenology of the way individuals were described, the way evidence was presented, and the movement of bodies and objects in the courtroom, to show how King's gender was read (transphobically) as a flagrant provocation, an incitement to violence, in a way that radically foreclosed the possibility of her anonymity.

17 On the estimated prevalence of "proactive" DFSA (cases in which the rapist has administered a drug to a victim without her knowledge or by force), see Janice Du Mont et al.'s Canadian study from 2009.

18 In early 2014 three teenage boys were sentenced to thirty or forty-five days in juvenile detention after pleading guilty to sexual assault (including digital penetration) of Audrie Pott.

19 See ABCNews 2013.

20 In both the Steubenville and Pott cases there are connections with the popular iconography of dead nonhuman animals that I don't have space to explore: the Steubenville victim was slung and carried like a slaughtered animal, while the drawing on Pott's body is reminiscent of the labeling of animal carcasses as "cuts"—an image that is often carried over (critically or not) to the labeling of women's naked bodies. See Adams 2003 for examples and discussion.

21 For a reproduction of the Cyrus image and links to other visual examples mentioned here, see Cochran 2014.

22 Black women have a homicide rate of 11.8 per population of 100,000, compared with 2.8 for twenty-two-year-old white women (see Smith and Cooper 2013).

23 Although Maryann Pearce's database captures cases from as long ago as the 1950s, the large majority are from the past twenty-five years. Some 25 percent of the missing or murdered women are identified as Aboriginal/First Nation/Inuit/Métis, although these categories account for only 2–3 percent of the Canadian population. See also A. Simpson 2016.

24 Toronto criminal defense lawyer Edward Prutschi is commenting on *R. v. J. A.* For discussion of judges' preoccupation with the hypothetical "sleeping spouse" in sexual assault cases, see Gotell 2012, 374–75.

THREE Down and Out

Parts of this chapter were published as "Anaesthetics of Existence" in Lisa Folkmarson Käll and Kristin Zeiler, eds., *Feminist Phenomenology and Medicine* (Albany, NY: SUNY Press, 2014).

1 Keynes says this in his essay "Economic Possibilities for Our Grandchildren" ([1930] 1963, 367). Thompson 1967, 95. For a historical analysis of the twentieth-century debates about the future of work and leisure, see Granter 2008; Schor 1991.

2 Bierria 2014 also makes this point, footnoting Code 2000; Lugones 2003; and Scales-Trent 1999. See also Berlant 2007; Povinelli 2011.

3 The 2012 edition of *The Politics of Piety* includes a new preface. There Mahmood discusses how the book might be reread in light of political upheavals in Egypt since the original publication.

4 In making this point Mahmood is drawing on a tradition of decolonial thought that stresses the limits of voluntarist understandings of agency in contexts of subaltern resistance. For example, Gayatri Spivak famously challenges the intellectual as Mahmood challenges the poststructuralist feminist. Intellectuals—including Western feminist intellectuals—must understand the Hindu widow as passive victim of her culture, the ultimate antiagent, upon whose body their analyses are written so that their own agency can be represented (and through whose agency the subaltern woman might be saved, including from herself) ([1988] 2010). Saidiya Hartman interprets African American slave culture

through the question of how agency can be understood when the slave as object of property is defined as a negation—a not-part of the human community and, indeed, the object on which the community's continued functioning depends. As she points out, "Generally, the representation of the performative has been inscribed in a repressive problematic of consensual and voluntarist agency that reinforces and romanticizes social hierarchy" (1997, 52). In other words, the slaves' performance of obedience, hard work, and (apparently apolitical) cultural production embodies (in the minds of their dominators) their willingness to be part of the social system that enslaves them. As long as agency can be understood only as "consensual and voluntarist," then much of the slaves' everyday apparent complicity with domination is the closest to agency they get. More troubling even than this tired rationalization of domination is the corollary belief even among critical interpreters that all that can count as an act of resistance is the overt rejection of slave life—the slave who runs away, who talks back and is beaten, who kills the overseer. Think too of James Scott's well-known work on subaltern resistance (1990).

FOUR Anaesthetic Time

Parts of this chapter were published as "Anaesthetics of Existence" in Lisa Folkmarson Käll and Kristin Zeiler, eds., *Feminist Phenomenology and Medicine* (Albany, NY: SUNY Press, 2014).

1   Here there is far more to say about the Heideggerian distinction between objective time and existential temporality that I bracket for the purposes of this book.

2   See Baraitser 2017 for a psychosocial account of temporality and care that uses different philosophical vocabulary to make a related argument.

3   There is an interesting debate about the use of the older term "melancholia" and its cognates as stand-ins for the more contemporary term "depression" that I won't engage here. See Radden 2003.

4   See responses to Wyllie by Broome 2005; Kupke 2005; Matthews 2005; and Fuchs 2005. See also Fuchs 2001, 2013.

5   Ratcliffe (2015) offers a more nuanced account of the depressive's relation to action and temporality. Distinguishing loss of "conative drive" (following Fuchs, a "disposition toward activity" that involves "feeling drawn towards a meaningful future" [178]) from loss of "practical significance" (the loss of the "sense that anything is potentially relevant to any kind of project. Everything the person encounters is stripped of the possibilities for action that is was previously imbued with" [166]), he identifies three configurations of depressive lived experience, desire to act, and temporality. The first seems to be much like Wyllie's: both conative drive and practical significance are lost. The second involves the persistence of conative drive (the world can still seem "enticing"), but without any concomitant practical significance—including any organization of action toward future goals. This looks like a kind of manic, undirected desire to remain

busy, moving, doing, but without any sense of purposive, personally meaningful projects. In the third state, the world is unenticing and lacks significance, but "the person still 'wants' to act, but in ways that she experiences as impossible; the world does not draw her in—it appears somehow alien to the possibility of action. This can involve retention of something that contributes to 'drive' or 'conation' but is insufficient to summon action on its own" (182). Developing a more nuanced account of "disordered" temporality and its relation to different modes of acting or failing to act could fill some of the lacunae in the political debates about agency that underlie this book; I'll leave some of that project for another time.

6 A reviewer suggested I delve deeper into the Heideggerian literature on temporality, including his analysis of boredom, which I was already aware had resonances with my analysis of anaesthetic time. Because I am not a Heidegger scholar, I have decided to leave this suggestion hanging, but for a good overview of Heidegger on relevant points, see Freeman and Elpidorou 2015.

7 There is even an addiction-memoir literary canon, which features narratives by Western men whose addiction has facilitated their creativity and success. See De Quincey [1821] 2013; Cocteau 1933; Trocchi 1960; Burroughs 1977. In the psychological literature on addiction and the self, see also Gray 2005; Shinebourne and Smith 2009.

8 There is no literature on the phenomenology of addiction to benzos and similar drugs, nor on compulsive eating or sugar addiction. (The very idea of a sugar addiction as a biological and experiential analogue to drug addiction attracts a literature but is still contested. See, for example, Gearhardt et al. 2011.)

9 So pervasive is the "women and wine" association, there is now a burgeoning journalistic and self-help literature that more systematically addresses the personal and political dangers of (representing) constant wine consumption for women to relieve stress and anger as a normal or harmless part of bourgeois life. See Coulter 2017; Glaser 2013; Turner and Rocca 2014. For a powerful memoir of alcoholism that tells the story of a high-functioning woman who mostly drinks wine (and thus breaks the mold of the masculinist addiction memoir as well as showing the dangers of trivializing "women and wine"), see Knapp 1996.

10 http://www.madhousewifecellars.com/our-story/, no longer available. Last archived capture at https://web.archive.org/web/20181101120024/http://www.madhousewifecellars.com/our-story/.

11 On punitive actions against pregnant women for allegedly fetus-harming behavior, see also Pollitt 1998; Kukla 2005, 105–43; and Benoit et al. 2014. There is also well-known media and publication bias in favor of studies that show that particular substances are harmful to fetuses, as opposed to those that show low or no risk. See Koren at al. 1989.

12 I am grateful to an anonymous reviewer for Duke University Press who rightly urged me to say more about the biopolitics of population, who used the phrase "post-disciplinary post-subjects," and who pointed me toward Bourgois and

Schonberg, as well as other useful references. What follows is a necessarily brief expansion of the argument into an area that deserves longer treatment.

13 I am thinking here of work such as Deutscher 2017; Povinelli 2011; Puar [2007] 2017; and Schotten 2018.

14 Interview with Bec Fary for *Sleeptalker* podcast, broadcast December 28, 2017, https://drive.google.com/file/d/1nvK3xJqtlTIy6sohzWmoFLsHovbxMAlf/view.

15 Except for those unlucky individuals who experience anaesthetic awareness—a condition in which the patient is conscious during the surgical experience (sometimes including being conscious to pain) but completely unable to move or indicate their consciousness to medical staff. See Cole-Adams 2017 for an extended treatment of the epistemic and ethical problems raised by anaesthesia in general and anaesthetic awareness in particular.

16 Quoted in Jon Henley, "Larger Than Life," *Guardian*, March 16, 2000, http://www .guardian.co.uk/theguardian/2000/mar/16/features11.g2.

17 http://www.momswhoneedwine.com/about/, no longer available. Last archived capture on April 20, 2016, at https://web.archive.org/web/20160420045225 /http://www.momswhoneedwine.com/about/.

FIVE Child, Birth

An earlier version of this chapter was published as "Child, Birth: An Aesthetic" in Lisa Folkmarson Käll, ed., *Dimensions of Pain: Humanities and Social Science Perspectives* (London: Routledge, 2012).

1 Some collections of birth stories and discussion of the genre and its politics include Crane and Moore 2008; see Hinsliff 2018 and associated articles on the *Guardian* website about the effects of sharing childbirth stories, which are alleged by one researcher to contribute to tocophobia (pathological fear of childbirth).

2 The reporting on Walsh's comments takes them out of the context of the research he was being interviewed about. His larger point in that work is that the medicalization of birth leads many contemporary women to see epidural anaesthesia as the only way of coping with the experience, despite the risks and losses it entails (of which those same women are typically unaware). This is surely a lack of choice and autonomy that need not imply women are lacking in moral fiber or that pain is a necessary preparation for parenthood (see Walsh 2009).

3 See Walter Channing's rebuttals of this tendency (1849, 135–57).

4 Anonymous physician, Boston, January 22, 1848, quoted in Channing 1849, 142. Negative moral effects on the physician might include an increased risk of sexual impropriety: women laboring under anaesthesia were sometimes sexually disinhibited, while male physicians sometimes took advantage of their vulnerability to sexually assault them (see my discussion in chapter 2). This could also be a foreshadowing of the later more widespread use of anaesthesia to erase the inconveniently conscious and complaining woman from the male doctor's experience.

5 The relation between pain, femininity, and masochism in Deutsch and more broadly is clearly hugely complex and extends through and beyond the psychoanalytic tradition to writing on sadomasochistic sex, including to masochistic practice as a limit-experience.

6 Indeed, this is one of Walsh's claims. See Walsh 2009, 91–92. It is also a claim heavily mediated by the medical system and by culture. In the United Kingdom, for example (the national context from which Walsh is writing), I speculate that stoicism in the face of suffering is more culturally valued and a nationalized health care system in which midwife-attended birth is the norm incentivizes minimal medical intervention into normal births. In the United States, by contrast, physical pain is more commonly understood as something to be avoided wherever possible, while an insurance-based system in which birth is managed by obstetricians incentivizes the use of epidurals and C-sections. In my experience (having lived in and received medical treatment in all three countries), Canada has a health system more like the United Kingdom and a culture more like the United States. The obvious gap between how pain is managed and how patients are expected to engage pain is one of the things that makes this philosophical reflection possible.

7 The best-known pain scale to use adjectives in this way is the McGill Pain Questionnaire, developed in 1971. More contemporary approaches to evaluating pain use analogue scales, in which the patient is asked to rate their pain from one to ten, or say which of a range of expressive faces captures their experience.

8 See Burney [1812] 1995; Frey 2003, 61–71. Frey's account raises the interesting epistemic twist of being largely fabricated while posing as a memoir; see Rybak 2003.

9 I am grateful to an anonymous reviewer who helped me clarify this point.

10 There are, of course, many contexts in which social stratification influences obstetric and midwifery perinatal care provision. In my own context, the lack of perinatal health care services for those who live in Canada's north or otherwise remote rural regions—who are of course disproportionately citizens of First Nations or Inuit—is of particular concern. Many Indigenous women must fly to major centers in advance of their due date, and give birth without family, friends, or familiar health care personnel in attendance; discrimination against Indigenous women in Canada's health care system is also commonplace, if underdescribed in the health sciences literature. For a qualitative discussion of the rural communities birth evacuation policy, see Lawford, Giles, and Bourgeault 2018; for a study of differences in prenatal care comparing First Nations and settler women in British Columbia, see Riddell, Hutcheon, and Dahlgren 2016; for a larger quantitative analysis of infant mortality rates in Indigenous populations in Canada, see Smylie, Fell, and Ohlsson, 2010.

11 A similar point is made by Rachel Benmayor in her testimony to Katherine Cole-Adams (2017), albeit in a much more destructive and dramatic situation. Benmayor experienced full anaesthetic awareness, including almost fatal pain, during a cesarean section birth.

1 Cited in this book, see Lafargue 1883; A. Simpson 2017; Weeks 2011. The traditions of autonomist Marxism and feminism provide critiques of work that connect with this point (for accessible overviews, see Frase 2013; Wandavra 2013), while the politics of passive resistance is most associated with Gandhi's independence movement in India. Although the categories "nonviolent resistance" and "civil resistance" are not obviously "passive," they also have important connections with the points about action made here (see Garton Ash and Roberts 2009 for a wide-ranging collection of analytic case studies). In "North America," a politics of refusal is also associated with Indigenous resurgence and the refusal to participate in nation-state structures (ideological and material) that presuppose the claims to sovereignty being advanced (e.g., Coulthard 2014). Finally, although "Slow" movements (Slow Food, Slow Cities, Slow Sex, etc.) are often annoyingly depoliticized, they provide another link with the politics of temporality and the imperatives of normative forms of action (e.g., Parkins and Craig 2006).

REFERENCES

ABCNews. 2013. "Steubenville Social Media: By the Numbers." March 21. https://abcnews.go.com/blogs/technology/2013/03/steubenville-social-media-by-the-numbers/.

Adams, Carol. 2003. *The Pornography of Meat*. New York: Continuum.

Ahmed, Sara. 2006. *Queer Phenomenology: Orientations, Objects, Others*. Durham, NC: Duke University Press.

Alcoff, Linda Martín. 1996. "Dangerous Pleasures: Foucault and the Politics of Pedophilia." In *Feminist Interpretations of Michel Foucault*, edited by Susan J. Hekman, 99–135. University Park: Pennsylvania State University Press.

Alcoff, Linda Martín. 2000. "Phenomenology, Post-Structuralism, and Feminist Theory on the Concept of Experience." In *Feminist Phenomenology*, edited by Linda Fisher and Lester Embree, 39–56. Dordrecht, Germany: Kluwer.

Alcoff, Linda Martín. 2006. *Visible Identities: Race, Gender, and the Self*. New York: Oxford University Press.

Alcoff, Linda Martín. 2014. "Sexual Violations and the Question of Experience." *New Literary History* 45 (3): 445–62.

Alcoff, Linda Martín. 2018. *Rape and Resistance: Understanding the Complexities of Sexual Violation*. Cambridge: Polity Press.

Allen, Amy. 2008. *The Politics of Our Selves: Power, Autonomy, and Gender in Contemporary Critical Theory*. New York: Columbia University Press.

Al-Saji, Alia. 2010a. "Bodies and Sensings: On the Uses of Husserlian Phenomenology for Feminist Theory." *Continental Philosophy Review* 43:13–37.

Al-Saji, Alia. 2010b. "The Racialization of Muslim Veils: A Philosophical Analysis." *Philosophy and Social Criticism* 36 (8): 875–902.

Al-Saji, Alia. 2014. "A Phenomenology of Hesitation: Interrupting Racializing Habits of Seeing." In *Living Alterities: Phenomenology, Embodiment, and Race*, edited by Emily S. Lee, 133–72. Albany, NY: SUNY Press.

Antony, Louise. 2013. "Healthy Advice That Sends a Dangerous Message." *New York Times*, October 24. http://www.nytimes.com/roomfordebate/2013/10/23/young -women-drinking-and-rape/advising-women-against-drinking.

Arendt, Hannah. (1958) 1998. *The Human Condition*. Chicago: University of Chicago Press.

Arnett, Dugan. 2013. "Nightmare in Maryville: Teens' Sexual Encounter Ignites a Firestorm against Family." *Kansas City Star*, October 12. http://www.kansascity .com/news/special-reports/maryville/article329412/Nightmare-in-Maryville -Teens%E2%80%99-sexual-encounter-ignites-a-firestorm-against-family.html.

Backhouse, Constance. 2008. *Carnal Crimes: Sexual Assault Law in Canada, 1900–1975*. Toronto: Osgoode Society for Canadian Legal History by Irwin Law.

Ball, Kelly H. 2013. "'More or Less Raped': Foucault, Causality, and Feminist Critiques of Sexual Violence." *philoSOPHIA: A Journal of Continental Feminism* 3 (1): 52–68.

Baraitser, Lisa. 2009. *Maternal Encounters: The Ethics of Interruption*. Hove, Sussex: Routledge.

Baraitser, Lisa. 2017. *Enduring Time*. London: Bloomsbury.

Bartky, Sandra Lee. 1990. *Femininity and Domination: Studies in the Phenomenology of Oppression*. New York: Routledge.

Bartky, Sandra Lee. 2009. "Iris Young and the Gendering of Phenomenology." In *Dancing with Iris: The Philosophy of Iris Marion Young*, edited by Ann Ferguson and Mechthild Nagel, 41–51. New York: Oxford University Press.

Bazelon, Emily. 2013. "Horrifying Maryville Rape Case Follows Familiar Pattern. Why Does This Keep Happening?" *Slate*, October 14. https://slate.com/human -interest/2013/10/maryville-rape-case-the-horrifying-details-of-what-happened -to-daisy-coleman-feel-all-too-familiar.html.

Beauvoir, Simone de. (1970) 1972. *Coming of Age* [*La Veilleisse*]. New York: Putnam's.

Benedet, Janine. 2010. "The Sexual Assault of Intoxicated Women." *Canadian Journal of Women and the Law* 22 (2): 435–62.

Benedet, Janine, and Isabel Grant. 2007. "Hearing the Sexual Assault Complaints of Women with Mental Disabilities: Consent, Capacity and Mistaken Belief." *McGill Law Journal* 52:243–89.

Benedet, Janine, and Isabel Grant. 2010. "R. v. A. (J.): Confusing Unconsciousness with Autonomy." *Criminal Reports* 74 (6): 80–85.

Benoit, Cecilia, Camille Stengel, Lenora Marcellus, Helga Hallgrimsdottir, John Anderson, Karen MacKinnon, Rachel Phillips, Pilar Zazueta, and Sinead Charbonneau. 2014. "Providers' Constructions of Pregnant and Early Parenting Women Who Use Substances." *Sociology of Health and Illness* 36 (2): 252–63.

Berlant, Lauren. 2007. "Slow Death (Sovereignty, Obesity, Lateral Agency)." *Critical Inquiry* 33 (summer): 754–80.

Berlant, Lauren. 2010. "Risky Bigness: On Obesity, Eating, and the Ambiguity of 'Health.'" In *Against Health: How Health Became the New Morality*, edited by Jonathan Metzl and Anna Kirkland, 26–39. New York: New York University Press.

Bierria, Alisa. 2014. "Missing in Action: Violence, Power, and Discerning Agency." *Hypatia* 29 (1): 129–45.

Binswanger, Ludwig. 1960. *Melancholie und Manie: Phänomenologische Studien*. Pfullingen, Germany: Neske.

Binswanger, Ludwig, with Michel Foucault. (1930) 1993. *Dream and Existence*. Edited by Keith Hoeller. Atlantic Highlands, NJ: Humanities Press.

Bourgois, Philippe, and Jeff Schonberg. 2009. *Righteous Dopefiend*. Berkeley: University of California Press.

Bourke, Joanna. 2007. *Rape: A History from 1860 to the Present Day*. London: Virago.

Bourke, Joanna. 2014. "Childbirth in the UK: Suffering and Citizenship before the 1950s." *Lancet* 383:1288–89.

Boyd, Susan. 2004. *From Witches to Crack Moms: Women, Drug Law, and Policy*. Durham, NC: Carolina Academic Press.

Brison, Susan. 2002. *Aftermath: Violence and the Remaking of a Self*. Princeton, NJ: Princeton University Press.

Brodsky, Phyllis L. 2008. *The Control of Childbirth: Women versus Medicine through the Ages*. Jefferson, NC: McFarland.

Broome, Matthew R. 2005. "Suffering and Eternal Recurrence of the Same: The Neuroscience, Psychopathology, and Philosophy of Time." *Philosophy, Psychiatry, and Psychology* 12 (3): 187–94.

Brown, Wendy. 2015. *Undoing the Demos: Neoliberalism's Stealth Revolution*. New York: Zone.

Brownmiller, Susan. 1999. *In Our Time: Memoir of a Revolution*. New York: Dial Press.

Buck-Morss, Susan. 1992. "Aesthetics and Anaesthetics: Walter Benjamin's *Artwork* Essay Reconsidered." *October* 62 (autumn): 3–41.

Burleigh, Nina. 2013. "Sexting, Shame, and Suicide: A Shocking Tale of Sexual Assault in the Digital Age." *Rolling Stone*, September 17. http://www.rollingstone.com/culture/news/sexting-shame-and-suicide-20130917.

Burney, Frances. (1812) 1995. "A Mastectomy." In *Medicine and Western Civilization*, edited by David J. Rothman, Steven Marcus, and Stephanie A. Kiceluk, 383–89. New Brunswick, NJ: Rutgers University Press.

Burroughs, William S. 1977. *Junky*. New York: Penguin.

Butler, Judith. 2002. "What Is Critique? An Essay on Foucault's Virtue." In *The Political*, edited by David Ingram, 212–26. Malden, MA: Blackwell.

Butler, Judith. 2004. *Undoing Gender*. New York: Routledge.

Butler, Judith. 2006. *Precarious Life: The Powers of Mourning and Violence*. London: Verso.

Cahill, Ann. 2001. *Rethinking Rape*. Ithaca, NY: Cornell University Press.

Cahill, Ann. 2012. *Overcoming Objectification: A Carnal Ethics*. New York: Routledge.

Campbell, Denis. 2009. "It's Good for Women to Suffer the Pain of a Natural Birth, Says Medical Chief." *Observer*, July 11. http://www.guardian.co.uk/lifeandstyle /2009/jul/12/pregnancy-pain-natural-birth-yoga.

CBC News. 2013. "Dr George Doodnaught Guilty of 21 Sex Assaults of Patients." November 19. http://www.cbc.ca/news/canada/toronto/dr-george-doodnaught -guilty-of-21-sex-assaults-of-patients-1.2431679.

CBC News. 2014. "Cpl. Derrick Gallagher Faces 18 New Charges in Sex Assault Probe." April 18. http://www.cbc.ca/news/canada/ottawa/cpl-derrick-gallagher -faces-18-new-charges-in-sex-assault-probe-1.2613423.

Channing, Walter. 1849. *A Treatise on Etherization in Childbirth: Illustrated by Five Hundred and Eighty-One Cases*. Boston: Ticknor.

Chisholm, Dianne. 2008. "Climbing Like a Girl: An Exemplary Adventure in Feminist Phenomenology." *Hypatia* 23 (1): 9–40.

Christman, John. 2009. *The Politics of Persons: Individual Autonomy and Socio-Historical Selves*. Cambridge: Cambridge University Press.

Cochran, Kira. 2014. "How Female Corpses Became a Fashion Trend." *Guardian*, January 9. https://www.theguardian.com/lifeandstyle/womens-blog/2014/jan /09/female-corpses-fashion-trend-marc-jacobs-miley-cyrus.

Cocteau, Jean. 1933. *Opium: The Diary of an Addict*. London: Allen and Unwin.

Code, Lorraine. 2000. "The Perversion of Autonomy and the Subjection of Women: Discourses of Social Advocacy at Century's End." In *Relational Autonomy: Feminist Perspectives on Autonomy, Agency, and the Self*, edited by Catriona Mackenzie and Natalie Stoljar, 181–209. New York: Oxford University Press.

Cole-Adams, Katherine. 2017. *Anesthesia: The Gift of Oblivion and the Mystery of Consciousness*. Berkeley, CA: Counterpoint Press.

Combahee River Collective. (1977) 1983. "A Black Feminist Statement." In *Home Girls: A Black Feminist Anthology*, edited by Barbara Smith, 210–18. New York: Kitchen Table Women of Color Press.

Coulter, Kristi. 2017. "'Wine. Immediately.' The Depressing Reason So Many Women Drink." *Vox*, August 25. https://www.vox.com/2016/8/23/12584530/women -alcohol-wine.

Coulthard, Glen. 2014. *Red Skin, White Masks: Rejecting the Colonial Politics of Recognition*. Minneapolis: University of Minnesota Press.

Crane, Dede, and Lisa Moore, eds. 2008. *Great Expectations: Twenty-Four True Stories about Childbirth*. Toronto: House of Anansi.

Crary, Jonathan. 2013. *24/7: Terminal Capitalism and the Ends of Sleep*. London: Verso.

Crawford, Lucas. 2017. "Slender Trouble: From Berlant's Cruel Figuring of Figure to Sedgwick's Fat Presence." *GLQ* 23 (4): 447–72.

Dean, Jodi. 2009. *Democracy and Other Neoliberal Fantasies: Communicative Capitalism and Left Politics*. Durham, NC: Duke University Press.

De Quincey, Thomas. (1821) 2013. *Confessions of an English Opium-Eater and Other Writings*. Oxford: Oxford University Press.

Deutsch, Hélène. 1945. *The Psychology of Women: A Psychoanalytic Interpretation*. New York: Grune and Stratton.

Deutscher, Penelope. 2017. *Foucault's Futures: A Critique of Reproductive Reason*. New York: Columbia University Press.

de Warren, Nicolas. 2010. "The Inner Night: Towards a Phenomenology of (Dreamless) Sleep." In *On Time—New Contributions to the Husserlian Phenomenology of Time*, edited by D. Lohmar and I. Yamaguchi, 273–94. Dordrecht, Germany: Springer.

Dillon, Stephen. 2018. *Fugitive Life: The Queer Politics of the Prison State*. Durham, NC: Duke University Press.

Dilts, Andrew. 2011. "From 'Entrepreneur of the Self' to 'Care of the Self': Neoliberal Governmentality and Foucault's Ethics." *Foucault Studies* 12:130–46.

Du Mont, Janice, Sheila Macdonald, Nomi Rotbard, Eriola Asllani, Deidre Bainbridge, and Marsha M. Cohen. 2009. "Factors Associated with Suspected Drug-Facilitated Sexual Assault." *Canadian Medical Association Journal* 180 (5): 513–19.

Durkin, Erin. 2018. "Bill Crosby Sentenced to Three to 10 Years for Sexual Assault." *Guardian*, September 25. https://www.theguardian.com/world/2018/sep/25/bill-cosby-sentence-sexual-assault-judge.

Ehrenreich, Barbara, and Dierdre English. (1973) 2010. *Witches, Midwives, and Nurses: A History of Women Healers*. 2nd ed. New York: Feminist Press.

Elson, Vicki. 2009. *Laboring Under an Illusion: Mass Media Childbirth vs. the Real Thing*. Conway, MA: Vicki Elson. http://www.birth-media.com/.

Evans, Elrena, and Caroline Grant, eds. 2008. *Mama, PhD: Women Write about Motherhood and Academic Life*. New Brunswick, NJ: Rutgers University Press.

Fanon, Frantz. (1952) 1967. *Black Skin, White Masks*. New York: Grove.

Ferguson, Michaele L. 2009. "Resonance and Dissonance: The Role of Personal Experience in Iris Marion Young's Feminist Phenomenology." In *Dancing with Iris: The Philosophy of Iris Marion Young*, edited by Ann Ferguson and Mechthild Nagel, 53–68. New York: Oxford University Press.

Fielding, Helen, and Dorothea Olkowski, eds. 2017. *Feminist Phenomenology Futures*. Bloomington: Indiana University Press.

Finch, Emily, and Vanessa E. Munro. 2007. "The Demon Drink and the Demonized Woman: Socio-Sexual Stereotypes and Responsibility Attribution in Rape Trials Involving Intoxicants." *Social and Legal Studies* 16 (4): 591–614.

Fisher, Linda, and Lester Embree, eds. 2000. *Feminist Phenomenology*. Dordrecht, Germany: Springer.

Fleming, Peter. 2009. *Authenticity and the Cultural Politics of Work: New Forms of Informal Control*. Oxford: Oxford University Press.

Florence, Maurice [Michel Foucault]. (1984) 1998. "Foucault." In *Michel Foucault, Aesthetics, Method and Epistemology*, edited by James D. Faubion and translated by Robert Hurley et al., 459–63. New York: New Press.

Flynn, Thomas R. 2004a. *A Poststructuralist Mapping of History*. Vol. 2, of *Sartre, Foucault, and Historical Reason*. Chicago: University of Chicago Press.

Flynn, Thomas R. 2004b. "Sartre and Foucault: A Cross-Generational Exchange." *Sartre Studies International* 10 (2): 47–55.

Foltyn, Jacque Lynn. 2011. "Corpse Chic: Dead Models and Living Corpses in Fashion Photography." In *Fashion Forward*, edited by Alissa de Witt-Paul and Mira Crouch, 379–92. Oxford: Interdisciplinary Press.

Foucault, Michel. 1954. *Maladie mentale et personnalité*. Paris: Presses Universitaires de France. Out of print. Original French available at http://generation-online.org /p/fp-foucault.pdf.

Foucault, Michel. (1966) 1970. *The Order of Things*. New York: Random House.

Foucault, Michel. (1962) 1976. *Mental Illness and Psychology*. Translated by Alan Sheridan. New York: Harper and Row. Translation of *Maladie mentale et psychologie*.

Foucault, Michel. 1976. *Histoire de la sexualité: La volonté de savoir*. Paris: Gallimard.

Foucault, Michel. 1977. "Nietzsche, Genealogy, History." In *Language, Counter-Memory, Practice: Selected Essays and Interviews by Michel Foucault*, edited and introduction by Donald F. Bouchard, 139–64. Ithaca, NY: Cornell University Press.

Foucault, Michel. (1975) 1977. *Discipline and Punish: The Birth of the Prison*. New York: Random House.

Foucault, Michel. (1976) 1978. *The History of Sexuality, Volume 1: An Introduction*. Translated by Robert Hurley. New York: Pantheon.

Foucault, Michel. (1981) 1982. "Conversation entre Werner Schroeter et Michel Foucault." In *Werner Schroeter*, edited by Gérard Courant. Paris: Goethe-Institut. http://www.gerardcourant.com/index.php?t=ecrits&e=162.

Foucault, Michel. (1984) 1988a. "The Concern for Truth." In *Politics, Philosophy, Culture*, edited by Lawrence D. Kritzman, translated by A. Sheridan, 255–67. New York: Routledge.

Foucault, Michel. (1981) 1988b. "Practicing Criticism." In *Politics, Philosophy, Culture*, edited by Lawrence D. Kritzman, translated by A. Sheridan, 152–56. New York: Routledge.

Foucault, Michel. (1984) 1990. *The History of Sexuality, Volume 2: The Use of Pleasure*. Translated by Robert Hurley. New York: Vintage.

Foucault, Michel. (1984) 1996a. "An Aesthetics of Existence." In *Foucault Live: Collected Interviews, 1961–1984*, edited by Sylvère Lotringer, 450–54. New York: Semiotext(e). April 25, 1984, interview in French with Alessandro Fontana, translated by John Johnston.

Foucault, Michel. 1996b. "An Ethics of Pleasure." In *Foucault Live: Collected Interviews, 1961–1984*, edited by Sylvère Lotringer, 371–81. New York: Semiotext(e).

Foucault, Michel. (1975) 1996c. "Sade: Sargeant of Sex." In *Foucault Live: Collected Interviews, 1961–1984*, edited by Sylvère Lotringer, 186–89. New York: Semiotext(e).

Foucault, Michel. (1983) 1997a. "On the Genealogy of Ethics: An Overview of Work in Progress." In *Michel Foucault, Ethics, Subjectivity, and Truth*, edited by Paul Rabinow, 253–80. New York: New Press.

Foucault, Michel. (1982) 1997b. "An Interview by Stephen Riggins." In *Michel Foucault, Ethics, Subjectivity, and Truth*, edited by Paul Rabinow, 121–33. New York: New Press. June 22, 1982, interview in English.

Foucault, Michel. (1982) 1997c. "Sex, Power, and the Politics of Identity." In *Michel Foucault, Ethics, Subjectivity, and Truth*, edited by Paul Rabinow, 163–73. New York: New Press. June 1982, interview in English with B. Gallagher and A. Wilson in Toronto.

Foucault, Michel. (1983) 1997d. "Sexual Choice, Sexual Act." In *Michel Foucault, Ethics, Subjectivity, and Truth*, edited by Paul Rabinow, 141–56. New York: New Press.

Foucault, Michel. (1981) 1997e. "The Social Triumph of the Sexual Will." In *Michel Foucault, Ethics, Subjectivity, and Truth*, edited by Paul Rabinow, 157–62. New York: New Press. October 20, 1981, interview in French with G. Barbedette.

Foucault, Michel. (1978) 1997f. "What Is Critique?" In *The Politics of Truth*, edited by Sylvère Lotringer, 41–81. Los Angeles: Semiotexte.

Foucault, Michel. (1984) 1997g. "What Is Enlightenment?" In *Michel Foucault, Ethics, Subjectivity, and Truth*, edited by Paul Rabinow, 303–19. New York: New Press.

Foucault, Michel. (1963) 1998. "A Preface to Transgression." In *Michel Foucault, Aesthetics, Method and Epistemology*, edited by James D. Faubion and translated by Robert Hurley et al., 69–87. New York: New Press.

Foucault, Michel. 1999. *Les Anormaux: Cours au Collège de France (1974-1975)*. Edited by Valerio Marchetti and Antonella Salomoni. Paris: Gallimard.

Foucault, Michel. (1979) 2000a. "For an Ethic of Discomfort." In *Michel Foucault, Power*, edited by James D. Faubion and translated by Robert Hurley et al., 443–48. New York: New Press.

Foucault, Michel. (1978) 2000b. "An Interview with Michel Foucault." In *Michel Foucault, Power*, edited by James D. Faubion and translated by Robert Hurley et al., 239–97. New York: New Press. Interview by D. Trombadori, late 1978.

Foucault, Michel. (1999) 2003. *Abnormal: Lectures at the Collège de France, 1974-1975*. Edited by Valerio Marchetti and Antonella Salomoni. Translated by Graham Burchell. New York: Picador.

Foucault, Michel. 2005. *The Hermeneutics of the Subject: Lectures at the Collège de France, 1981-1982*. Edited by Frédéric Gros, Francois Ewald, and Alessandro Fontana. Translated by Graham Burchell. New York: Palgrave Macmillan.

Foucault, Michel. (2004) 2008. *The Birth of Biopolitics: Lectures at the Collège de France, 1978-1979*. Edited by Michel Senellart. Translated by Graham Burchell. New York: Picador.

Frase, Peter. 2013. "Post-work: A Guide for the Perplexed." *Jacobin*, February. https://jacobinmag.com/2013/02/post-work-a-guide-for-the-perplexed/.

Fraser, Nancy. 2003. "From Discipline to Flexibilization? Rereading Foucault in the Shadow of Globalization." *Constellations* 10 (2): 160–71.

Freedman, Karyn L. 2014. *One Hour in Paris: A True Story of Rape and Recovery*. Calgary: Freehand Books.

Freeman, Elizabeth. 2010. *Time Binds: Queer Temporalities, Queer Histories*. Durham, NC: Duke University Press.

Freeman, Lauren, and Andreas Elpidorou. 2015. "Affectivity in Heidegger II: Temporality, Boredom, and Beyond." *Philosophy Compass* 10 (10): 672–84.

Freud, Sigmund. 1884. "Über Coca." Reproduced and translated in *Journal of Substance Abuse Treatment* 1:206–7.

Frey, James. 2003. *A Million Little Pieces*. New York: Random House.

Fricker, Miranda. 2006. "Powerlessness and Social Interpretation." *Episteme: A Journal of Social Epistemology* 3 (1): 96–108.

Friedman, Ann. 2013. "When Rape Goes Viral," *Newsweek*, July 24. http://www.newsweek.com/2013/07/24/when-rape-goes-viral-237742.html.

Fuchs, Thomas. 2001. "Melancholia as a Desynchronization: Towards a Psychopathology of Interpersonal Time." *Psychopathology* 34:179–86.

Fuchs, Thomas. 2005. "Implicit and Explicit Temporality." *Philosophy, Psychiatry, and Psychology* 12:195–98.

Fuchs, Thomas. 2013. "Temporality and Psychopathology." *Phenomenology of Cognitive Science* 12:75–104.

Garton Ash, Timothy, and Adam Roberts, eds. 2009. *Civil Resistance and Power Politics: The Experience of Non-violent Action from Gandhi to the Present*. Oxford: Oxford University Press.

Gauntlett-Gilbert, Jeremy, Anna Keegan, and Jenny Petrak. 2004. "Drug-Facilitated Sexual Assault: Cognitive Approaches to Treating the Trauma." *Behavioural and Cognitive Psychotherapy* 32:215–23.

Gearhardt, Ashley N., Carlos M. Grilo, Ralph J. DiLeone, Kelly D. Brownell, and Marc N. Potenza. 2011. "Can Food Be Addictive? Public Health and Policy Implications." *Addiction* 106:1208–12.

Geniusas, Saulius. 2015. "Between Phenomenology and Hermeneutics: Paul Ricoeur's Philosophy of Imagination." *Human Studies* 38:223–41.

Glaser, Gabrielle. 2013. *Her Best-Kept Secret: Why Women Drink—And How They Can Regain Control*. New York: Simon and Schuster.

Glennie, Paul, and Nigel Thrift. 1996. "Reworking E. P. Thompson's 'Time, Work-Discipline and Industrial Capitalism.'" *Time and Society* 5 (3): 275–99.

Glucklich, Ariel. 2003. *Sacred Pain: Hurting the Body for the Sake of the Soul*. New York: Oxford University Press.

Goldberg-Hiller, Jonathan. 2019. "Is There a Right to Sleep?" *Theory and Event* 22 (4): 951–83.

Gotell, Lise. 2012. "Governing Heterosexuality through Specific Consent: Interrogating the Governmental Effects of *R. v J.A.*" *Canadian Journal of Women and the Law* 24 (2): 359–88.

Granter, Edward. 2008. "A Dream of Ease: Situating the Future of Work and Leisure." *Futures* 40:803–11.

Gray, Mary Tod. 2005. "The Shifting Sands of Self: A Framework for the Experience of Self in Addiction." *Nursing Philosophy* 6:119–30.

Guenther, Lisa. 2006. *The Gift of the Other: Levinas and the Politics of Reproduction*. Albany, NY: SUNY Press.

Guenther, Lisa. 2013. *Solitary Confinement: Social Death and Its Afterlives*. Minneapolis: University of Minnesota Press.

Gutting, Gary. 2005. *Foucault: A Very Short Introduction*. Oxford: Oxford University Press.

Hadot, Pierre. 1992. "Reflections on the Notion of 'The Cultivation of the Self.'" In *Michel Foucault: Philosopher: Essays Translated from the French and German*, edited by Timothy J. Armstrong, 225–31. New York: Routledge.

Halberstam, Judith [Jack]. 2011. *The Queer Art of Failure*. Durham, NC: Duke University Press.

Halperin, David. 1995. *Saint Foucault: Towards a Gay Hagiography*. New York: Oxford University Press.

Harrison, Paul. 2009. "In the Absence of Practice." *Environment and Planning D: Society and Space* 27:987–1009.

Hartman, Saidiya. 1997. *Scenes of Subjection: Terror, Slavery, and Self-Making in Nineteenth-Century America*. New York: Oxford University Press.

Hatch, Anthony Ryan, and Kym Bradley. 2016. "Prisons Matter: Psychotropics and the Trope of Silence in Technocorrections." In *Mattering: Feminism, Science, and Materialism*, edited by Victoria Pitts-Taylor, 224–41. New York: New York University Press.

Hess, Amanda. 2014. "Rehtaeh Parsons Was the Most Famous Victim in Canada. Now, Journalists Can't Even Say Her Name." *Slate*, September 29. http://www.slate.com/blogs/xx_factor/2014/09/29/rehtaeh_parsons_canadian_journalists_can_t_print_her_name_as_a_suspect_pleads.html.

Heyes, Cressida J. 2003. "Feminist Solidarity after Queer Theory: The Case of Transgender." *Signs: Journal of Women in Culture and Society* 28 (4): 1093–120.

Heyes, Cressida J. 2007. *Self-Transformations: Foucault, Ethics, and Normalized Bodies*. New York: Oxford University Press.

Heyes, Cressida J. 2009. "Changing Race, Changing Sex: The Ethics of Self-Transformation." In *You've Changed: Sex Reassignment and Personal Identity*, edited by Laurie Shrage, 135–54. New York: Oxford University Press.

Heyes, Cressida J. 2013. "Foucault and Feminist Philosophy Now." *Foucault Studies* 16:3–14.

Heyes, Cressida J. (2002) 2016. "Identity Politics." *Stanford Encyclopedia of Philosophy*. 4th rev. ed. http://plato.stanford.edu/.

Heyes, Cressida J. 2017. "I'll Sleep When I'm Dead: Work and Agency in Political Imagination." Paper given in the Department of Sociology speakers' series, Carleton University, September 26.

Heyes, Cressida J. 2018. "Two Kinds of Awareness: Foucault, the Will, and Freedom in Somatic Practice." *Human Studies: A Journal for Philosophy and the Social Sciences* 41 (4): 527–44.

Heyes, Cressida J. Forthcoming. "Practices of Justification: From Philosophy to Pluralism." In *Civic Freedom in an Age of Diversity: James Tully's Public Philosophy*, edited by Dimitrios Karmis and Jocelyn Maclure.

Highmore, Ben. 2004. "Homework: Routine, Social Aesthetics, and the Ambiguity of Everyday Life." *Cultural Studies* 18 (2/3): 306–27.

Hinsliff, Gaby. 2018. "'Yes He's Alive but I'm Not OK': The Bloody Truth about Childbirth." *Guardian*, September 19. https://www.theguardian.com /lifeandstyle/2018/sep/19/yes-hes-alive-but-im-not-ok-the-bloody-truth-about -childbirth?CMP=Share_iOSApp_Other.

Hochschild, Arlie. 2012. *The Outsourced Self: Intimate Life in Market Times*. New York: Metropolitan Books.

Hoy, David Couzens. 2012. *The Time of Our Lives: A Critical History of Temporality*. Cambridge, MA: MIT Press.

Huffer, Lynne. 2010. *Mad for Foucault: Rethinking the Foundations of Queer Theory*. New York: Columbia University Press.

Huffer, Lynne, and Elizabeth Wilson. 2010. "Mad for Foucault: A Conversation." *Theory, Culture, and Society* 27 (7–8): 324–38.

Hurst, Rachel Alpha Johnston, and Luna Dolezal. 2018. "Cosmetic Surgery as 'Cut-Up': The Body and Gender in Breyer P-Orridge's Pandrogeny." *Configurations* 26 (4): 389–409.

Janack, Marianne. 2012. *What We Mean by Experience*. Stanford, CA: Stanford University Press.

Jay, Martin. 2005. *Songs of Experience: Modern American and European Variations on a Universal Theme*. Berkeley: University of California Press.

Jones, Meredith. 2005. *Makeover Culture: Landscapes of Cosmetic Surgery*. PhD diss., University of Western Sydney.

Jones, Meredith. 2008. "Sleeping Beauties: Lolo Ferrari and Anaesthesia." In *Skintight: An Anatomy of Cosmetic Surgery*, 129–49. Oxford: Berg.

Käll, Lisa Folkmarson, and Kristin Zeiler, eds. 2014. *Feminist Phenomenology and Medicine*. Albany, NY: SUNY Press.

Kemp, Ryan. 2009. "The Temporal Dimension of Addiction." *Journal of Phenomenological Psychology* 40:1–18.

Keynes, John Maynard. 1923. *A Tract on Monetary Reform*. London: Macmillan.

Keynes, John Maynard. (1930) 1963. "Economic Possibilities for Our Grandchildren." In *Essays in Persuasion*, 358–73. New York: Norton.

Kirkland, Anna. 2011. "The Environmental Account of Obesity: A Case for Feminist Skepticism." *Signs: Journal of Women in Culture and Society* 36 (2): 463–85.

Knapp, Caroline. 1996. *Drinking: A Love Story*. New York: Random House.

Koren, Gideon, Karen Graham, Heather Shear, and Tom Einarson. 1989. "Bias against the Null Hypothesis: The Reproductive Hazards of Cocaine." *Lancet*, December 16, 1440–42.

Kristeva, Julia. 1981. "Women's Time." Translated by Alice Jardine and Harry Blake. *Signs: Journal of Women in Culture and Society* 7 (1): 13–35.

Kruks, Sonia. 1995. "Identity Politics and Dialectical Reason: Beyond an Epistemology of Provenance." *Hypatia* 10 (2): 1–22.

Kukla, Rebecca. 2005. *Mass Hysteria: Medicine, Culture, and Mother's Bodies.* Lanham, MD: Rowman and Littlefield.

Kupke, Christian. 2005. "Lived Time and to Live Time: A Critical Comment on a Paper by Martin Wyllie." *Philosophy, Psychiatry, and Psychology* 12 (3): 199–203.

Lafargue, Paul. 1883. *The Right to Be Lazy.* Marxist Internet Archive. http://www.marxists.org/archive/lafargue/1883/lazy/index.htm.

Laqueur, Thomas Walter. 1992. *Making Sex: Body and Gender from the Greeks to Freud.* Cambridge, MA: Harvard University Press.

Latham, J. R., Suzanne Fraser, Renae Fomiatti, David Moore, Kate Seear, and Campbell Aitken. 2019. "Men's Performance and Image-Enhancing Drug Use as Self-Transformation: Working Out in Makeover Culture." *Australian Feminist Studies* 34 (100): 149–64.

Lawford, Karen M., Audrey R. Giles, and Ivy L. Bourgeault. 2018. "Canada's Evacuation Policy for Pregnant First Nations Women: Resignation, Resilience, and Resistance." *Women and Birth* 31 (6): 479–88.

Leder, Drew. 1990. *The Absent Body.* Chicago: University of Chicago Press.

Lee, Emily S., ed. 2014. *Living Alterities: Phenomenology, Embodiment, and Race.* Albany, NY: SUNY Press.

Lenson, David. 1995. *On Drugs.* Minneapolis: University of Minnesota Press.

Levy, Ariel. 2013. "Trial by Twitter." *New Yorker,* August 5. http://www.newyorker.com/reporting/2013/08/05/130805fa_fact_levy.

Lindberg, Tracey, Priscilla Campeau, and Maria Campbell. 2011. "Indigenous Women and Sexual Assault in Canada." In *Sexual Assault Law: Practice and Activism in a Post-Jane Doe Era,* edited by Elizabeth A. Sheehy, 87–109. Ottawa: University of Ottawa Press.

Lowe, Pam, Cathy Humphreys, and Simon J. Williams. 2007. "Night Terrors: Women's Experiences of (Not) Sleeping Where There Is Domestic Violence." *Violence Against Women* 13:549–61.

lowendtheory. 2012. "A Love Letter to Radical Graduate Students, Present, Former, Future: Part One." lowendtheory (blog), March 12. http://www.lowendtheory.org/post/19214802546/a-love-letter-to-radical-graduate-students.

Lugones, Maria. 2003. *Pilgrimages: Peregrinajes: Theorizing Coalition against Multiple Oppressions.* Lanham, MD: Rowman & Littlefield.

Mackenzie, Catriona. 2008. "Imagination, Identity, and Self-Transformation." In *Practical Identity and Narrative Agency,* edited by Kim Atkins and Catriona Mackenzie, 121–14. New York: Routledge.

MacLean, Lorna. 2002. "'Deserving' Wives and 'Drunken' Husbands: Wife Beating, Marital Conduct, and the Law in Ontario, 1850–1910." *Histoire sociale / Social History* 35:69, 59–81.

Mahmood, Saba. (2005) 2012. *The Politics of Piety: The Islamic Revival and the Feminist Subject.* 2nd ed. Princeton, NJ: Princeton University Press.

Mann, Bonnie. 2009. "Iris Marion Young: Between Phenomenology and Structural Injustice." In *Dancing with Iris: The Philosophy of Iris Marion Young*, edited by Ann Ferguson and Mechthild Nagel, 79–91. New York: Oxford University Press.

Masson, Erin M. 1997. "The Woman's Christian Temperance Union, 1874–1898: Combatting Domestic Violence." *William and Mary Journal of Women and the Law* 3 (1): 163–88.

Matthews, Eric. 2005. "The Relevance of Phenomenology." *Philosophy, Psychiatry, and Psychology* 12 (3): 205–7.

May, Todd. 2006. "Foucault's Relation to Phenomenology." In *The Cambridge Companion to Foucault*, edited by Gary Gutting, 284–311. Cambridge: Cambridge University Press.

Mbembe, Achille. 2003. "Necropolitics." Translated by Libby Meintjes. *Public Culture* 15 (1): 11–40.

McIntosh, Tania. 2012. *A Social History of Maternity and Childbirth*. Abingdon, UK: Routledge.

McKenna, Stacey. 2013. "'We're Supposed to Be Asleep?' Vigilance, Paranoia, and the Alert Methamphetamine User." *Anthropology of Consciousness* 24 (2): 172–90.

McNay, Lois. 2009. "Self as Enterprise: Dilemmas of Control and Resistance in Foucault's *The Birth of Biopolitics*." *Theory, Culture, and Society* 26 (6): 55–77.

McTighe, Laura. 2012. "The War on Drugs Is a War on Relationships: Crossing the Borders of Fear, Silence, and HIV Vulnerability in the Prison-Created Diaspora." In *Walls and Cages: Prisons, Borders, and Global Crisis*, edited by Andrew Burridge, Jenna Loyd, and Matt Mitchelson, 301–13. Athens: University of Georgia Press.

McWhorter, Ladelle. 1999. *Bodies and Pleasures: Foucault and the Politics of Sexual Normalization*. Bloomington: Indiana University Press.

Meinbresse, Molly, Lauren Brinkley-Rubinstein, Amy Grassette, Joseph Benson, Carol Hall, Reginald Hamilton, Marianne Malott, and Darlene Jenkins. 2014. "Exploring the Experiences of Violence among Individuals Who Are Homeless Using a Consumer-Led Approach." *Violence and Victims* 29 (1): 122–36.

Merleau-Ponty, Maurice. (1945) 2002. *Phenomenology of Perception*. London: Routledge.

Metzl, Jonathan. 2003. *Prozac on the Couch: Prescribing Gender in the Era of Wonder Drugs*. Durham, NC: Duke University Press.

Milanovic, Branko. 2016. *Global Inequality: A New Approach for the Age of Globalization*. Cambridge, MA: Belknap Press of Harvard University Press.

Miller, Chanel. 2019. *Know My Name: A Memoir*. New York: Penguin Random House.

Miller, James. 1993. *The Passion of Michel Foucault*. New York: Doubleday.

Minkowski, Eugène. (1933) 1970. *Lived Time: Phenomenological and Psychopathological Studies*. Translated by Nancy Metzel. Evanston, IL: Northwestern University Press.

Mohanty, Chandra Talpade. 1992. "Feminist Encounters: Locating the Politics of Experience." In *Destabilizing Theory: Contemporary Feminist Debates*, edited by Michele Barrett and Anne Phillips, 74–92. Stanford, CA: Stanford University Press.

Morris, David B. 1991. *The Culture of Pain*. Berkeley: University of California Press.

Morris, Theresa, and Katherine McInerney. 2010. "Media Representations of Pregnancy and Childbirth: An Analysis of Reality Television Programs in the United States." *Birth* 37 (2): 134–40.

Moscoso, Javier. 2012. *Pain: A Cultural History*. Basingstoke, UK: Palgrave Macmillan.

Murphy, Michelle. 2017. *The Economization of Life*. Durham, NC: Duke University Press.

Nancy, Jean-Luc. 2009. *The Fall of Sleep*. New York: Fordham University Press.

Navarro, Vicente, ed. 2007. *Neoliberalism, Globalization, and Inequalities: Consequences for Health and Quality of Life*. Amityville, NY: Baywood.

Neimanis, Astrida. 2017. *Bodies of Water: Posthuman Feminist Phenomenology*. London: Bloomsbury.

Oksala, Johanna. 2004. "Anarchic Bodies: Foucault and the Feminist Question of Experience." *Hypatia* 19 (4): 97–119.

Oksala, Johanna. 2010. "Sexual Experience: Foucault, Phenomenology and Feminist Theory." *Hypatia* 25 (1): 2–17.

Oksala, Johanna. 2016. *Feminist Experiences: Foucauldian and Phenomenological Investigations*. Evanston, IL: Northwestern University Press.

O'Leary, Timothy. 2002. *Foucault and the Art of Ethics*. London: Continuum.

O'Leary, Timothy. 2009. *Foucault and Fiction: The Experience Book*. London: Continuum.

Oliver, Kelly. 2012. *Knock Me Up, Knock Me Down: Images of Pregnancy in Hollywood Films*. New York: Columbia University Press.

Oliver, Kelly. 2016. *Hunting Girls: Sexual Violence From* The Hunger Games *to Campus Rape*. New York: Columbia University Press.

Ortega, Mariana. 2016. *In-Between: Latina Feminist Phenomenology, Multiplicity, and the Self*. Albany, NY: SUNY Press.

Padmanabhanunni, Anita, and David Edwards. 2013. "Treating the Psychological Sequelae of Proactive Drug-Facilitated Sexual Assault: Knowledge Building through Systematic Case Based Research." *Behavioural and Cognitive Psychotherapy* 41:371–75.

Parkins, Wendy, and Geoffrey Craig. 2006. *Slow Living*. Oxford: Berg.

Paul, L.A. 2014. *Transformative Experience*. Oxford: Oxford University Press.

Pearce, Maryanne. 2013. "An Awkward Silence: Missing and Murdered Vulnerable Women and the Canadian Justice System." PhD diss., University of Ottawa.

Pearce, Matt. 2014. "No Prison Time for Man Convicted of Drugging, Raping Wife." *LA Times*, May 19. http://www.latimes.com/nation/nationnow/la-na-nn -indianapolis-rape-sentence-20140519-story.html.

Plaza, Monique. 1978. "Nos dommages et leurs intérêts." *Questions Féministes* 3 (May): 93–103.

Pollan, Michael. 2018. *How to Change Your Mind: What the New Science of Psychedelics Teaches Us about Consciousness, Dying, Addiction, Depression, and Transcendence*. New York: Penguin.

Pollitt, Katha. 1998. "'Fetal Rights:' A New Assault on Feminism." In *"Bad" Mothers: The Politics of Blame in Twentieth-Century America*, edited by Molly Ladd-Taylor and Lauri Umansky, 285–98. New York: New York University Press.

Povinelli, Elizabeth A. 2011. *Economies of Abandonment: Social Belonging and Endurance in Late Liberalism*. Durham, NC: Duke University Press.

Povinelli, Elizabeth, Mathew Coleman, and Kathryn Yusoff. 2017. "An Interview with Elizabeth Povinelli: Geontopower, Biopolitics and the Anthropocene." *Theory, Culture and Society* 34 (2–3): 169–85.

Powell, Anastasia, and Nicola Henry. 2017. *Sexual Violence in a Digital Age*. London: Palgrave Macmillan.

Prutschi, Edward. 2011. "Crimes of (Unconscious) Passion." SLAW: *Canada's Online Legal Magazine*, May 27. http://www.slaw.ca/2011/05/27/crimes-of-unconscious-passion/.

Puar, Jasbir K. (2007) 2017. *Terrorist Assemblages: Homonationalism in Queer Times*. Durham, NC: Duke University Press.

Radden, Jennifer. 2003. "Is This Dame Melancholy? Equating Today's Depression and Past Melancholia." *Philosophy, Psychiatry, and Psychology* 10 (1): 37–52.

Ramey, Valerie A., and Neville Francis. 2009. "A Century of Work and Leisure." *American Economic Journal: Macroeconomics* 1 (2): 189–224.

Ratcliffe, Matthew. 2015. *Experiences of Depression: A Study in Phenomenology*. New York: Oxford University Press.

Reiss, Benjamin. 2017. *Wild Nights: How Taming Sleep Created Our Restless World*. New York: Basic Books.

Reith, Gerda. 1999. "In Search of Lost Time: Recall, Projection, and the Phenomenology of Addiction." *Time and Society* 8 (1): 99–117.

Riddell, Corinne A., Jennifer A. Hutcheon, and Leanne S. Dahlgren. 2016. "Differences in Obstetric Care among Nulliparous First Nations and Non-First Nations Women in British Columbia, Canada." *Canadian Medical Association Journal* 188 (2): E36–43.

Rodemeyer, Lanei M. 2017. "Husserl and Queer Theory." *Continental Philosophy Review* 50:311–34.

Rodemeyer, Lanei M. 2018. *Lou Sullivan Diaries (1970–1980) and Theories of Sexual Embodiment*. Cham, Switzerland: Springer.

Rosa, Hartmut. 2003. "Social Acceleration: Ethical and Political Consequences of a Desynchronized High-Speed Society." *Constellations* 10 (1): 3–33.

Rosa, Hartmut. 2013. *Social Acceleration: A New Theory of Modernity*. Translated by Jonathan Trejo-Mathys. New York: Columbia University Press.

Rybak, Deborah Caulfield. 2003. "Taking Liberties: Memoir Writers Walk a Wavy Line between Reality and Invention." *Minneapolis Star Tribune*. July 27.

Sabot, Phillipe. 2013. "Foucault et Merleau-Ponty: Un dialogue impossible?" *Les Études philosophiques* 3 (106): 317–32.

Sacks, Oliver. 2012. *Hallucinations*. Toronto: Knopf.

Salamon, Gayle. 2006. "'The Place Where Life Hides Away': Merleau-Ponty, Fanon, and the Location of Bodily Being." *differences* 17 (2): 96–112.

Salamon, Gayle. 2010. *Assuming a Body: Transgender and Rhetorics of Materiality.* New York: Columbia University Press.

Salamon, Gayle. 2012. "The Phenomenology of Rheumatology: Disability, Merleau-Ponty, and the Fallacy of Maximal Grip." *Hypatia* 27 (2): 243–60.

Salamon, Gayle. 2018. *The Life and Death of Latisha King: A Critical Phenomenology of Transphobia.* New York: New York University Press.

Samuels, Alexandra. 2016. "Father of Student Convicted of Rape: Steep Price for '20 Minutes of Action'." *USA Today,* June 6. https://www.usatoday.com/story /college/2016/06/06/father-of-student-convicted-of-rape-steep-price-for-20 -minutes-of-action/37418253/.

Sawicki, Jana. 2005. Review of Michel Foucault, *Abnormal: Lectures at the Collège de France, 1974–1975. Notre Dame Philosophical Reviews.* http://ndpr.nd.edu/news /23977/?id=1581.

Scales-Trent, Judy. 1999. "Oppression, Lies, and the Dream of Autonomy." *William and Mary Law Review* 40 (3): 857–68.

Scarry, Elaine. 1985. *The Body in Pain: The Making and Unmaking of the World.* New York: Oxford University Press.

Schor, Juliet. 1991. *The Overworked American: The Unexpected Decline of Leisure.* New York: Basic Books.

Schotten, C. Heike. 2018. *Queer Terror: Life, Death, and Desire in the Settler Colony.* New York: Columbia University Press.

Schube, Sam, and Benjy Hansen-Bundy. 2018. "The New Status Symbols: How to Be Better Than Everyone Else in 2018." *GQ* 88: 34.

Schües, Christina, Dorothea Olkowski, and Helen Fielding, eds. 2011. *Time in Feminist Phenomenology.* Bloomington: Indiana University Press.

Scott, James C. 1990. *Domination and the Arts of Resistance: Hidden Transcripts.* New Haven, CT: Yale University Press.

Scott, Joan W. 1991. "The Evidence of Experience." *Critical Inquiry* 17 (4): 773–97.

Scott, Joan W. 2001. "Fantasy Echo: History and the Construction of Identity." *Critical Inquiry* 27 (2): 284–304.

Shabot, Sara Cohen. 2016. "Making Loud Bodies 'Feminine': A Feminist-Phenomenological Analysis of Obstetric Violence." *Human Studies* 39:231–47.

Shabot, Sara Cohen. 2017. "Constructing Subjectivity through Labour Pain: A Beauvoirian Analysis." *European Journal of Women's Studies* 24 (2): 128–42.

Shabot, Sara Cohen, and Keshet Korem. 2018. "Domesticating Bodies: The Role of Shame in Obstetric Violence." *Hypatia* 33 (3): 384–401.

Shabot, Sara Cohen, and Christinia Landry. 2018. *Rethinking Feminist Phenomenology: Theoretical and Applied Perspectives.* London: Rowman and Littlefield.

Sharma, Sarah. 2013. *In the Meantime: Temporality and Cultural Politics.* Durham, NC: Duke University Press.

Sheehy, Elizabeth A. 2011a. "Judges and the Reasonable Steps Requirement: The Judicial Stance on Perpetration against Unconscious Women." In *Sexual Assault*

Law: Practice and Activism in a Post-Jane Doe Era, edited by Elizabeth Sheehy, 483–540. Ottawa: University of Ottawa Press.

Sheehy, Elizabeth A., ed. 2011b. Sexual Assault Law: Practice and Activism in a Post-Jane Doe Era. Ottawa: University of Ottawa Press.

Shinebourne, Pnina, and Jonathan A. Smith. 2009. "Alcohol and the Self: An Interpretative Phenomenological Analysis of the Experience of Addiction and Its Impact on the Sense of Self and Identity." Addiction Research and Theory 17 (2): 152–67.

Simpson, Audra. 2016. "The State Is a Man: Theresa Spence, Loretta Saunders, and the Gender of Settler Sovereignty." Theory and Event 19 (4). https://www.muse.jhu.edu/article/633280.

Simpson, Audra. 2017. "The Ruse of Consent and the Anatomy of 'Refusal': Cases from Indigenous North America and Australia." Postcolonial Studies 20 (1): 18–33.

Simpson, James Young. (1849) 1995. "Answer to the Religious Objections Advanced against the Employment of Anaesthetic Agents in Midwifery and Surgery," excerpted from Anaesthesia, or the Employment of Chloroform and Ether in Surgery, Midwifery, Etc., in Medicine and Western Civilization, edited by David J. Rothman, Steven Marcus, and Stephanie A. Kiceluk, 398–401. New Brunswick, NJ: Rutgers University Press.

Sluga, Hans. 2006. "Foucault's Encounter with Heidegger and Nietzsche." In The Cambridge Companion to Foucault, edited by Gary Gutting, 210–39. Cambridge: Cambridge University Press.

Small, Peter. 2013. "Dr. George Doodnaught: Woman Recalls Forced Oral Sex during Surgery." Toronto Star, February 21. http://www.thestar.com/news/crime/2013/02/21/dr_george_doodnaught_woman_recalls_forced_oral_sex_during_surgery.html.

Smith, Andrea. 2005. Conquest: Sexual Violence and American Indian Genocide. Cambridge, MA: South End Press.

Smith, Daniel. 2015. "Foucault on Ethics and Subjectivity: 'Care of the Self' and 'Aesthetics of Existence.'" Foucault Studies 19:135–50.

Smith, Erica L., and Alexia Cooper. 2013. "Homicide in the U.S. Known to Law Enforcement, 2011." U.S. Department of Justice, Bureau of Justice Statistics, December. http://www.bjs.gov/content/pub/pdf/hus11.pdf.

Smylie, Janet, Deshayne Fell, and Arne Ohlsson. 2010. "A Review of Aboriginal Infant Mortality Rates in Canada: Striking and Persistent Aboriginal/Non-Aboriginal Inequities." Canadian Journal of Public Health 101 (2): 143–48.

Snow, Stephanie J. 2006. Operations without Pain: The Practice and Science of Anaesthesia in Victorian Britain. Basingstoke, UK: Palgrave Macmillan.

Spivak, Gayatri. (1988) 2010. "Can the Subaltern Speak?" In Can the Subaltern Speak? Reflections on the History of an Idea, edited by Rosalind C. Morris, 21–80. New York: Columbia University Press.

Springer, Kristen W. 2010. "The Race and Class Privilege of Motherhood: The New York Times Presentations of Pregnant Drug-Using Women." Sociological Forum 25 (3): 476–99.

Stewart, Kathleen. 2007. *Ordinary Affects*. Durham, NC: Duke University Press.

Stoller, Silvia. 2009. "Phenomenology and the Poststructural Critique of Experience." *International Journal of Philosophical Studies* 17 (5): 707–37.

St. Pierre, Joshua. 2018. "Fluency Machines: Semiocapitalism, Disability, and Action." PhD diss., University of Alberta.

Svendsen, Lars. 2005. *A Philosophy of Boredom*. London: Reaktion.

Taylor, Chloë. 2010. "Fanon, Foucault, and the Politics of Psychiatry." In *Fanon and the Decolonization of Philosophy*, edited by Elizabeth A. Hoppe and Tracey Nicholls, 55–76. Lanham, MD: Lexington Books.

Taylor, Chloë. 2013. "Infamous Men, Dangerous Individuals, and Violence against Women: Feminist Re-readings of Foucault." In *A Companion to Foucault*, edited by Christopher Falzon, Timothy O'Leary, and Jana Sawicki, 419–35. Oxford: Blackwell.

Taylor, Chloë. 2018. *Foucault, Feminism, and Sex Crimes: An Anti-Carceral Analysis*. New York: Routledge.

Thacker, Andrew. 1993. "Foucault's Aesthetics of Existence." *Radical Philosophy* 63:13–21.

TheSublimeDegree. 2013. "CNN Grieves That Guilty Verdict Ruined 'Promising' Lives of Steubenville Rapists." March 17. *YouTube*. https://www.youtube.com/watch?v=MvUdyNko8LQ.

Thompson, E. P. 1967. "Time, Work-Discipline, and Industrial Capitalism." *Past and Present* 38:56–97.

Tokumitsu, Miya. 2018. "Tell Me It's Going to Be OK." *The Baffler*, no. 41. https://thebaffler.com/salvos/tell-me-its-going-to-be-ok-tokumitsu.

Tone, Andrea. 2009. *The Age of Anxiety: A History of America's Turbulent Affair with Tranquilizers*. New York: Basic Books.

Tremain, Shelley. 2013. "Educating Jouy." *Hypatia* 28 (4): 801–81.

Tremain, Shelley. 2017. *Foucault and Feminist Philosophy of Disability*. Ann Arbor: University of Michigan Press.

Trocchi, Alexander. 1960. *Cain's Book*. New York: Grove Press.

Turner, Sarah, and Lucy Rocca. 2014. *The Sober Revolution: Calling Time on Wine O'Clock*. Cardiff, Wales: Accent Press.

Valverde, Mariana. 2004. "Experience and Truth Telling in a Post-Humanist World: A Foucauldian Contribution to Feminist Ethical Reflections." In *Feminism and the Final Foucault*, edited by Dianna Taylor and Karen Vintges, 67–90. Champaign: University of Illinois Press.

Vandervort, Lucinda. 2011. "Lawful Subversion of the Criminal Justice Process? Judicial, Prosecutorial, and Police Discretion in *Edmondson, Kindrat*, and *Brown*." In *Sexual Assault Law: Practice and Activism in a Post-Jane Doe Era*, edited by Elizabeth Sheehy, 111–50. Ottawa: University of Ottawa Press.

Vetlesen, Arne. 2009. *A Philosophy of Pain*. London: Reaktion Books.

Vintges, Karen. 2001. "'Must We Burn Foucault?' Ethics as Art of Living: Simone de Beauvoir and Michel Foucault." *Continental Philosophy Review* 34:165–81.

Wade, Simeon, with Heather Dundas. 2017. "Michel Foucault in Death Valley: A *Boom* Interview with Simeon Wade." *Boom California*, September 10. https://boomcalifornia.com/2017/09/10/michel-foucault-in-death-valley-a-boom-interview-with-simeon-wade/.

Walsh, Denis. 2009. "Pain and Epidural Use in Normal Childbirth." *Evidence Based Midwifery* 7 (3): 89–93.

Wandavra. 2013. "Work and the Politics of Refusal." *The Disorder of Things* (blog), June 13. https://thedisorderofthings.com/2013/06/13/work-and-the-politics-of-refusal/.

Weeks, Kathi. 2011. *The Problem with Work: Feminism, Marxism, Antiwork Politics, and Postwork Imaginaries.* Durham, NC: Duke University Press.

Weiss, Gail. 1999. *Body Images: Embodiment as Intercorporeality.* New York: Routledge.

Weiss, Gail. 2008. *Refiguring the Ordinary.* Bloomington: Indiana University Press.

Whyte, Kyle Powys. 2017. "Our Ancestors' Dystopia Now: Indigenous Conservation and the Anthropocene." In *The Routledge Companion to the Environmental Humanities,* edited by Ursula K. Heise, Jon Christensen, and Michelle Niemann, 206–15. New York: Routledge.

Williams, Raymond. 1983. "Experience." In *Keywords: A Vocabulary of Culture and Society,* 126–29. London: Fontana.

Wittgenstein, Ludwig. 1953. *Philosophical Investigations.* Oxford: Blackwell.

Wolf, Jacqueline H. 2009. *Deliver Me from Pain: Anesthesia and Birth in America.* Baltimore, MD: Johns Hopkins University Press.

Wolin, Richard. 1994. "Foucault's Aesthetic Decisionism." In *Michel Foucault: Critical Assessments,* vol. 3, edited by Barry Smart, 251–71. London: Routledge.

World Health Organization (WHO). 2015. "The Prevention and Elimination of Disrespect and Abuse during Facility-Based Childbirth." http://www.who.int/reproductivehealth/topics/maternal_perinatal/statement-childbirth/en/.

Wortham, Simon Morgan. 2013. *The Poetics of Sleep: From Aristotle to Nancy.* London: Bloomsbury.

Wyllie, Martin. 2005. "Lived Time and Psychopathology." *Philosophy, Psychiatry, and Psychology* 12 (3): 173–85.

Yeatman, Anna. 2014. "Feminism and the Technological Age." *Australian Feminist Studies* 29 (79): 85–100.

Yoffe, Emily. 2013. "College Women: Stop Getting Drunk." *Slate*, October 5. http://www.slate.com/articles/double_x/doublex/2013/10/sexual_assault_and_drinking_teach_women_the_connection.html.

Young, Hilary. 2010. "*R. v. A. (J.)* and the Risks of Advance Consent to Unconscious Sex." *Canadian Criminal Law Review* 14:273–306.

Young, Iris Marion. (1980) 2005. *On Female Body Experience: "Throwing Like a Girl" and Other Essays.* New York: Oxford University Press.

Zerilli, Linda. 2005. *Feminism and the Abyss of Freedom.* Chicago: Chicago University Press.

INDEX

women (*continued*)
  violence); and wine, 109–15, 123, 155n9.
  See also experience: in feminist thought;
  experience: women's experience; time: and
  women; work: women's work
work, 7, 21, 75–76, 81–82, 91, 126, 144, 158n1;
  and aesthetics of existence, 2–7, 95–96; and

leisure, 79–80, 153n1; sexual harassment at,
  32; and time, 77–78, 81–82, 85–88, 103, 107,
  116; women's work, 80–84, 109–13, 124; work
  ethic, 44–45, 78–89
Wyllie, Martin, 103–5, 154n5

Yeatman, Anna, 83–84, 87